Synergy in Polycentric Cities

Complementarity, organising capacity and critical mass

Evert Meijers

The series **Sustainable Urban Areas**
is published by IOS Press under the imprint Delft University Press

IOS Press BV
Nieuwe Hemweg 6b
1013 BG Amsterdam
The Netherlands
Fax +31-20-6870019
E-mail: info@iospress.nl

Sustainable Urban Areas is edited by
Delft Centre for Sustainable Urban Areas
C/o OTB Research Institute for Housing, Urban and Mobility Studies
Delft University of Technology
Jaffalaan 9
2628 BX Delft
The Netherlands
Phone +31 15 2783005
Fax +31 15 2784422
E-mail mailbox@otb.tudelft.nl
http://www.otb.tudelft.nl

Synergy in Polycentric Urban Regions

Complementarity, organising capacity and critical mass

PROEFSCHRIFT

ter verkrijging van de graad van doctor
aan de Technische Universiteit Delft,
op gezag van de Rector Magnificus prof. dr. ir. J.T. Fokkema,
voorzitter van het College voor Promoties,
in het openbaar te verdedigen op dinsdag 13 maart 2007 om 10.00 uur
door

Evert Jan MEIJERS
Doctorandus in de planologie

geboren te Veere

Dit proefschrift is goedgekeurd door de promotor:
Prof. dr. ir. H. Priemus

Samenstelling promotiecommissie:
Rector Magnificus, voorzitter
Prof. dr. ir. H. Priemus, Technische Universiteit Delft, promotor
Prof. dr. P.J. Boelhouwer, Technische Universiteit Delft
Prof. dr. R.C. Kloosterman, Universiteit van Amsterdam
Prof. dr. F. van Oort, Universiteit Utrecht
Prof. dr. W.G.M. Salet, Universiteit van Amsterdam
Dr. ir. M. Spaans, Technische Universiteit Delft
Dr. W.A.M. Zonneveld, Technische Universiteit Delft
Prof. dr. W.K. Korthals Altes, Technische Universiteit Delft, reservelid

Synergy in Polycentric Urban Regions:
Complementarity, organising capacity and critical mass
Evert Jan Meijers
Thesis Delft University of Technology, Delft, the Netherlands

The author wishes to acknowledge the financial assistance of the Dutch government through the Habiforum Program Innovative Land Use and Delft University of Technology through the Delft Centre for Sustainable Urban Areas.

Design: Cyril Strijdonk Ontwerpburo, Gaanderen
DTP: Yvonne Alkemade, Delft
Cover photo: Victor Abellón
Printed in the Netherlands by: Haveka, Alblasserdam

ISSN 1574-6410; 13
ISBN 978-1-58603-724-6
NUGI 755

Subject headings: polycentricity, interurban relationships, urban networks, complementarity, organising capacity, critical mass

This is my Truth, Tell me Yours
Manic Street Preachers, 1998

Contents

Preface

The foundations for this thesis were laid during the work on the Interreg IIc project named EURBANET in which I participated between 2000 and 2002. This project focused on four polycentric urban regions in North West Europe and explored the practical value of this kind of a region as a planning concept. The subject of polycentric urban regions caught my great personal interest and it was only a matter of course that such regions would become the focus of my PhD research, the EURBANET project providing a jump-start.

Although writing a PhD thesis is foremost meant to be a demonstration of an individual's capability of doing academic research, it could not have been accomplished without the help of others. This holds particularly for professor Hugo Priemus and dr. Marjolein Spaans. Both Hugo and Marjolein have accurately read, discussed and commented on numerous versions of research papers, not only those that are included in this thesis. I feel privileged to have such an experienced and distinguished promoter as Hugo Priemus. Many thanks for the efforts to get my research proposal funded, but above all for sharing your experience in doing academic research and of the rigors of getting published with me. In addition, I greatly value the relative freedom – as I experienced it – I was given to further develop the research as a sign of having confidence in a good ending. Marjolein is to be credited for making the process of doing PhD research have many 'ups' and few 'downs'. Many thanks for putting me on the track, for keeping me there and for safeguarding my interest in the process.

The members of the OTB-department of Urban and Regional Development should be credited for the pleasant, harmonious and stimulating working atmosphere. Next to the occasional chat over coffee or lunch, for me, this also includes the well-established academic orientation of our work. Thanks to the department co-ordinators Robert Kloosterman, Wil Zonneveld and Kees Maat for safeguarding this. Special thanks goes to Arie Romein, who co-authored one of the papers in this thesis. The publication of this paper has very much encouraged me to proceed in writing a thesis based on a collection of papers. I also very much enjoyed working with him and my other colleagues Bart Lambregts, Bas Waterhout, Dominic Stead, Eric Hoppenbrouwer and Wil Zonneveld on several international research projects within the frameworks of Interreg IIc and ESPON, as well as the NOVEM-project on integral policy making. Working on these projects meant a welcome distraction from the PhD research and allowed for a much richer research experience.

OTB Research Institute for Housing, Urban and Mobility Studies provides researchers with many opportunities and few constraints. Important for me in particular was the opportunity to pursue research on issues that were driven by my own personal interests, as well as according to their theoretical and practical relevance. I am indebted to many people in the institute who have contributed in some way to the completion of this thesis. I very much appreciated the comments and advice of the late Frans Dieleman. Thanks go to Henny Coolen and Sylvia Jansen for their methodological advice and to Herman Toneman for drawing up several figures. Roommates are important in making a nice working atmosphere. In that sense I owe much to Eric Hoppenbrouwer, Reinout Kleinhans and now Wendy Bohte for the fun, interest and encouragement.

Help was also provided by people outside OTB Research Institute for Housing, Urban and Mobility Studies. This includes the participants in the EURBANET project as Chapter 5 builds on its results. Thanks go to the managers of hospitals and universities for professional education for their willingness to be interviewed for parts of the field research. In addition, many organisations have been willing to provide me with data and figures. Peter Schmitt assisted greatly in acquiring German data. Rachel Heap skilfully and accurately edited my English.

No research without funding. Funding for this research was kindly provided by the Dutch government through the Habiforum Program Innovative Land Use and by Delft University of Technology through the Delft Centre for Sustainable Urban Areas. Furthermore, I acknowledge the financial assistance for purchasing data by the Deltametropolis Association.

Enjoying the warmth and support of my parents, sister, 'in-laws' and friends has been very important to me. Special thanks goes to Joris Bekkers and Martijn van Berkum for their support as paranimfs. Immeasurable thanks and love go to my pillar in life, Lonneke. Being with you, and our children, is a wonderful experience that I value dearly. Finally, Veerle, Casper and Wessel; while your actual geographical worlds are still so small, learning about other countries and peoples brings the most magical associations and great fantasies. I sincerely hope that when we explore our world together, or you on your own, you will enjoy and care for what is out there.

1 Introduction

1.1 Cities and networks

Cities cannot be studied in isolation. Each human settlement is connected to other settlements in many different ways and through many different actors. These connections include flows of information, capital, goods and persons, which travel along such infrastructures as roads, railways, waterways, airlines and increasingly telecommunications. While actors such as companies, institutes, households or individual persons maintain these connections, on a more abstract level it is also possible to distinguish relationships between cities (see also Pred, 1977; Taylor, 2003). These intercity relationships can be considered the aggregates of all the multifarious types of flows between the many urban actors.

Contemporary urban studies put much emphasis on the significance of these relationships in explaining the economic, social and cultural functioning of cities. As Gottmann (1984:1) puts it, 'to understand the evolution of the contemporary ways of the world, networks of cities are fundamental.' Similarly, Massey *et al.* (1999:2) state that 'it is impossible to tell the story of any individual city without understanding its connections to elsewhere. Cities are essentially open; they are meeting places, the focus of the geography of social relations.' Also Castells (1996) defines cities as networked phenomena. He postulates that the really significant feature is the network, not the particular status or functions and roles cities perform. Cities are the nodes of the 'space of flows'. Consequently, research on these intercity relationships has taken off in the last decade with a strong emphasis on exploring networks of cities on the global scale (for instance Sassen, 2002; Taylor, 2003). With the work of the Globalisation and World Cities Study Group and Network (GaWC) the still considerable 'evidential crisis' (Taylor, 2003:32) in the research of such global networks is diminishing. While this focus on the external linkages of world cities or global city regions seems justifiable given the fact that both globalisation and the transformation to an informational economy tend to increase the importance of cities at the top, it does not mean that intercity relationships on a regional scale are of less importance. On the contrary, as territorial competition has been scaled down from the nation-state to the city region as the principal geographic platform (see for instance Storper, 1995; Scott, 1998), and as the spatial configuration and internal linkages between a regional set of cities also determine a region's competitiveness, these regional intercity relationships constitute another important field of research. Such regional intercity relationships stand central in this thesis.

1.2 Polycentric urban regions

This research on regional intercity relationships is focused on a particular type of region: the polycentric urban region, or PUR. PURs can be defined as collections of historically distinct and both administratively and politically independent cities located in close proximity, well connected through infrastructure and lacking one dominating city in political, economic, cultural and other aspects (see Kloosterman and Lambregts, 2001). Parr (2004) presents several conditions that define a PUR. A PUR can be distinguished from other regions as the cities are more clustered, not located too far from each other – say within one hour travel time – nor too close as in the case of conurbations, while none of the cities dominates the others in terms of population, and the level of interaction between the urban centres and of specialisation is higher than in other not polycentric regions (Parr, 2004). These definitions imply that PURs of varying size can be identified. Examples of the PUR are most widespread in North West Europe. Large-scale examples include the Randstad region in the Netherlands, which serves as the classic archetype example of a PUR (Hohenberg and Lees, 1985; Batten, 1995), but the RheinRuhr Area (see Blotevogel, 1998; Knapp, 1998) and Central Belgium or the 'Flemish Diamond' (Albrechts, 1998, 2001) are also often mentioned. Also, parts of northern Italy, for instance the Veneto region have been identified as PURs, next to large Asian examples as the Japanese Kansai area (Batten, 1995) or the Pearl River Delta (see for instance Yeh, 2001). The San Francisco Bay Area qualifies as well. A much larger number of PURs of a more modest size are also widely found across the world. In addition, ideas resembling the PUR concept have emerged on an even higher spatial scale, sometimes referred to as Mega-City-Regions, for instance the Delta region in North West Europe cornered by the three PURs Randstad, RheinRuhr and Flemish Diamond (see Dieleman and Faludi, 1998a; Priemus and Hall, 2004).

As the terms 'polycentric development' and 'polycentricity' are applied to a variety of scales, ranging from the European scale to the local scale of individual cities, and as the meaning of such terms differs between scales (Kloosterman and Musterd, 2001; Davoudi, 2003), it is essential here to distinguish the concept of the PUR from interpretations of polycentricity at other scales, in particular the intra-urban or city scale. Polycentric urban patterns on the latter scale arise from the development of centres alongside the traditional inner city or central business district within a city region consisting of a city and its smaller suburban satellites. This has led to a more spatially specialised metropolitan layout incorporating many different types of centres (Roberts *et al.*, 1999; Hall, 2001). It is widely acknowledged nowadays that all post-industrial cities are in fact polycentric. However, polycentric urban regions are comprised of several such polycentric cities. As a result of processes of, amongst others, increased connectedness, and the scaling-up of business activities and people's daily urban systems, they have coalesced or 'fused' (Champion, 2001) both functionally and morphologically into larger regional urban systems (Dieleman and Faludi, 1998b). PURs therefore represent polycentricity at the regional inter-urban spatial scale, between cities that used to be relatively independent from each other.

In the literature several rather synonymous terms referring to the PUR circulate. Recent examples include 'city networks' (Camagni and Salone, 1993), 'multicore city-regions' (Westin and Östhol, 1994), 'network cities' (Batten, 1995) and 'polynucleated metropolitan regions' (Dieleman and Faludi, 1998b). The recent concept of the 'polycentric mega-city region' (Hall and Pain, 2006) is insufficiently specified for our purposes as it lumps PURs and single polycentric cities together.

In recent years, the concept of the PUR has gained considerable interest in academic literature. Many of the contributions have been primarily focused on either establishing the concept of the PUR in the academic and policy debate, on its defining characteristics and on research agenda-setting (see for instance Batten 1995; Dieleman and Faludi, 1998b; Kloosterman and Musterd, 2001; Parr, 2004), on its relevance for, or its potential application to specific PURs (Priemus, 1994; Albrechts, 1998; Bailey and Turok, 2001; Turok and Bailey, 2004). Considerable attention has also been paid to capacity building and governance in such regions (Albrechts, 2001; Mueller, 2001; Knapp *et al.*, 2004; Albrechts and Lievois, 2004; Lambregts and Zonneveld, 2004). Less attention has so far been paid to empirically substantiating the PUR concept, including the many assumptions addressing the economic significance of PURs circulating. These assumptions often refer to the PUR's specific spatial-functional layout. Due to their specific spatial structure, PURs would have the potential for superior economic performance, as they allegedly enjoy economies of scale, scope and complexity similar to their monocentric counterparts, without, however, incurring the same costs or agglomeration diseconomies that the latter entail. The latter includes for instance congestion, lack of space and high land prices, criminality and environmental pollution. Some validity may be hidden in the latter argument as many of the benefits of urban concentration can also be accessed from locations well outside the agglomeration. At the same time, agglomeration diseconomies remain largely confined to the agglomeration (Parr, 2002). In addition, the general idea presented is that, taken together, PURs are at least able to develop new sources of competitive advantage and market their city-regions better internationally. However, as some of the authors on PURs argue, the focus in the discussion on PURs should now turn to empirically substantiating and validating the many claims and assumptions that have been made for the PUR (Kloosterman and Musterd, 2001; Parr, 2004; Turok and Bailey, 2004). Filling parts of this lacuna is the aim of this thesis.

1.3 Polycentric urban regions on the policy agenda

These calls for empirical sophistication of the PUR concept have become increasingly more relevant and urgent now that throughout Europe policy-makers are developing policies to foster the spatial, economic and social development of PURs. This reflects the large potential policy-makers attribute to such regions. They assume that taking a set of relatively small or medium-sized cities together opens up possibilities for regional economic growth. Taken individually, these cities fear being overlooked, but taken together they would be able to 'play in the major leagues' of international competition (Priemus, 1994). This latter ambition can be considered the main rationale behind this policy interest, although occasionally it may also be rooted in the objective to control urbanisation (Lambregts and Zonneveld, 2004). Furthermore, increased functional relationships between a cluster of cities also raises the need for planning at a higher scale.

At present, explicit planning for PURs is a feature of strategic regional development strategies in many European countries, albeit that such regional clusters of cities are generally not referred to as PURs. Rather, policy makers often refer to them as 'urban networks' or 'city networks'. Use is made of the network metaphor to emphasise the alleged or desired complex and strong relationships between the cities and as such the coherence and unity of the region. The inclusion of the PUR concept in the European Spatial Development Perspective (CEC, 1999), albeit in different terms, can be considered one of the accelerators of its spread across Europe (Davoudi, 2003). Table 1.1 lists several European countries in which PURs have been identified as an objective of strategic policy-making, also giving examples of networks and the policy label given to the PUR.

Planning for PURs in many cases involves planning on a relatively new scale, based upon new starting points and taking on board new strategic objectives (Lambregts, 2000). Some of these new rationales become apparent in implicit and explicit assumptions found in policy documents about the spatial-functional structure of PURs, which includes understandings of intercity relationships. Two examples from the low countries can illustrate this. The Spatial Structure Plan for Flanders (Ministerie van de Vlaamse Gemeenschap, 1997) introduced the concept of the Flemish Diamond (cornered by Brussels-Antwerp-Ghent-Leuven) as an 'international competitive urban network' (see also Albrechts, 1998; 2001). The document suggests that urban networks – 'complementary and coherent entities' – replace the traditional historically grown hierarchy of cities: 'the significance of a city is no longer determined by the size of the population of the city and its immediate hinterland, but by the city's position in the European or global network of cities' (Ministerie van de Vlaamse Gemeenschap, 1997:49, author's translation). Such urban networks were also introduced in Dutch planning, for the first time in the Fifth Memorandum on Spatial Planning (Ministerie van VROM, 2002). According to this document, the strength of urban networks is that 'cities in networks do not duplicate each other, but exploit chances to complement each other and co-ordinate a certain division of labour. Amsterdam, Rotterdam, The Hague

Table 1.1 Planning for polycentric urban regions in European countries

Country	Concept	Examples
Belgium (Flanders)	'urban network'	e.g. Flemish Diamond (Brussels-Antwerp-Ghent-Leuven)
Denmark	'regions of competence', polycentric 'national centres'[1]	Struer-Holstebro-Herning-Ikast; Middelfart-Kolding-Vejle-Fredericia
Estonia	'urban network'	Ida-Viru county: Jõhvi-Kohtla-Järve-Narva
France	'réseaux des villes' (urban networks)	e.g. Normandie Métropole (Caen-Le Havre-Rouen)
Germany	'European metropolitan region'[1], 'städtenetze' (urban networks)	e.g. RheinRuhr (Bonn-Cologne-Düsseldorf-Essen-Dortmund); Bergisches city triangle (Remscheid-Solingen-Wuppertal); Sachsendreieck (Dresden-Leipzig-Chemnitz/Zwickau)
Greece	'twin poles' or 'bi-poles'	e.g. Larissa-Volos
Italy	'city network', 'multicentric metropolitan system'	e.g. Veneto (Padua-Venice-Treviso)
Ireland	'linked gateways'	Letterkenny-Derry; Athlone-Tullamore-Mullingar
Lithuania	'metropolis Vilnius-Kaunas'	Vilnius-Kaunas
The Netherlands	'urban networks'	e.g. Randstad (Amsterdam-Rotterdam-The Hague-Utrecht); Brabantstad (Breda-Tilburg-Den Bosch-Eindhoven-Helmond)
Poland	'duopols'	Warsaw-Lodz; Toruń-Bydgoszcz
Switzerland	'vernetzte Städtesystem', 'polycentric system'	Northern part of the country (among which Zürich-Basel-Bern-Winterthur-Luzern)

1 This concept is not specifically developed for polycentric urban regions, but in its elaboration it also identifies polycentric urban regions.

and Utrecht together with the other cities in the Delta Metropolis have much more to offer when taken together instead of individually and should be further developed in a coherent and co-ordinated way' (Ministerie van VROM, 2002:32, authors translation). Furthermore, '[i]t is not the individual cities, but the metropolitan areas and urban networks that offer a complete range of living/working environments, services, parks and transport systems' (Ministerie van VROM, 2002:33, English summary version). This idea sets aside the previously dominant idea in Dutch planning of 'complete cities' (see Zonneveld and Verwest, 2005). Due to the fall of the Dutch government in 2002, the policy of the Fifth Memorandum was never ratified. However, the new government maintained the concept of urban networks in its successor, the National Spatial Strategy 'Nota Ruimte' (Ministerie van VROM, 2005), which emphasises the co-operative aspects of urban networks comparably more. However, it is expected that exactly through this co-operation in urban networks the spatial-functional structure of PURs will change after some time: 'co-operation must enhance the competitive power of all cities in the network and ensure the presence of an attractive (international) location environment and a large diversity of urban functions. The cities and centres in the network complement and mutually enforce one another as together they are able to deliver more than taken individually. The government expects the cities to co-ordinate tasks to allow for specialisation and complementarities' (Ministerie van VROM, 2005:70). The document distinguishes six urban networks considered to be of national and international importance due to their size, dynamics and position and therefore eligible for additional investments by the central government, the extent to which is, however, dependent on the ability of actors in the urban network to draw up spatial programmes and plans in mutual consultation and to set aside competition.

What is clear in both the Flemish and Dutch policies is the belief of policy-makers that a certain specific spatial structure would be beneficial for the region. This is particularly true for the presence of complementarity through a division of labour. This is to be achieved through co-operation and should allow for specialisation. The support base or critical mass of the region would then be based on the entire network of cities rather than the individual constituting cities. This thesis explores whether such assumptions on synergetic relationships between cities empirically hold.

1.4 Intercity relationships in theory

Relationships between cities are often defined in terms of hierarchy. This is particularly true for urban systems research, but even when this field of research declined, from the mid-1980s on, many researchers continued discussing intercity relationships in terms of hierarchy, for instance in the case of the literature on 'World Cities' (Friedmann, 1986, 1995) and 'Global Cities' (Sassen, 1991, 2001), while this dominance becomes also evident in the many rankings of cities that are made (see Beaverstock *et al.*, 1999 for an overview). The prominence of the idea of hierarchy finds its origin in central place theory, which has dominated academic thought on the spatial organisation of urban systems for many decades over the last century. Ever since the seminal work of Christaller (1933) and Lösch (1944) on the size and spacing of cities the essence of this theory in terms of intercity relationships has remained the same. In the first place, the theory emphasises the presence of one-sided hierarchical relationships between different classes of hierarchically ordered central places. 'One-sided' means that the lower class of central places is dependent on the higher class of central places for the provision of increasingly specialised urban functions. In the second place, the theory postulates that horizontal relationships between cities in the same class (thus of similar size) would be non-existent and also redundant, as these cities provide the same amenities and services. Though in the heyday of urban systems research many enhancements and refinements of the initial work by Christaller and Lösch were introduced by authors such as Berry, Dacey, Mulligan, Beckmann, Beguin, Parr and others (see Berry *et al.*, 1988 and Coffey *et al.*, 1998 for an overview) the idea of hierarchical intercity relationships has not been contested. However, this perseverance is in part the reason for the decline of the popularity of central place theory as increasingly often the idea of hierarchy could not explain the patterns found in practice. For instance, because higher order functions were found in lower-order central places, or because strong relationships existed between central places of similar size. Nowadays it is generally acknowledged that real city systems in advanced economies have departed in many respects from the Christallerian pattern of a nested hierarchy of centres and markets. While these and other deficiencies of the central place model have often been highlighted, no other set of clearly defined hypotheses has replaced those of central place theory (Camagni, 1993).

However, from the early 1990s on, some researchers hinted at the development of a new model of spatial organisation, which is generally referred to as a 'network model' (see Camagni, 1993; Batten, 1995; Van der Knaap, 2002). This model is essentially the opposite of the central place model. While the central place system emphasises, amongst other things, centrality, size dependency, a tendency towards primacy, a dominance of one-way flows, a fixed number of spatial scales, economic functions raising with and linked to scale and an even territorial distribution of urban population, the network model, on the contrary, emphasises nodality, size neutrality, a tendency towards complementarity, two-way flows, a variable number of spatial scales, variable sets of functions on the same scale and an uneven territorial distribution of urban population (Batten, 1995; Van der Knaap, 2002). In terms of intercity relationships, the network model stresses the presence of horizontal relationships, thus between relatively similar-sized cities, of a complementary nature and resulting from the division in functions between cities, next to the hierarchical vertical-type of relationships. However, rather than replacing the central place model with a network model, authors suggest a sequential link between both models. Whereas the central place model seems most typical for industrial economies, the network model seems more applicable to economies that have become more service-sector dominated (Camagni and Salone, 1993; Batten, 1995; Van der Knaap, 2002).

The discourse on an alternative model to the central place model was informed by some early observations of alternative spatial patterns. This includes Burton's work on the 'Dispersed City', a group of rather similar-sized politically discrete cities, separated by tracts of open land, but functioning economically as a single urban unit (Burton, 1963). In addition, Gottmann (1961) opposed the dominant view of hierarchical relationships in his analysis of the polycentric urbanised north-eastern seaboard of the US, which he termed the

'Megalopolis'. Both examples underline the presence of complementary, rather than hierarchical, relationships between cities, also between cities of a relatively similar size. Both Burton and Gottmann refer to a clustering of rather similar-sized cities. Others have also suggested that it is particularly in such a spatial setting of a group of relatively similar-sized close-by cities that the central place model would not hold true (Camagni, 1993; Capello, 2000; Davies, 1998; Van der Knaap, 2002). Conversely, the network model would be most applicable for such regional clusters of similar-sized cities. However, while the theoretical framework of the network model paradigm seems relatively well established, research demonstrating its empirical validity is largely non-existent (Capello, 2000). This thesis aims to fill parts of this lacuna.

1.5 Research aims and questions

The aim of this thesis is to fill part of the two lacunas in our understanding of PURs and intercity relationships identified at the end of the sections 1.2 and 1.4. In the first place, this implies that the research aims to provide further theoretical clarification and empirical assessment of the PUR concept and in particular the claims and assumptions that have been made with regard to their spatial-functional structure, with an emphasis on regional intercity relationships. Secondly, the research aims to theoretically explicate the features of the network model further and to provide an empirical assessment of its validity as a description of the spatial-functional structure of PURs. Both aims will appear to be strongly linked as the claims and assumptions made with respect to the spatial-functional structure of PURs are largely in concordance with the basic ideas of the network model of spatial organisation. The overarching research theme that frames this research is the extent to which cities constituting a PUR relate to each other in a synergetic way. In other words, to what extent are they more than the sum of the parts?

Both this research theme and the underlying two research agendas are very broad and the research is therefore necessarily focused on particular issues on these agendas. Therefore, the overarching central research theme is broken down into three research questions relating to three dominant issues that arise on both research agendas:

1. complementarity
2. organising capacity
3. critical mass.

Each of these issues is addressed by a separate research question:

1. *To what extent is the complementary development of cities within polycentric urban regions happening and worthwhile pursuing?*

2. *What is the potential of a regional co-ordinated planning approach in PURs and what factors foster or hamper the development of regional organising capacity in such regions?*
3. *To what extent does the polycentric spatial layout of PURs influence their support base for urban functions?*

1.6 Outline of the thesis

The thesis takes the shape of a collection of related research papers on the three issues of complementarity, organising capacity and critical mass. Most of them address one particular research issue, with the exception of the first paper in Chapter 2 that combines both the issues of complementarity and organising capacity. The attention given to these three issues is not evenly distributed. The issue of complementarity has received most attention and is addressed in Chapters 2, 3 and 4. The issue of organising capacity stands central in Chapters 2 and 5. Finally, the issue of critical mass is the theme of Chapter 6. As the papers in Chapters 2-6 were designed as separate publications, there are some unavoidable overlaps and gaps between the chapters. However, the overlap remains largely limited to accounts of research methods and introductory texts on the concept of PURs. In addition, slight differences occur in spelling and set-up of the different chapters. This reflects the preferences of the journal in which they have been published or have been accepted for publication.

1. Complementarity: *To what extent is the complementary development of cities within polycentric urban regions happening and worthwhile pursuing?*

Concerning the research agenda of whether there is a trend towards a network model of spatial organisation in PURs, here, the focus will be on only one, but important feature of this model: complementarity. Complementarity refers to the situation in which different cities fulfil different and mutually beneficial roles (Hague and Kirk, 2003), for instance through providing different sets of economic functions and services. Complementarity is a multifaceted concept in that it can be applied to a wide variety of phenomena, including both activities (economic functions, services, amenities) and places (business environments, residential environments). The focus in this research has been on activities, or urban functions, as suggestions of complementarity are commonly linked to these (e.g. Camagni and Salone, 1993; Van der Knaap, 1994). Complementarity results from the differentiation between centres or cities in terms of urban functions, thus on the supply side, while these urban functions should be provided, at least partly, for the same geographical demand market. Complementarity can be considered a main feature of the network model as it positively enhances the presence of other characteristics of the network model, for instance two-way flows, horizontal accessibility, nodality and size neutrality. Given these links between the features of the network model of spatial organisation, it seems that the feature of complementarity provides an excellent starting point for the comprehensive research agenda to test the empirical validity of the network model of spatial organisation. Moreover, the assumption that cities complement each other, and will do so even more in the future, is widespread in the policy and academic debates on PURs.

As an analytical model a micro-macro scheme was applied (see Coleman, 1990) (see Figure 1.1).

The question of whether there is a trend towards complementarity, thus a change in the spatial-functional structure of urban regions, is obviously phrased on a macro level (macro-macro relation). However, whether there is such a trend is dependent on the choices and actual location behaviour of actors such as businesses and households (the micro-level). Their choice-set is conditioned by the opportunities and constraints following from the current spatial-functional structure, as well as economic, social, cultural and political developments in society at large or in the regions (macro-micro relations). Given this choice-set, the effective locational behaviour of businesses and households is determined by their own particular rationales (micro-micro). The behavioural decisions at the micro-level then aggregate to macro-level developments in, amongst others, the urban structure (micro-macro). The circle repeats itself continuously.

Chapters 2-4 present the research on complementarity. The overarching research question of this thesis is most prominently addressed in Chapter 2, as is evidenced by the title of the paper: 'Polycentric Urban Regions and the Quest for Synergy: Is a Network of Cities more than the Sum of the Parts?' The paper was published in *Urban Studies* in 2005 and acts as an introductory text for the complementarity as well as the co-operation issue. The paper explores economic network theories on synergy and transforms the findings to spatial phenomena such as PURs in the sense of them being networks of cities. It was found that synergy in PURs will derive from two major synergy-mechanisms: complementarity and co-operation. This theoretical exploration gives insight into the value that should be attributed to the issue of complementarity in PURs and therefore answers the part of the research question on the worthiness of complementarity. Furthermore, it presents an analysis of the trends in economic profiles of a collection of 14 cities in the Dutch Randstad area, also distinguishing between the North Wing and the South Wing of this area. The analysis remains on the macro-level. Correspondence analysis is presented as an appropriate method to determine such complementarities. Correspondence analysis is a technique to analyse the association between rows and columns of a table or a matrix by representing the rows and columns as points

Figure 1.1 Macro-micro analytical model

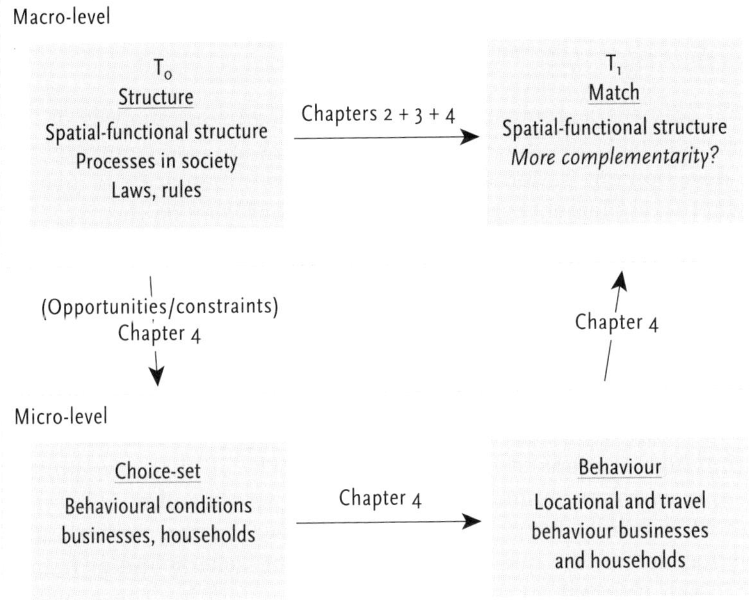

in a low-dimensional Euclidean space (in practice often a two-dimensional plot). Though often used as a tool to enable graphic interpretation of complex data, correspondence analysis also provides a single statistic that describes the extent of differentiation in profiles of a group of cities. This statistic, called the total inertia, is the weighted average of the squared χ^2 distances between the scores on the column and row variables and the average scores. If all cities host exactly the same activities, the total inertia-statistic would be 0, thus representing maximum duplication. If all cities would host completely dissimilar activities, then the total inertia would be equal to the dimensionality of the problem (in practice the number of cities –1). In reality, values will be far from this maximum, as cities have a large component of employment in non-tradeable economic activities, for instance schools, supermarkets etc. To allow for comparisons between PURs with different numbers of constituent cities, it is possible to normalise the score on the total inertia statistic by dividing it by the maximum possible score on the total inertia statistic.

Correspondence analysis is also employed in Chapter 3, which presents a paper entitled 'Clones or Complements? The Division of Labour between the Main Cities of the Randstad, the RheinRuhr and Flemish Diamond', accepted for publication in *Regional Studies* (to be published mid 2007). As the title suggests, the paper presents an international comparison between three well-known examples of PURs – the Dutch Randstad region, the RheinRuhr in Germany and the Flemish Diamond in Belgium. The extent to which the major cities within these regions complement each other in terms of business and consumer services is compared. Again this concerns an analysis of complementarity on solely the macro-level. The findings are also compared to polycentric development patterns found on the intra-urban scale of polycentric cities, where complementarity between centres has been on the rise.

The micro-level aspects of a possible trend towards complementarity in PURs are addressed in Chapter 4. The chapter features a paper entitled 'From Central Place to Network Model: Theory and Evidence of a Paradigm-Change', which was published in the *Tijdschrift voor Economische en Sociale Geografie (Journal of Economic and Social Geography)* in spring 2007. Two types of urban facilities, hospitals and universities of professional education (*hogescholen*), are studied in depth to find out whether there is a trend towards complementarity within organisations of hospitals and hogescholen that have multiple locations spread over a number of close-by cities. As a result of mergers, these facilities increasingly function on a regional level in the Netherlands. The analysis focuses on the question of what are the driving and/or hampering factors in the possible process towards complementarity. These factors are found as much on the macro as on the micro level. Therefore, the research covers the building blocks of the entire macro-micro scheme.

2. Organising capacity: *What is the potential of a regional co-ordinated planning approach in PURs and what factors foster or hamper the development of regional organising capacity in such regions?*

A vast amount of literature has appeared dealing with aspects of co-operation and organising capacity on the regional scale, an administrative scale that in many countries is lacking although spatial trends have made this particular spatial scale more important than ever before. The research effort on this regional deficit in this volume was concentrated on the development of what was termed 'regional organising capacity' in PURs. The analysis of network theories in Chapter 2 provided the starting point as co-operation turned out to be a major synergy generating mechanism for PURs. The value of co-operation was well articulated by Capineri and Kamann (1998:42): '[A]ctors have the choice between independent 'stand alone' strategies where they perform all activities themselves usually at higher costs resulting in lower performance and strategies of co-operation which result in the transfer of activities and/or resources to other actors increasing a large range of types of dependencies but also improving their performance'.

Chapter 5 presents a paper published in *European Urban and Regional Studies* in 2003 with the title 'Realising Potential: Building Regional Organising Capacity in Polycentric Urban Regions'. The paper explores the potentialities of regional planning in PURs. While the advantages of regional planning seem widely acknowledged by local, regional and national planners and stakeholders, in practice successful examples of proclaimed PURs developing networks for regional co-ordination and action are rather thin on the ground. The paper presents an analysis of factors that foster or hamper this development of regional organising capacity. This includes spatial-functional, political-institutional and cultural factors. The argument is based on evidence from four PURs in North West Europe: the Randstad, the RheinRuhr, the Flemish Diamond and Central Scotland. Most of the evidence was collected within the framework of the Interreg IIc project EURBANET.

3. Critical mass: *To what extent does the polycentric spatial layout of PURs influence their support base for urban functions?*

The network model of spatial organisation predicts a further integration between the cities of a PUR. Bailey and Turok (2001) explore the alleged links between integration and competitiveness. One of the ideas is that the integration of cities in PURs may provide for greater agglomeration or external economies as the assets of a region are pooled together. This applies for instance to the benefits of sharing major facilities as seaports and airports and an enlarged labour market (Priemus, 1994), or specialised services as higher education or R&D (Lambooy, 1998). Many advanced or rare high-level urban amenities need a considerable minimum market size as regards both demand for the amenities offered and the supply for the necessary human capital. Therefore, a certain critical mass is deemed necessary for businesses, urban amenities and services to be able to diversify and function smoothly. Not surprisingly, the highest valued economic activities and the widest variety in economic and cultural functions are found within the largest agglomerations. As Capello (2000:1926) argues, 'the limit that the medium-sized cities come up against, and which often makes them succumb vis-à-vis the great metropolis, is the limit of critical mass and centrality'. It is a strategic issue whether such activities 'can also be realised in polynuclear urban structures, which lack the critical mass of large cities with agglomeration economies' (Lambooy, 1998:459).

Therefore, assumptions relating to the support base of a PUR are explored in Chapter 6, which features a research paper entitled 'Summing Small Cities does not make a Metropolis: Polycentric Urban Regions and the Provision of Cultural, Leisure and Sports Amenities' and that is currently being submitted for publication. The support base is considered an important manifestation of the critical mass that is organised in PURs. If cities related to each other in a synergetic way, it is expected that the support base of a PUR is equivalent to other, monocentric regions of similar size. This is an assumption echoing from many policy documents on PURs, often implicitly hidden in the statement that the total number of inhabitants of a particular PUR is similar to some competing monocentric metropoles. This implicitly suggests comparability between the regions. The research question is examined, looking at the provision of cultural, leisure and sports amenities. Their presence in 42 Dutch regions, which constitute functionally coherent entities according to local administrators' views, is expressed as an index. This index serves as the dependent variable in a multiple regression model. One of the independent variables is the extent of mono- or polycentricity of each of the 42 regions. This indicator is based on the size distribution of cities in each region. Other independent variables entered in the model include population size, the number of external visitors and the average household income.

To summarise, Chapters 2, 3 and 4 explore the research issue of complementarity from different perspectives, Chapters 2 and 5 address the issue of organising capacity and Chapter 6 the issue of critical mass. Finally, the concluding synthesis in Chapter 7 presents an overall conclusion, a discussion of the results, shows implications for regional development strategies in PURs and directions for further research.

References

Albrechts, L. (1998) The Flemish Diamond: Precious Gem and Virgin Area, *European Planning Studies*, 6, pp. 411-424.

Albrechts, L. (2001) How to Proceed from Image and Discourse to Action: As Applied to the Flemish Diamond, *Urban Studies*, 38, pp. 733-745.

Albrechts, L. and G. Lievois (2004) The Flemish diamond: urban network in the making?, *European Planning Studies*, 12, pp. 351-370.

Bailey, N. and I. Turok (2001) Central Scotland as a polycentric urban region: useful planning concept or chimera?, *Urban Studies*, 38, pp. 697-715.

Batten, D.F. (1995) Network Cities: Creative Urban Agglomerations for the 21st Century, *Urban Studies*, 32, pp. 313-327.

Beaverstock, J.G., P. Taylor, and R.G. Smith (1999) A Roster of World Cities, *Cities*, 16, pp. 445-458.

Berry, B.J.L., J.B. Parr, B.J. Epstein, A. Ghosh and R.H.T. Smith (1988) *Market Centers and Retail Location. Theory and Applications*. Englewood Cliffs: Prentice Hall.

Blotevogel, H.H. (1998) The Rhine-Ruhr metropolitan region: reality and discourse, *European Planning Studies*, 6, pp. 395-410.

Burton, I. (1963) A restatement of the dispersed city hypothesis, *Annals of the Association of American Geographers*, 63, pp. 285-289.

Camagni, R. (1993) From city hierarchy to city networks: reflections about an emerging paradigm, in: T.R. Lakshmanan and P. Nijkamp (Eds) *Structure and change in the Space Economy: Festschrift in honour of Martin Beckmann*, pp. 66-87. Berlin: Springer Verlag.

Camagni, R. and C. Salone (1993) Network Urban Structures in Northern Italy: Elements for a Theoretical Framework, *Urban Studies*, 30, pp. 1053-1064.

Capello, R. (2000) The City Network Paradigm: Measuring Urban Network Externalities, *Urban Studies*, 37, pp. 1925-1945.

Capineri, C. and D.J.F. Kamann (1998) Synergy in Networks: Concepts, in: K. Button, P. Nijkamp and H. Priemus (Eds) *Transport Networks in Europe*, pp. 35-56. Cheltenham/Northampton: Edward Elgar.

Castells, M. (1996) *The Rise of the Network Society*. Oxford: Blackwell.

CEC, Commission of the European Communities (1999) *European Spatial Development Perspective: Towards Balanced and Sustainable Development of the Territory of the EU*. Luxembourg: Office for Official Publications of the European Communities.

Champion, A.G. (2001) A Changing Demographic Regime and Evolving Polycentric Urban Regions: Consequences for the Size, Composition and Distribution of City Populations, *Urban Studies*, 38, pp. 657-677.

Christaller, W. (1933) *Die zentralen Orte in Süddeutschland*. Jena: Fischer.

Coffey, W.J., L.S. Bourne, J.E. Randall, W.K.D. Davies and R. White (1998) Urban systems research: past, present, and future. A panel discussion. *Canadian Journal of Regional Science*, XXI, pp. 327-364.

Coleman, J.S. (1990) *Foundations of Social Theory*. Cambridge (MA): The Belknap Press of Harvard University Press.

Davies, W.K.D. (1998) Urban Systems Research: Unfulfilled Promises? *Canadian Journal of Regional Science*, XXI, pp. 349-356.

Davoudi, S. (2003) Polycentricity in European Spatial Planning: From an Analytical Tool to a Normative Agenda, *European Planning Studies*, 11, pp. 979-999.

Dieleman, F.M. and A. Faludi (1998a) Randstad, Rhine-Ruhr and Flemish Diamond as one Polynucleated Macro-Region?, *Tijdschrift voor Economische en Sociale Geografie*, 89, pp. 320-327.

Dieleman, F.M. and A. Faludi (1998b) Polynucleated Metropolitan Regions in Northwest Europe: Theme of the Special Issue, *European Planning Studies*, 6, pp. 365-377.

Friedman, J. (1986) The World City Hypothesis, *Development and Change*, 17, pp. 69-83.

Friedman, J. (1995) Where we Stand: A Decade of World City Research, in: P.L. Knox and P.J. Taylor (Eds) *World Cities in a World-System*. Cambridge: Cambridge University Press.

Gottmann, J. (1961) *Megalopolis, The urbanized Northeastern Seaboard of the United States*. New York: The Twentieth Century Fund.

Gottmann, J. (1984) *Orbits: The Ancient Mediterranean Tradition of Urban Networks*. Oxford: Leopard's Head Press.

Hague, C. and K. Kirk (2003) *Polycentricity Scoping Study*. London: Office of the Deputy Prime Minister.

Hall, P. (2001) Global City-Regions in the Twenty-first Century, in: A.J. Scott (ed.) *Global City Regions - Trends, Theory, Policy*, pp. 57-77. Oxford: Oxford University Press.

Hall, P. and K. Pain (Eds) (2006) *The Polycentric Metropolis: Learning from mega-city regions in Europe*. London: Earthscan.

Hohenberg, P.M. and L.H. Lees (1985) *The Making of Urban Europe: 1000-1950*. Cambridge, MA: Harvard University Press.

Kloosterman, R.C. and B. Lambregts (2001) Clustering of Economic Activities in Polycentric Urban Regions: The Case of the Randstad, *Urban Studies*, 38, pp. 717-732.

Kloosterman, R.C. and S. Musterd (2001) The Polycentric Urban Region: Towards a Research Agenda, *Urban Studies*, 38, pp. 623-633.

Knaap, G.A. van der (1994) *Ruimtelijke complexen en schaalspanning op de stedenring*, EGI-onderzoekspublikatie 19. Rotterdam: Erasmus Universiteit Rotterdam.

Knaap, G.A. van der (2002) *Stedelijke bewegingsruimte, over veranderingen in stad en land*. The Hague: Sdu uitgevers.

Knapp, W. (1998) The Rhine–Ruhr Area in Transformation: Towards a European Metropolitan Region?, *European Planning Studies*, 6, pp. 379-394.

Knapp, W., K.R. Kunzmann and P. Schmitt (2004) A cooperative spatial future for RheinRuhr, *European Planning Studies*, 12, pp. 323-349.

Lambooy, J.G. (1998) Polynucleation and Economic Development: The Randstad, *European Planning Studies*, 6, pp. 457-466.

Lambregts, B. (2000) *Background study and theoretical framework for the Eurbanet project*, EURBANET Report to the European Commission. Delft: OTB Research Institute.

Lambregts, L. and W. Zonneveld (2004) From Randstad to Deltametropolis: Changing Attitudes Towards the Scattered Metropolis, *European Planning Studies*, 12, pp. 299-321.

Lösch, A. (1944) *Die raumliche Ordnung der Wirtschaft*. 2nd Edition. Jena: Fischer.

Massey, D., J. Allen and S. Pile (Eds) (1999) *City Worlds*. London: Routledge.

Ministerie van de Vlaamse Gemeenschap (1997) *Ruimtelijk Structuurplan Vlaanderen. Integrale versie*. Brussel: Ministerie van de Vlaamse Gemeenschap.

Ministerie van Volkshuisvesting, Ruimtelijke Ordening en Milieubeheer (VROM) (2002) *Vijfde Nota over de Ruimtelijke Ordening 2000/2020, Ruimte maken, ruimte delen*, PKB deel 3: kabinetsstandpunt. The Hague: Ministerie van VROM.

Ministerie van Volkshuisvesting, Ruimtelijke Ordening en Milieubeheer (VROM) (2004) *Nota Ruimte, Ruimte voor Ontwikkeling*, deel 3: kabinetsstandpunt. The Hague: Ministerie van VROM.

Ministerie van Volkshuisvesting, Ruimtelijke Ordening en Milieubeheer (VROM) (2005) *Nota Ruimte, Ruimte voor Ontwikkeling*, deel 4: tekst na parlementaire instemming. The Hague: Ministerie van VROM.

Ministry of Housing, Spatial Planning and the Environment (2001) *Summary: Making Space, Sharing Space*. The Hague: Ministerie van VROM.

Mueller, B. (2001) Urban Networks and Polycentric Spatial Development in Europe – the Case of Germany, *EUREG*, 9, pp. 40-46.

Parr, J.B. (2002) Agglomeration economies: ambiguities and confusions, *Environment and Planning A*, 34, pp. 717-731.

Parr, J.B. (2004) The Polycentric Urban Region: A Closer Inspection, *Regional Studies*, 38, pp. 231-240.

Pred, A. (1977) *City-Systems in Advanced Economies*. London: Hutchinson.

Priemus, H. (1994) Planning the Randstad: Between Economic Growth and Sustainability, *Urban Studies*, 31, pp. 509-534.

Priemus, H. and P. Hall (2004) Multifunctional Urban Planning of Mega-City Regions, *Built Environment*, 30, pp. 338-349.

Roberts, M., T. Lloyd-Jones, B. Erickson and S. Nice (1999) Place and Space in the Networked City: Conceptualizing the Integrated Metropolis, *Journal of Urban Design*, 4, pp. 51-66.

Sassen, S. (1991) *The Global City*. Princeton, NJ: Princeton University Press.

Sassen, S. (2001) *The Global City*, 2nd edition. Princeton, NJ: Princeton University Press.

Sassen, S. (ed) (2002) *Global Networks, Linked Cities*. London: Routledge.

Scott, A.J. (1998) *Regions and the world economy, the coming shape of global production, competition and political order*. Oxford: Oxford University Press.

Storper, M. (1995) The resurgence of regional economies, ten years later: the Region as a Nexus of Untraded Interdependencies, *European Urban and Regional Studies*, 2, pp. 191-221.

Taylor, P.J. (2003) *World City Network: a Global Urban Analysis*. London: Routledge.

Turok, I. and N. Bailey (2004) The Theory of Polynuclear Urban Regions and its Application to Central Scotland, *European Planning Studies*, 12, pp. 371-389.

Westin, L. and A. Östhol (1994) Functional Networks, Infrastructure and Regional Mobilization, in: L. Lundqvist and O. Persson (Eds) *Northern Perspectives on European Integration*, pp. 43-57. Stockholm: NordREFO.

Yeh, A.G.O. (2001) Hong Kong and the Pearl River Delta: Competition or Co-operation?, *Built Environment*, 27, pp. 129-145.

Zonneveld, W. and F. Verwest (2005) *Tussen droom en retoriek, de conceptualisering van ruimte in de Nederlandse planning*. Rotterdam/The Hague: NAi Uitgevers/Ruimtelijk Planbureau.

2 Polycentric urban regions and the quest for synergy:

Is a network of cities more than the sum of the parts?

Meijers, E. (2005) Polycentric Urban Regions and the Quest for Synergy: Is a Network of Cities More than the Sum of the Parts?, in: *Urban Studies*, 42 (4), pp. 765-781.

Abstract

Polycentric urban regions, or urban networks, are often associated with the notion of synergy, the assumption being that the individual cities in these collections of distinct but proximally-located cities relate to each other in a synergetic way, making the whole network of cities more than the sum of its parts. Drawing on economic network theories, an analysis of the presence of synergy is carried out for the Randstad region in the Netherlands, which is often considered a classic example of a polycentric urban region. The analysis focuses on the synergy-mechanisms of co-operation and in particular complementarity. The results are mixed. In terms of co-operation, the Randstad has become more synergetic. However, less complementary economic roles of the cities caused a reverse effect.

2.1 Introduction

Interest in polycentric urban regions has increased rapidly during the last decade. This can be partly explained by the emerging belief that regions in general are becoming the most important spatial level of international territorial competition. In addition, polycentric urban regions are believed to be the next stage in the expansion of urban living space, particularly in densely populated countries or regions. The daily urban space of actors would not only cover the city, its suburbs and its surrounding rural area, but extends to include other cities as well. In polycentric urban regions, cities seem to have coalesced in functional and morphological terms into larger and more dispersed regional urban systems. In the literature, polycentric urban regions are often defined as collections of historically distinct and both administratively and politically independent cities located in close proximity and well connected through infrastructure (see Kloosterman and Lambregts, 2001). However, as the literature on polycentric urban regions is still limited and therefore rather unconsolidated (Bailey and Turok, 2001), a diversity of concepts is applied, which are largely synonymous with the polycentric urban region concept used here. Recent examples include 'multicore city-regions' (Westin and Östhol, 1994), 'network cities' (Batten, 1995), 'city networks'[1] (Camagni and Salone, 1993), or 'polynucleated metropolitan regions' (Dieleman and Faludi, 1998a). Moreover, in terms of ideas on spatial structure and interurban relationships, the polycentric urban region concept builds on older concepts such as the 'dispersed city' (Burton (1963), 'Megalopolis' (Gottmann, 1961) or the ideas of Stein and Mumford on 'The Regional City' (Stein, 1964).

The interest in polycentric urban regions has also increased among politicians and urban planners, as evidenced by their appearance as planning concepts in planning policies in a wide variety of European countries including Belgium ('urban networks'), Denmark (polycentric 'National Centres'), Estonia ('urban networks'), France ('*réseaux des villes*'), Germany ('*Metropolregionen*'; '*Städtenetze*'), Greece ('Twin poles'), Italy ('city networks'), Ireland ('linked gateways'), Lithuania ('Metropolis Vilnius-Kaunas'), the Netherlands ('urban networks'), Poland ('*duopols*') and Switzerland ('*vernetzte Städtesystem*'). Interestingly, planning policy concepts referring to polycentric urban regions often make use of the network metaphor. This is by no means a coincidence. The metaphor of the network emphasises the complex and strong relationships between the cities and as such the coherence and unity of the region. Moreover, networks are associated with economies of scale, critical mass and syn-

1 The term 'city networks' is generally applied to: systems of distant cities linked to each other by some functional characteristic; and, a system of proximal cities more or less located within each others' functional hinterland. Polycentric urban regions are city networks in the latter meaning.

ergy. Not surprisingly, the network metaphor has become part of the standard vocabulary of administrators, planners and other policy-makers promoting or otherwise dealing with polycentric urban regions. In particular the idea of synergy, or 'being more than the sum of the parts' is a central objective in many policies for polycentric urban regions. Examples are manifold, but can for instance be found in the Flanders Structural Outline (Ministerie van de Vlaamse Gemeenschap, 1997) which introduces the concept of the Flemish Diamond (see also Albrechts, 1998) and in the proposals for a new national spatial policy in the Netherlands in which the concept of 'urban networks' (for instance, the Randstad region) plays a prominent role (Ministerie van Volkshuisvesting, Ruimtelijke Ordening en Milieubeheer, 2004). The perhaps rather loose collection of cities in both regions would suddenly turn into a metropolis, and planners have suggested that the Randstad and Flemish Diamond could compete with the highest-level metropolitan agglomerations such as London and Paris, claiming that they provide economies of scale without incurring the costs or agglomeration diseconomies that these large metropolises entail.

This article addresses the more theoretical underpinning of this quest for synergy by policy-makers. Its aim is to explore whether there is a theoretical basis for assuming the presence of synergy in polycentric urban regions and, building on that, to develop a conceptual model to analyse the presence of synergy in polycentric urban regions. Subsequently, the presence of synergy in the Randstad region is explored. The structure of this article is as follows. First, an overview of economic network theories in relation to the principle of synergy is presented. Assuming that polycentric urban regions may be considered as a network in some sense, this may shed some light on how synergy within such regions can be achieved as the same network fundamentals and synergy principles are likely to apply. The third section addresses this issue of synergy in polycentric urban regions, resulting in a conceptual model to analyse the presence of synergy. Before applying this model to the Randstad in sections five and six in order to establish whether there is synergy developing, the fourth section introduces this 'prime' or 'classic' example of a polycentric urban region (Hohenberg and Lees, 1985; Batten, 1995).

2.2 Synergy in networks

The concept of networks is strongly linked to the notion of synergy. The aim of this section is to present some fundamental knowledge on network synergies, drawing on recent analysis of synergy in economic theory. The networks considered in these analyses are mainly networks between firms, transport networks and communication networks.

The word 'synergy' comes from the Greek (syn+ergos) and refers to a situation in which the effect of two or more co-operating or combined bodies or functions is larger than the sum of the effects each body or function alone can achieve. Synergy is often popularly formulated as 1 + 1 > 2, which, however, emphasises well that synergy can be expressed as the rise in performance of a network through efficient and effective interaction. Although widely used in economic theory, synergy is a rather fuzzy concept as it hides different mechanisms from which synergy is derived. Capello and Rietveld, analysing the synergy-concept in a variety of economic theories on micro-, meso- and macro-level arrive at three distinct meanings:

- 'Synergy means that when two or more actors co-operate, there is a positive result for both of them;
- synergy means that when co-operative behaviour is implemented in order to exploit complementarity in the production of a particular good, advantages are obtained by economic actors taking place in a group;
- synergy means that when individuals or firms 'voluntarily and non-voluntarily' are part of a group, externalities may be present and exploited by these individuals or groups in conducting their economic activity' (Capello and Rietveld, 1998:64).

The presence of one of these three synergy-releasing mechanisms - co-operation, complementarity or externality - combined with network behaviour generates synergy and hence economic benefits for the actors.

Next to these different mechanisms, the type of network is also relevant. Different synergy-mechanisms play a role in the various types of networks. Networks in general are made up of nodes (cities, households, firms, organisations, individuals), linkages between the nodes (infrastructure, relationships, ties), flows (people, goods, information, capital etc.) and meshes.

Networks can be labelled as being of the 'club' type or of the 'web' type (Capineri and Kamann, 1998). In club networks, actors share a common objective, activity or service, while also having parallel interests and transaction-chains. A classic but telling example is the tennis club. Members of such a club cannot afford the common objective – facilities for tennis – on their own, but by organising themselves they can. More members lead to positive externalities such as lower membership fees or extended opening hours. Negative externalities arise, however, when all members want to play tennis at the same time. Web networks, on the other hand, are characterised by different activities of the actors. These are complementary instead of similar and are linked in a serial way. A typical example is a chain of enterprises or business units each undertaking a certain phase in the production of a product.

Distinguishing between club and web networks is relevant as synergy in both networks is achieved in different ways. In club networks so-called 'horizontal synergy' can be achieved; in web networks, 'vertical synergy'. In the case of horizontal synergy, the synergy derives from co-operation leading to economies of scale and so-called positive network externalities. Characteristic of these economies of scale is that they apply only to participants in the network. Externalities are present when the costs of participating in the network are less than the benefits of the co-operation. The value of co-operation is well articulated by Capineri and Kamann (1998:42): 'Actors have the choice between independent 'stand alone' strategies where they perform all activities themselves usually at higher costs resulting in lower performance and strategies of co-operation which result in the transfer of activities and/or resources to other actors increasing a large range of types of dependencies but also improving their performance.'

Vertical synergy is the surplus value following from agglomeration or specialisation effects. Complementarity is the key synergy mechanism here. The synergy results from a specialisation process, redistributing resources and activities among the participating actors according to their competence. This means that the individual performance of actors improves as they can focus their efforts on their core activities, abandoning non-core activities unnecessarily absorbing energy (Capineri and Kamann, 1998). Classic network development theories also point to specialisation as the outcome of a process of rationalisation of the network structure once it has achieved a considerable level of complexity.

To summarise, synergy is achieved through the mechanisms of co-operation, complementarity and externalities linked to them. Co-operation leads to horizontal synergy possibly achieved in club type networks, complementarity to vertical synergy possibly achieved within web type networks. Externalities are present in both. They represent the most important economic advantage of network behaviour: 'It is ... a matter of exploiting scale economies in complementary relationships and synergic effects in co-operative activities, achieved through participation in the network' (Capello, 2000:1927).

2.3 Synergy in polycentric urban regions

Transferring the concept of synergy to cities does not seem too difficult. In fact, the first cities emerged because of synergy, developing from the advantages that arose from agglomeration economies. Living and working in cities entails advantages such as the supply of public services, specialised products and services, a large and diversified urban market and easy exchange and availability of information. The question, however, is how such agglomeration economies can also be organised in a network of cities.

This brief analysis of the synergy concept and some network fundamentals sheds some light on the way synergy can be achieved in polycentric urban regions. The cities making up a polycentric urban region can be considered the nodes in a network that is further made up by infrastructure, interurban relationships and flows. A city in itself is an accumulation of many other nodes such as households, firms, individuals, organisations, each one connected to other nodes by infrastructure, flows and interdependencies. So, in a polycentric urban region a multitude of other networks can be found, by no means restricted to the scale of the polycentric urban region. However, here we focus on a macro-level, thus on the polycentric urban region as a network of cities.

As it can be assumed that polycentric urban regions are networks indeed (there are nodes, linkages, flows and meshes), it is likely that the same basic knowledge of synergy in networks applies to these spatial phenomena.[2] Depending on whether polycentric urban regions are networks of the club or the web type, the same mechanisms will lead to synergy. This means that also in polycentric urban regions, synergy is established through the mechanisms of co-operation and complementarity (and externalities involved in both).

Two important questions remain. The first is whether a polycentric urban region is a club or a web type network. The second is how these two mechanisms should be given a translation relevant to spatial phenomena such as polycentric urban regions. Categorising a network of cities as a club or web type network seems a fruitless endeavour, given its complex nature. In fact, Capineri and Kamann (1998) state that, in real life, networks will have both club-type aspects and web-type dimensions. This is also the case with polycentric urban regions, which opens up different ways through which synergy can be established. Polycentric urban regions may be characterised as club networks when cities having similar characteristics join forces to achieve some kind of a common objective or common interests. This co-operation then generates economies of scale. Examples include for instance co-operation between cities performing similar economic roles, e.g. port cities or tourist cities. But cities can also co-operate when facing similar urban problems or challenges - for instance relating to segregation, a weak economic base, the need for efficient public transportation or waste disposal. On the other hand, polycentric urban regions resemble web networks when the individual cities perform different economic roles and host complementary urban facilities, activities, residential and working environments. Comparable to the distinction of club type networks and web type networks, is the classification of city networks by Camagni and Salone (1993). They refer to club-type urban networks as 'synergy networks', while web-type networks are labelled 'complementarity networks'. Although both club-type networks and web-type networks can be present in polycentric urban regions, it seems that web-type networks are of particular relevance for polycentric urban regions. With these, proximity matters in the sense that market areas overlap. Club-type networks can play a role, but they are also important in networks among distant cities (think for instance of club-

2 A comparable analogy between firm networks and urban networks is for instance drawn by Dematteis (1991), Emanuel (1990) and Camagni (1993).

type networks as METREX or Eurocities which build on common interests).

The second question to be answered is how co-operation and complementarity (and the externalities involved) should be interpreted in the context of polycentric urban regions to provide a meaningful framework for analysis. As mentioned before, our focus is on the network on a macro-level in polycentric urban regions - that is, a network between the cities rather than between firms, organisations or persons located in these cities. Consequently, co-operation is interpreted as co-operation between cities. Public administration tends to be organised in a territorial hierarchy. However, many spatial issues these days call for an approach that is formulated and implemented at multiple scales and across several administrative tiers. Additionally, an increasing number of spatial issues are, or preferably should be, addressed through a governance rather than a governmental mode. This requires the involvement of multiple public, private and organised interest groups, thereby taking into account that different issues call for different alliances with different spatial competencies and different life spans (see Boelens, 2000). Seen from this perspective, a focus on co-operation between cities seems too narrow. What is needed is regional organising capacity - that is, the ability to regionally co-ordinate developments through a more or less institutionalised framework of co-operation, debate, negotiation and decision-making in pursuit of regional interests in which a multitude of public and private stakeholders participate (Meijers and Romein, 2003). The externalities that may arise depend on the utilisation and functioning of such frameworks. Synergy requires a high level of interaction which will generate the necessary network cohesion to make up for the increased interdependency (see Capello and Nijkamp, 1993). Moreover, actors must be willing and able to adjust their internal profile and external behaviour. Free-rider behaviour is to be avoided. To establish whether synergy has developed, we need to consider the extent to which such frameworks are present in polycentric urban regions.

Though some previous work on conceptualising 'complementarity' as an interurban relationship has been done (Ullmann, 1956; Lambooy, 1969; Camagni and Salone, 1993), the concept has remained rather vague, despite its increasingly frequent, but often casual, appearance in both academic writings and policy documents. This lack of conceptual clarity probably explains why the concept has so far not been empirically analysed.

In urban regions, complementarity refers to the specific nature of a relationship between two or more relatively similar activities or places. 'Activities' include economic activities, such as commercial services, or urban facilities such as education, culture and medical care. 'Places' on the other hand refer to business milieus or residential milieus. As places make up cities and most activities take place within cities, it is also expedient to refer at a macro-level to cities complementing each other. For activities and places (or indirectly cities) to be complementary, they need to satisfy two important preconditions relating to supply and demand:

1. There must be differentiation in the supply of activities and/or places;
2. The geographical markets of demand for these activities or places must at least partly overlap.

To give some examples, two universities are complementary if they offer different academic education, while they are at the same time recruiting their students from more or less the same region. Similarly, two hospitals are complementary when they provide for different medical specialisations, or specialise in different kinds of treatment – for instance, standardised routine operations versus specialised knowledge-intensive care whilst serving more or less the same region. Two or more residential areas are complementary when they offer different residential milieus, thus providing alternatives to match the different preferences of a regional population (see Musterd and Van Zelm, 2001). At a macro-level, two cities are complementary when one specialises in, for instance, financial services and the other one in transportation and logistical services, each also providing these services to businesses or citizens located in the other city.

Complementarity often leads to spatial interaction. In fact, Ullmann (1956), who describes complementarity as differentiation, argues that complementarity is the main explanation for the development of spatial interaction. Similarly, Batten (1995) states that links between the cities in a polycentric urban region (or 'network city' as he terms it) are forged on the basis of complementary functions rather than on the basis of distance or demand thresholds. However, mere complementarity does not suffice for spatial interaction to occur. Following Stouffer (1940), Ullmann (1956) points to the role of intervening opportunities (intervening sources of supply), as well as the role of transferability (the costs of interaction) in determining whether or not spatial interactions arise from complementarity. So, spatial interactions only partly reveal the complementarity relationships present.

One of the ideas behind the polycentric urban region concept is that it is not one city that provides a complete array of economic functions, urban facilities or residential and business environments, but rather the whole system of cities within a region. Such a situation would provide for externalities. When two cities complement each other, then the citizens and companies in one place can take advantage of the various functions the other city has to offer. These functions can then be more specialised, as the demand market on which they build is larger given the overlapping of hinterlands. In such a way, companies, citizens and tourists can choose from a larger, more specialised and diverse collection of urban functions (public services, facilities, business services), businesses milieus and residential milieus. In other words, complementarity is strongly linked to agglomeration economies.

To sum up, synergy in polycentric urban regions is generated through:

- co-operation (regional organising capacity or frameworks for co-operation

and their functioning leading to horizontal synergy);
- complementarity (differentiation in the economic roles of cities, in urban facilities, in business and residential milieus coupled with a regional demand leading to vertical synergy).

In the next section, this conceptual model will be applied to the Randstad region in order to establish whether there is synergy present and developing.

2.4 The Randstad: Is it more than the sum of the parts?

The Randstad provides an excellent case for analysing the extent of synergy in a polycentric urban region, not only because many authors have claimed that it is a classic stereotype of such a network of cities (see for instance Stein, 1964; Hohenberg and Lees, 1985; Batten, 1995), but also because several authors have suggested the presence of synergy. For instance, Camagni and Salone (1993) refer to the Randstad as an example of a complementary network made up of specialised and complementary centres. This is fully endorsed by Van der Knaap (1994) who states that in the Dutch context there seems to be a dominance of complementary networks, based on vertical integration, spatial specialisations and complementary urban centres. This would be particularly exemplified in the Randstad, where it is mainly expressed in the relations between the larger and smaller cities. After briefly introducing the Randstad region, we will analyse whether such claims can be based on empirical evidence.

The Randstad is the horseshoe-shaped urban constellation in the western part of the Netherlands (see Figure 2.1). The Dutch word 'Rand' means 'rim' and refers to the position of the Randstad encircling a green open area called the Green Heart. Seven million people live in the Randstad (44% of the Dutch population) and 45% of the national employment is located on what is less than 20% percent of Dutch territory. The anchors of the Randstad are formed by the four largest cities of the Netherlands: Amsterdam, Rotterdam, The Hague and Utrecht. Together with some dozens of other medium-sized and smaller cities and the absence of one predominant centre, the Randstad can be characterised as a stereotypical polycentric urban region. This polycentric pattern is basically inherited from the past, as fragmented political and administrative structures have prevailed in this area (in fact, in a large part of North West Europe) for centuries (Dieleman and Faludi, 1998b). However, the Randstad, as it is nowadays, is also the result of urban and regional planning, being, with its counterpart the Green Heart, at the core of Dutch planning policies since the 1950s (Zonneveld, 1991; Faludi and Van der Valk, 1994). A common division of the Randstad is into a North Wing (including Amsterdam, Utrecht and surrounding cities) and a South Wing (The Hague, Rotterdam and surrounding cities). Suggestions have been made that these two wings provide a more accurate definition of coherent urban regions than does the Randstad (Van der Laan, 1998; Kloosterman and Lambregts, 2001).

The Randstad region still dominates in Dutch planning. The proposals for a new national spatial policy introduce the concept of 'urban networks' and the Randstad is the most important one (Ministerie van Volkshuisvesting, Ruimtelijke Ordening en Milieubeheer, 2004). In order to increase the Randstad's competitiveness, emphasis is put on the need for synergy. This pursuit of synergy is also expressed by several other networks of relevant actors in the Randstad. For instance, the Delta Metropolis Association (see also next section) states as the first guiding principle for the development of the Randstad: 'In a European perspective, the development of the Delta Metropolis is aimed at the achievement of synergy in the activities of the people living there; more synergy is possible and needed in the light of social, economic and cultural activities and efforts aimed at a sustainable environment'[3] (Delta Metropolis Association, 2000:1). And, the 'Projectgroep Randstadinbreng Vijfde Nota' in which several provinces, regional authorities and the major cities in the Randstad were represented, has presented as a first major administrative outline that: 'The urbanised western part of our country needs a quality leap towards a Blue Green Delta Metropolis. This must be seen in the context of the pursuit to let the Randstad be more than the sum of the parts, in order to take a competitive position in Europe. Co-operation and fine-tuning between networked cities, each having their own specialties, and the wetlands of the Green Heart will give the Randstad as a whole added value and will increase the quality of life. The necessary increase in quality requires an extended support for facilities and amenities, distinct profiling of areas and an increase in diversity' (Bureau Regio Randstad, 2001:6).

The following sections present the results of an explorative analysis of synergy in the Randstad, addressing co-operation and complementarity. Most attention, however, will be paid to the synergy mechanism of complementarity for two reasons. First, it was argued that, compared to co-operation, this mechanism is most prominent in polycentric urban regions as proximity matters. Second, claims for the Randstad being a complementary network have been made (Camagni and Salone, 1993; Van der Knaap, 1994).

2.5 Co-operation or horizontal synergy in the Randstad

There are three administrative tiers in the Netherlands: national government, provinces and municipalities. The Randstad extends over four different prov-

3 'Delta Metropolis' is synonymous with 'Randstad'.

Figure 2.1 The Randstad

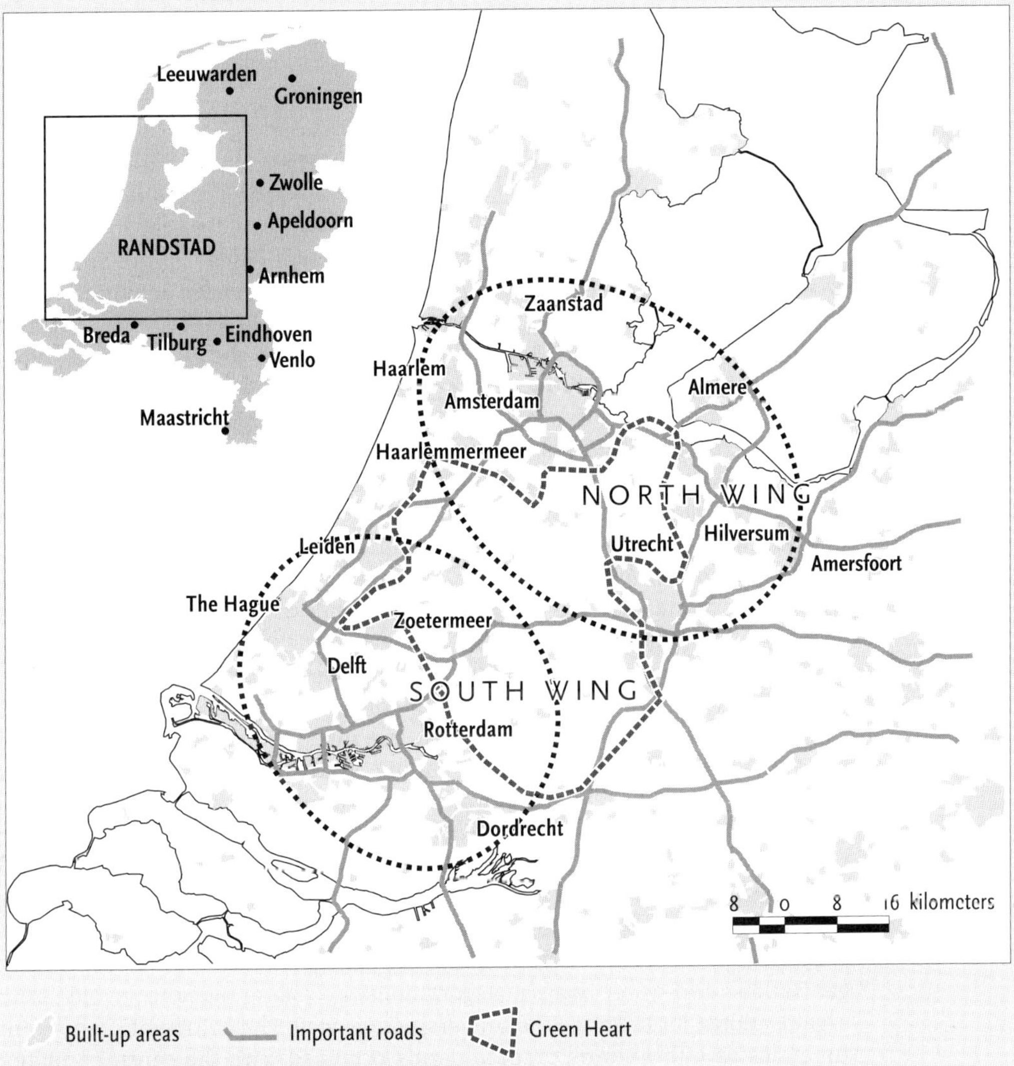

inces, which complicates the recognition of and dealing with the complex, multi-scalar interplay of spatial trends and forces in an integrated way. Although several attempts have been made to add a formal administrative tier, in particular at the supra-local scale, the existing framework has proved to be rather resistant to changes. It has become slowly apparent that multilevel governance requires co-operation across scales and across actors, including private actors.

In the Randstad, it seems that actors are increasingly aware of this need. A large variety of co-operation networks has emerged in this region in an attempt to overcome the lack of administrative layers between the municipal and provincial levels and between the provincial and national levels. Around the 4 largest Randstad cities, city-regions have been formed including the large cities and 10-20 adjacent municipalities. These co-operation platforms address issues such as transport, traffic, regional spatial development, housing, employment, economic affairs and youth welfare. Several more or less similar co-operation networks exist around smaller cities (Dordrecht, Leiden) or more or less homogeneous regions in terms of economic activities or location. At a higher spatial level, we find co-operation networks in the northern and southern wings of the Randstad. Compared with the North Wing, the co-operation in the South Wing is closer, probably due to a greater urgency for co-operation because of a lower level of economic development. The co-operation in the South Wing involves the municipalities of The Hague and Rotterdam, the province of South Holland and various co-operation platforms at the city-region level. Finally, also at the scale of the entire Randstad, two interesting co-operation networks have emerged in recent years. The first is a formal co-operation between the four provinces, four regional authorities (city-regions) and four major cities in the Randstad, together organising the 'Bureau Regio Randstad' (Randstad Agency). Their objectives are to foster a balanced and dynamic development of the western part of the Netherlands, the Randstad in particular, as an entity consisting of high-quality urban and rural environments and to strengthen the international competitiveness of the Randstad, in particular within Europe. Next to this formal co-operation between public actors, an informal co-operation platform has emerged: the Delta Metropolis Association. It was established in 2000 by twelve municipalities and four chambers of commerce from within the Randstad. Being an open network, the number of members has gradually grown and now also includes housing corporations, organisations of the agriculture and horticulture branches, an employer's organisation, the transport sector, environmental organisations and water boards. Negotiations are taking place to involve other organisations, for instance the universities, as well. The co-operation platform functions as a think-tank predominantly occupied with the central ambition to let the 'in principle yet present metropolis grow to full stature' (article 2 of the statutes of the Association). All in all, it can be typified as a lobby group for the interests of the Randstad region. Interestingly, all these co-operation networks were initiated by actors within the region, rather than dictated by a higher level of government.

The patchwork of co-operation networks in the Randstad provides for a considerable regional organising capacity in the Randstad. All these networks are examples of club networks as they share a common objective and have at least partly corresponding interests and together fund the organisation of the network. Thus synergy is likely to be achieved, although the development of externalities depends on the functioning of these often rather new co-operation networks. Interestingly, Capello (2000) has demonstrated the development of externalities for actors when participating in a co-operation network in an active and serious way. It needs to be said that this co-operation does not mean that the cities do not compete with each other. On the contrary, they have competed for centuries and will continue to contend in the future. However, the awareness that many issues call for a co-ordinated approach coupled with the idea that regions have become the principal geographic platform for competition (see for instance Storper, 1995; Scott, 1998) fuelled a reconsideration of the intra-regional interdependencies resulting in more co-operation. Interesting in this respect is that, at the level of the Randstad or its two wings, co-operation networks are formed between the larger cities, while the main competitors of these cities tend to be the nearby smaller (satellite) cities, who have profited from the process of selective outmigration of middle-class and higher-income households as well as economic activities (Van der Wouden and De Bruijne, 2001). Obviously, the co-operation networks in the Randstad still have to prove themselves, but some successes are already visible - for instance, the Randstad region office in Brussels which takes care of the region's interests in the European context, and the joint approach towards policy proposals, investment plans, etc. emanating from the national government. Perhaps the biggest success so far is that the Randstad region features prominently in spatial as well as in many sectoral national policies. Obviously, there is more horizontal synergy in the Randstad than there was before, even though this horizontal synergy is hard to quantify at this moment.

2.6 Complementarity or vertical synergy in the Randstad

The presence of complementarity in the Randstad has already been assumed by several authors (Camagni and Salone, 1993; Van der Knaap, 1994), although these assumptions lack strong empirical justification. We have seen that complementarity relates to differentiation in economic roles, urban facilities and business and residential environments. Moreover, a geographical overlapping of demand markets for these activities and places is also important. Consequently, analysing such a multi-faceted concept as complementarity is a complex undertaking. Here, the explorative analysis of the presence of complementarity in the Randstad is limited to one of these facets - namely the differentiation in economic roles, or economic profiles, of the main cities within the Randstad. Differentiation in economic roles also indicates to some extent the differentiation in business environments, as one city may provide better conditions for certain firms and this then becomes explicit in its economic profile. Economic profiles also present an indication of differentiation in urban facilities as these are part of a city's economic profile. Another reason for focusing on the macro level of economic roles of cities is that the extent of complementarity that is generally assumed to be present in the Randstad is usually linked to the division of labour between its main cities (see for example, Van der Wouden and De Bruijne, 2001). Of course, the need for selectivity here does not deny the fact that the issue of complementarity requires extended analysis and, consequently, this limits the significance of the results as regards the synergy derived from complementarity in the Randstad.

The economic profile of a city is made up by the number of jobs in that city classified by economic sector. For our analysis we used a dataset derived from the National Information System on Employment (LISA) database. This database is a registration of all the establishments in the Netherlands, including government and non-commercial organisations. An establishment in this database is defined as a location of a firm, organisation, institution or independent profession in which or from which an economic activity or independent liberal profession is being practiced by at least one employed person. Multi-establishment firms have separate recordings for each establishment. The economic activities are coded according to the European Union wide NACE Rev. 1 classification (*Nomenclature statistique des Activités économiques dans la Communauté Européenne*), which is, up to two-digits, similar to the ISIC Rev. 3.1 (International Standard Industrial Classification of all Economic Activities). The database has been updated annually since 1996. Our dataset contains the 1996 and 2002 data on the number of jobs classified according to two-digit NACE Rev. 1 classification of economic activities for the municipalities of Amsterdam, Rotterdam, The Hague and Utrecht. For reasons of comparison we also have datasets for the main cities in the North Wing (municipalities of Amsterdam, Haarlem, Zaanstad, Utrecht, Amersfoort, Almere, Haarlemmermeer and Hilversum) and South Wing (Rotterdam, The Hague, Leiden, Dordrecht, Zoetermeer and Delft).

In this paper correspondence analysis is used to analyse the differentiation in the economic roles of cities. Correspondence analysis is a technique to analyse the association between rows and columns of a table or matrix by representing the rows and columns as points in a low-dimensional Euclidean space (in practice, often a two-dimensional plot). Categories with similar distributions will be represented as points that are close in space, and categories that have very dissimilar distributions will be positioned far apart. For an extensive discussion of correspondence analysis, see Greenacre (1993) and Clausen (1998)[4]. Although often used as a tool to enable graphic interpretation of complex data, correspondence analysis also provides a single statistic that describes the extent of differentiation in the economic profiles of a group of cities. This statistic is called the total inertia. Total inertia is a measure of the extent to which the profile points are spread around a centroid, repre-

4 See Kloosterman and Lambregts (2001) for an earlier example of the application of correspondence analysis. Rather than analysing general economic profiles of cities, they focus on patterns of convergence in business start-up profiles of cities in the Randstad.

Table 2.1 Total inertia and complementarity ratios in the Randstad and spatial subdivisions in 1996 and 2002

	Total inertia		Complementarity ratio		
Polycentric urban region	1996	2002	1996	2002	Trend
Randstad (N=4)	0.170	0.148	5.7	4.9	- 12.9%
Randstad (N=14)	0.545	0.493	4.2	3.8	- 9.5%
North Wing (N=8)	0.489	0.440	7.0	6.3	- 10.0%
South Wing (N=6)	0.263	0.245	5.3	4.9	- 6.8%

N = Number of cities included

senting the average profile. The larger the distance of the category points to the centroid, the higher the inertia. The highest attainable inertia is equal to the dimensionality of the problem (in our case, the number of cities – 1). This maximum would be reached if all the cities have completely different economic profiles, whereas zero inertia is attained when they all have exactly the same economic profiles. In reality, values will be far from the maximum, as reaching the maximum value would imply - for example, that all schools are located in one city, all supermarkets in another one and all doctors in yet another one. In other words, cities have a large component of employment in non-tradeable economic activities. Correspondence analysis corrects for such activities in the sense that they do not, or hardly, contribute to the total inertia statistic. In order to enable a comparison of the inertia between polycentric urban regions, we defined a complementarity ratio for which we normalised the total inertia by dividing it by the maximum total inertia possible and multiplying this by 100, resulting in a value between 0 and 100.

Table 2.1 presents the results of our analysis, the total inertia and complementarity ratios for the Randstad and its North Wing and South Wing for 1996 and 2002. The table reveals clearly that the economic profiles of cities within the Randstad, or its South and North Wings, are becoming less differentiated. This trend towards more homogeneous economic roles for cities indicates a decreasing complementarity in terms of economic roles (on average, a decrease of nearly 10% in six years). The North Wing of the Randstad is the most complementary region, with a ratio of 6.3 in 2002. This is 29% higher than in its counterpart, the South Wing, and the Randstad as a whole when defined by the four cities. This is 66% higher than if the Randstad is defined using all the larger cities. However, the ratio in the North Wing is decreasing faster than in the South Wing, but not as fast as in the Randstad defined by the four largest cities.

One of the main advantages of correspondence analysis is that it graphically displays associations, thus enabling an easier interpretation of complex contingency tables. Here, we are interested in associating cities with economic activities (see Figure 2.2). The two dimensions displayed represent a reasonable 84.2 % of the total inertia. The two axes together indicate the origin (0.0), which resembles the average profile of the four cities. This plot requires careful interpretation. If two cities lie close together, then their economic profiles are more or less similar. The same condition applies to the economic activities. Economic activities lying close together are more or less similarly distributed between the cities. The distances between cities and economic activities are more complicated, since these are not defined as chi-square distances. All cities influence the location of an economic activity and, the other way around, all economic activities contribute to the location of a city. In general, cities and activities will be close to each other when the observed value for this pair of points in the table is larger than expected, and the distance will be large when the observed value is less than the expected value. For reasons of clarity, only those economic activities that contribute to at least 1% of the total inertia value are depicted. Economic activities that do not meet this threshold value are either insignificant in terms of the number of jobs, or because the distribution of jobs in this activity over the four cities is similar to the distribution of all jobs over these cities. This is for instance the case with retail trade, where the expected number of jobs in the four cities is more or less equal to the observed number.

In 2002, the three largest cities, Amsterdam, Rotterdam and The Hague seem to have relatively distinct profiles, while Utrecht has a more general and average profile and is, therefore, located closer to the origin. Still, Utrecht's economic profile is more similar to that of Amsterdam than to the other cities. Out of the origin it is possible to distinguish three axes in which a number of economic activities are grouped that are dominated by one of the three main cities. Amsterdam has a relatively dominant position in the commercial services sector, in particular in financial intermediation, Internet and communication technology, publishing and printing, recreation, culture and sports, as well as for hotels and restaurants. Rotterdam, on the other hand, holds a strong position in manufacturing and transport, undoubtedly related to its large port. This includes heavy industries such as the petrochemical and chemical industries, the manufacturing of fabricated metal products and of transport equipment. Not surprisingly, Rotterdam specialises in water transport and supporting and auxiliary transport activities. Finally, Rotterdam has relatively more jobs in the construction and public utilities sectors. The Hague, the seat of government, is particularly dominant in public administration. Moreover, it has a position in agriculture, but this seems predominantly due to the presence of a number of agricultural interest groups. The Hague shares, with Amsterdam and Utrecht, a strong position in activities of membership organisations and post and telecommunications. Utrecht is relatively more associated with wholesale trade and education. In general, it seems that there is a considerable division of labour between the three largest cities in the Randstad, each specialising in either commercial services (Amsterdam), manufacturing and transport (Rotterdam) or public administration (The Hague). The spread of economic activities over the four cities is to a large extent similar to the pattern observed for 1996.

Figure 2.3 presents the developments in the economic profile of the four

Figure 2.2 Cities associated with economic activities in the Randstad (N=4), 2002 (percentage of inertia explained: 84,2%)

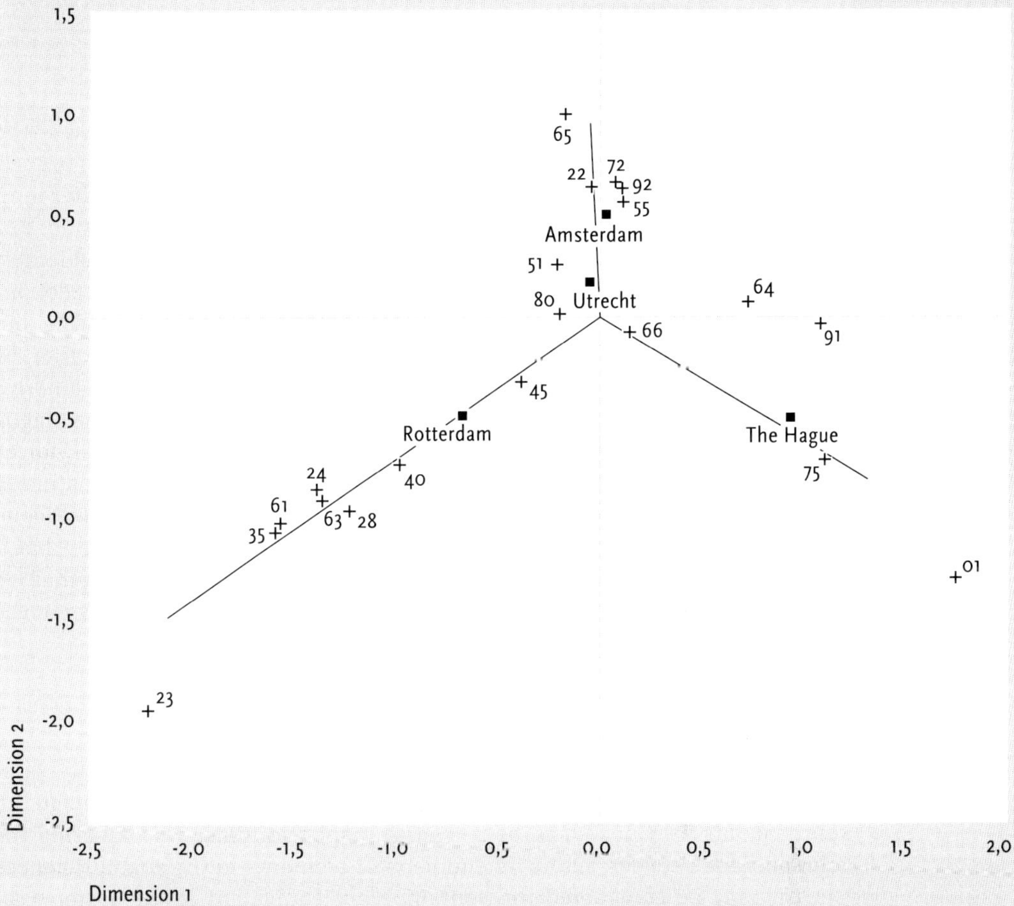

01 Agriculture, hunting and related service activities
22 Publishing, printing and reproduction of recorded media
23 Manufacture of coke, refined petroleum products and nuclear fuel
24 Manufacture of chemicals and chemical products
28 Manufacture of fabricated metal products
35 Manufacture of other transport equipment
40 Electricity, gas, steam and hot water supply
45 Construction
51 Wholesale trade and commission trade
55 Hotels and restaurants
61 Water transport
63 Supporting and auxiliary transport activities; travel agencies
64 Post and telecommunications
65 Financial intermediation, except insurance and pension funding
66 Insurance and pension funding
72 Computer and related activities
75 Public administration and defence; compulsory social security
80 Education
91 Activities of membership organisations n.e.c.
92 Recreational, cultural and sporting activities

main cities in the Randstad between 1996 and 2002. The origin here is the weighted average of the average economic profiles in 1996 and 2002.

Figure 2.3 provides an accurate picture of developments in the differentiation in economic profiles (roles) of the four main cities in the Randstad. Rotterdam accounts for the largest change in position as it became considerably less different in economic profile given its move towards the average economic profile. This could be due to the number of jobs in the manufacturing and transport sectors decreasing relative to other sectors. Alternatively, other cities may have seen a considerable increase in the number of jobs in economic activities associated with them. This is for instance the case for The Hague, which, contrary to Rotterdam, moved further away from the origin, indicating increased differentiation. The number of jobs in the public administration sector increased considerably in the 1996-2002 period. Similar to The Hague, Utrecht's economic role became more distinct, though trends indicate that it will converge with that of Amsterdam. Amsterdam's economic role remained more or less equally distinct. The overall conclusions regarding synergy in the Randstad will be presented in the conclusions.

2.7 Conclusions

The network metaphor first entered social sciences several decades ago. Recently, it has also proved to be a fruitful inspiration base for exploring the relationships between actors, phenomena or elements in the spatial sciences. Thus it may be considered the contemporary equivalent to the systems approach which, although still relevant, had its heyday in the 1970s and also directed research in a wide variety of fields of study. In urban and regional planning, the network metaphor has been increasingly applied to describe interurban relationships. Analysing the synergy concept in economic network theory and transferring the findings to spatial phenomena such as polycentric urban regions reveal that it is exactly these relationships between cities that determine whether or not synergy is present. In particular, it is the nature of these interurban relationships that is decisive when considering synergy. It was found that polycentric urban regions can indeed be more than the sum of their parts by means of co-operative and, in particular, complementary relationships and externalities arising from them.

The results of our explorative analysis of synergy in the Randstad are mixed. The first synergy mechanism, co-operation, seems to be increasingly present in the Randstad. The bottom-up establishment of both formal and informal frameworks for a regional co-ordination of regional issues and developments has led to more regional organising capacity than there was before. The wide variety of co-operating actors present in the two frameworks operating at the scale of the Randstad are even explicitly aiming for increased

Figure 2.3 Development in differentiation of economic roles of Randstad cities between 1996 and 2002 (percentage of inertia explained 79,4%)

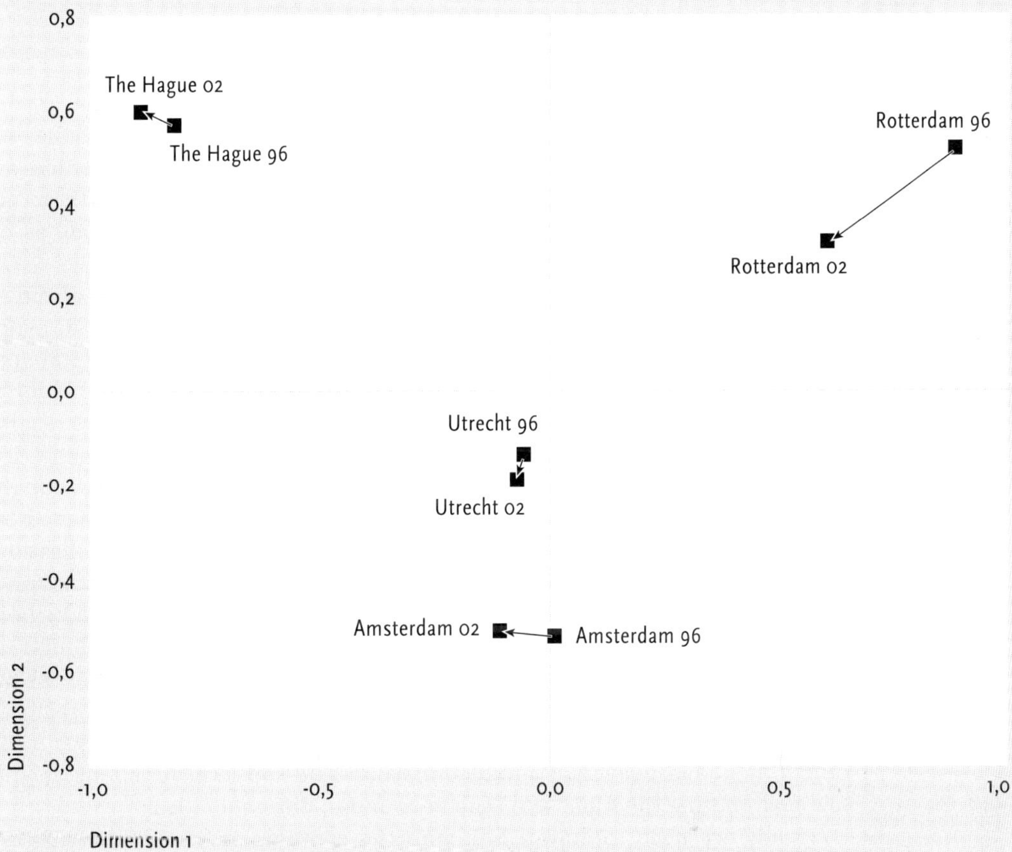

synergy. Although most partnerships at the moment do not yet have an extensive track record of successes, given their relatively recent establishment, it appears that these club-type networks provide much better conditions for achieving horizontal synergy than ever before. As such, it is likely that synergy has increased.

We argued that complementarity, the second synergy mechanism, is of particular relevance for polycentric urban regions. Our analysis here was limited to differentiation in the economic role performed by cities, which we inferred from the economic profile of cities within polycentric urban regions. The analysis revealed that the main cities in the Randstad perform distinct roles, each of them specialising in either commercial services, manufacturing and transport, public administration, or trade and education. At the same time, the extent of complementarity in economic roles diminished during the 1996-2002 period by almost 13%, leading to less synergy at the macro level of the cities in the Randstad. Following the common divide of the Randstad into a North Wing and a South Wing reveals that complementarity in the North Wing is substantially higher than in the South Wing. Whether or not the balance between both synergy-mechanisms is shifting to more or less synergy in the Randstad remains a crucial question. Answering it requires further research into other facets of complementarity at the micro level of certain activities and particular places, the extent to which differentiation in these activities and places is matched by a regional demand for them, as well as of the externalities present in the co-operation frameworks.

The decline in complementarity in terms of economic profiles of cities should be looked at in the proper perspective. Other research on developments in the sectoral composition of cities has shown that the sectoral specialisation of cities of all sizes has already been declining considerably for a long time (Duranton and Puga, 2003). From this viewpoint, our findings regarding the development in synergy through the mechanism of complementarity are perhaps not surprising nor as negative as they may seem. Interestingly, Duranton and Puga (2003) argue that cities are increasingly distinguished by their functional specialisation rather than by their sectoral specialisation. They demonstrate that, in US cities, headquarters and business services functions of manufacturing companies cluster in larger cities, whereas production functions cluster in smaller cities. Similar processes are likely to be found in the Randstad. Although the spread of sectoral economic activities over the region is becoming more homogeneous, it may well be that, within a sectoral economic activity, different functions (for instance, front-offices versus back-offices, headquarter versus production, high-skill top-level functions versus low-skill routine functions, etc.) can be found in different cities.

Finally, we need to draw a link with the contemporary and emerging debate on the changing spatial organisation of urbanised regions and in particular on the changing relations between cities. Whereas interurban relationships have long been defined in terms of hierarchy, it is increasingly assumed that these vertical Christaller-like type relationships are being replaced, or at least supplemented with more horizontal network-like relationships between cities such as complementarity and, at the institutional level, co-operation. This new model of spatial organisation is generally referred to as a network urban structure. From our analysis, it follows that the development of a network urban structure in urban regions is beneficial in terms of synergy as the horizontal network-like relationships between cities that build such a structure correspond exactly with the synergy-mechanisms.

Acknowledgement

The author would like to thank Hugo Priemus, Marjolein Spaans, Henny Coolen and Frans Dieleman for their helpful comments.

References

Albrechts, L. (1998) The Flemish Diamond: Precious Gem and Virgin Area, *European Planning Studies*, 6, pp. 411-424.

Bailey, N. and I. Turok (2001) Central Scotland as a polycentric urban region: useful planning concept or chimera?, *Urban Studies*, 38, pp. 697-715.

Batten, D.F. (1995) Network Cities: Creative Urban Agglomerations for the 21st Century, *Urban Studies*, 32, pp. 313-327.

Boelens, L. (2000) Inleiding, in: L. Boelens (Ed.) *Nederland Netwerkenland*, pp. 5-12. Rotterdam: NAi Uitgevers.

Bureau Regio Randstad (2001) *Naar een blauwgroene Deltametropool*. Utrecht: Bureau Regio Randstad.

Burton, I. (1963) A restatement of the dispersed city hypothesis, *Annals of the Association of American Geographers*, 63, pp. 285-289.

Button, K., P. Nijkamp and H. Priemus (Eds) (1998) *Transport Networks in Europe*. Cheltenham/Northampton: Edward Elgar.

Camagni, R. (1993) From city hierarchy to city networks: reflections about an emerging paradigm, in: T.R. Lakshmanan and P. Nijkamp (Eds) *Structure and change in the Space Economy: Festschrift in honour of Martin Beckmann*, pp. 66-87. Berlin: Springer Verlag.

Camagni, R. and C. Salone (1993) Network Urban Structures in Northern Italy: Elements for a Theoretical Framework, *Urban Studies*, 30, pp. 1053-1064.

Capello, R. (2000) The City Network Paradigm: Measuring Urban Network Externalities, *Urban Studies*, 37, pp. 1925-1945.

Capello, R. and P. Nijkamp (1993) *Measuring Network Externalities*, paper presented at the Nectar Cluster 2 Workshop, Certosa di Pontignano, Siena, 4-5 June.

Capello, R. and P. Rietveld (1998) The Concept of Network Synergies in Economic Theory: Policy Implications, in: K. Button, P. Nijkamp and H. Priemus (Eds) *Transport Networks in Europe*, pp. 57-83. Cheltenham/Northampton: Edward Elgar.

Capineri, C. and D.J.F. Kamann (1998) Synergy in Networks: Concepts, in: K. Button, P. Nijkamp and H. Priemus (Eds) *Transport Networks in Europe*, pp. 35-56. Cheltenham/Northampton: Edward Elgar.

Clausen, S-E. (1998) *Applied correspondence analysis: an introduction*, Sage University Papers Series on Quantitative Applications in the Social Sciences, 07-121. Thousand Oaks, CA: Sage.

Delta Metropolis Association (2000) *Hoofdlijnen ontwikkelingsconcept*. Delft: Vereniging Deltametropool.

Dematteis, G. (1991) Sistemi locali nucleari e sistemi a rete: un contributo geografico all'interpretazione delle dinamiche urbane, in: C.S. Bertuglia and A. la Bella (Eds) *I sistemi urbani, Vol. 1: Le teorie, il sistema e le reti*, pp. 417-441. Milan: Franco Angeli.

Dieleman, F.M. and A. Faludi (1998a) Polynucleated Metropolitan Regions in Northwest Europe: Theme of the Special Issue, *European Planning Studies*, 6, pp. 365-377.

Dieleman, F.M. and A. Faludi (1998b) Randstad, RhineRuhr and Flemish Diamond as One Polynucleated Macro-region, *Tijdschrift voor Economische en Sociale Geografie*, 89, pp. 320-327.

Duranton, G. and D. Puga (2003) *From sectoral to functional urban specialisation*, Center for Economic Policy Research Discussion Paper 2971.

Emanuel, C. (1990) Polimorfismo di imprese e di territorio: Una possibile convergenza disciplinare nellésame del caso italiano, *Rivista Geografica Italiana*, pp. 13-37.

Faludi, A. and A.G. van der Valk (1994) *Rule and Order: Dutch Planning Doctrine in the Twentieth Century*. Dordrecht: Kluwer Academic Publishers.

Gottmann, J. (1961) *Megalopolis, The urbanized Northeastern Seaboard of the United States*. New York: The Twentieth Century Fund.

Greenacre, M.J. (1993) *Correspondence analysis in practice*. London: Academic Press Limited.

Hohenberg, P.M. and L.H. Lees (1985) *The Making of Urban Europe: 1000-1950*. Cambridge, MA: Harvard University Press.

Kloosterman, R.C. and B. Lambregts (2001) Clustering of Economic Activities in Polycentric Urban Regions: The Case of the Randstad, *Urban Studies*, 38, pp. 717-732.

Knaap, G.A. van der (1994) *Ruimtelijke complexen en schaalspanning op de stedenring*, EGI-onderzoekspublikatie 19. Rotterdam: Erasmus Universiteit Rotterdam.

Laan, L. van der (1998) Changing Urban Systems: An Empirical Analysis at Two Spatial Levels, *Regional Studies*, 32, pp. 235-247.

Lambooy, J. (1969) City and city region in the perspective of hierarchy and complementarity, *Tijdschrift voor Economische en Sociale Geografie*, 60, pp. 141-154.

Meijers, E. and A. Romein (2003) Realizing potential: building regional organizing capacity in polycentric urban regions, *European Urban and Regional Studies*, 10, pp. 173-86.

Ministerie van de Vlaamse Gemeenschap (1997) *Ruimtelijk Structuurplan Vlaanderen. Integrale versie*. Brussel: Ministerie van de Vlaamse Gemeenschap.

Ministerie van Volkshuisvesting, Ruimtelijke Ordening en Milieubeheer (2004) *Nota Ruimte, Ruimte voor Ontwikkeling*, deel 3: kabinetsstandpunt. The Hague: Ministerie van VROM.

Musterd, S. and I. van Zelm (2001) Polycentricity, Households and the Identity of Places, *Urban Studies*, 38, pp. 679-696.

Scott, A.J. (1998) *Regions and the world economy, the coming shape of global production, competition and political order*. Oxford: Oxford University Press.

Stein, C.S. (1964) A regional pattern for dispersal, *Architectural Record*, September, pp. 205-206.

Storper, M. (1995) The resurgence of regional economies, ten years later: the Region as a Nexus of Untraded Interdependencies, *European Urban and Regional Studies*, 2, pp. 191-221.

Stouffer, S.A. (1940) Intervening Opportunities: A Theory Relating Mobility and Distance, *American Sociological Review*, 5, pp. 845-867.

Ullman, E.L. (1956) The Role of Transportation and the Bases for Interaction, in: W.L. Thomas (ed) *Man's Role in Changing the Face of Earth*, pp. 862-880. Chicago: The University of Chicago Press.

Westin, L. and A. Östhol (1994) Functional Networks, Infrastructure and Regional Mobilization, in: L. Lundqvist and O. Persson (Eds) *Northern Perspectives on European Integration*, pp. 43-57. Stockholm: NordREFO.

Wouden, R. van der and E. de Bruijne (2001) *De stad in de omtrek: problemen en perspectieven van de vier grootstedelijke gebieden in de Randstad*. The Hague: Sociaal en Cultureel Planbureau.

Zonneveld, W.A.M. (1991) *Conceptvorming in de ruimtelijke planning. Patronen en processen*. Amsterdam: Planologisch en Demografisch Instituut.

3 Clones or complements?

The division of labour between the main cities of the Randstad, the Flemish Diamond and the RheinRuhr Area

Meijers, E. (forthcoming), Clones or Complements? The division of labour between the main cities of the Randstad, the Flemish Diamond and the RheinRuhr Area. Accepted for publication in *Regional Studies*. To be published mid 2007.

Abstract

In the contemporary debate on the spatial organisation of urban regions much emphasis is put on the development of polycentric urban patterns on a variety of spatial scales. Polycentric development at the intra-urban scale of the polycentric city implies an unfolding of a spatial division of labour between the centres. This article analyses whether also on the inter-urban scale of polycentric urban regions such a trend towards complementarity can be found. Opposing trends occur, however, as the division of labour in service sector activities between the main cities of some prime examples of polycentric urban regions is diminishing.

3.1 Introduction

In the contemporary debate on the changing spatial organisation of urban regions much emphasis is put on the development of polycentric urban patterns. The concept of polycentricity basically means little more than the co-existence of a number of centres within a certain area and so can be applied to a wide variety of spatial scales. Polycentric urban patterns have been identified and conceptualised at the intra-urban scale and at the inter-urban scale (Kloosterman and Musterd, 2001a; Davoudi, 2003). An intra-urban polycentric urban pattern arises from the development of centres alongside the traditional inner city or central business district within a city region (a city and its smaller suburban satellites) and is labelled a 'polycentric city'. Nowadays, it is widely acknowledged that all post-industrial cities are in fact polycentric[1]. By polycentric urban patterns at the inter-urban scale, reference is made to regions in which a number of cities cluster together. These are often called polycentric urban regions: systems of historically distinct and administratively and politically independent cities located in close proximity and lacking a dominating city in political, economic, cultural and other aspects (Kloosterman and Lambregts, 2001). Though 'polycentric urban region' seems to have become one of the more common concepts for urban regions with these characteristics, a wide variety of more or less similar concepts is in circulation. Recent examples include 'city networks' (Camagni and Salone, 1993), 'multi-core city-regions' (Westin and Östhol, 1994), 'network cities' (Batten, 1995), or 'polynucleated metropolitan regions' (Dieleman and Faludi, 1998a). Several authors have suggested that the meaning of the concept of polycentricity differs between the intra-urban and inter-urban scale (Kloosterman and Musterd, 2001a; Davoudi, 2003). Kloosterman and Musterd (2001a) see four dimensions along which inter-urban polycentricity may be qualitatively different from intra-urban polycentricity: physical form, political entity; functional relationships and the economic dimension. In this paper, differences in functional relationships between the intra-urban level of the 'polycentric city' and the inter-urban level of 'polycentric urban regions' are explored.

In terms of functional relationships, Kloosterman and Musterd (2001a:627) argue that on the intra-urban scale '[t]he shift towards polycentricity in the context of one individual city implies an unfolding of a spatial division of labour where 'new' locations are being developed'. The balancing of agglomera-

1 Questions have been raised over whether the dominant form of the deconcentration of employment and urban functions indeed results in a clustering in centres, as some have found evidence, particularly in the US, for a dispersal over the urban territory in a non-centred way (Gordon and Richardson, 1996; Lang and LeFurgy, 2003). However, evidence for metropolitan areas in North West Europe justifies the term 'Polycentric City' as a process of 'concentrated deconcentration' rather than dispersal results in a polycentric structure (Halbert, 2004; Bogaerts *et al.*, 2005).

tive and dispersive forces by economic activities and urban functions has led to a more spatially specialised metropolitan layout incorporating many different types of centres (Roberts *et al.*, 1999, Hall, 2001). As each of them has some specific locational advantages, for instance relating to accessibility, rental prices, room for expansion etc., they together cater for the diversity in locational needs of these activities and functions. Though many of these centres are often labelled as *sub*centres, they are often the main centre in the region for the specific activities and functions found there. So, while a hierarchy remains, it is more appropriate to speak about a hierarchy between different locations in connection with a specific urban function or economic activity, rather than with a centre in general. This is a manifestation of a disconnection between the size and function of centres. The many different urban functions and economic activities each have their own hierarchy, which is reflected in different settlement patterns, the main centres of which often do not overlap, but rather tend to be spread over the variety of centres. Consequently a certain division of labour between the centres has developed (Halbert, 2004), leading to complementarity (Roberts *et al.*, 1999). On the higher scale of polycentric urban regions, Kloosterman and Musterd see two possible outcomes of further polycentric development. On the one hand, they speculate that a development similar to the development at the intra-urban level will take place, i.e. functional differentiation may be strengthened as cities specialise in specific urban functions, which they then provide for the entire region. On the other hand, the functional differentiation between the cities making up the polycentric urban region may erode, as the whole region becomes more of a homogeneous economic environment characterised as one large labour market or location for business. The first explanation has been accepted as the most likely outcome, for instance Hall (2001) suggests that within increasingly polycentric urban structures there is increasing specialisation, citing as an example the functional division of labour between the main cities of the Pearl River Delta region in China. So, as regards the dimension of functional relationships, the key issue is whether or not a division of labour is developing between centres or cities so that they increasingly complement each other.

Polycentric development processes at the intra-urban scale have been widely documented, for a recent analysis see for instance Halbert (2004). However, less is known about these processes at the inter-urban level. This paper explores whether we see a further division of labour also developing on the scale of polycentric urban regions. This question will be framed in a wider theoretical debate on the spatial organisation of polycentric urban regions, and in particular on the nature of the relationships between cities (Section 3.2). In Section 3.3 we present our analysis of these relationships on the inter-urban scale of polycentric urban regions. This includes details on methodology and data, as well as an introduction to our three case study regions, which are all prime examples of polycentric urban regions: the Randstad in the Netherlands, the Flemish Diamond in Belgium and the RheinRuhr Area in Germany. The results of the comparative analysis of the division of labour between the major cities of these regions are presented in Section 3.4. In the final section we compare our findings at the inter-urban level with polycentric urban development patterns at the intra-urban level.

3.2 Complementary relationships

In the contemporary debate on the spatial organisation of urban regions much emphasis is put on the nature of the functional relationships between the centres of urban regions. It is debated whether or not we are witnessing a transformation in spatial structure that can be labelled 'from hierarchy to network'. The pattern of centres within a city would then be increasingly less characterised by a hierarchy with the traditional downtown centre at the top and a number of subcentres. Often it is questionable whether subcentres are really that 'sub'. On a higher spatial scale, polycentric urban regions also seem to be at odds with the traditional Christallerian urban pattern emphasising hierarchical relationships (Camagni, 1993; Capello, 2000). The clustering of more or less similar-sized cities close together and the lack of a clear hierarchy between them seems to provide a completely different urban pattern. It has been suggested that this pattern is following a 'network model', which conflicts with the central place model (Batten, 1995; Van der Knaap, 2002). The unfolding of a division of labour between centres or cities in a region could be considered as a manifestation of the development of complementary relationships between them. Such complementary relationships are a key characteristic of this 'network model' of spatial organisation, the others being the overlapping of the functional hinterlands of cities resulting in functional integration and size neutrality, that is a relative disconnection between size and function of a city. The latter means that the population number of a city no longer determines its basis for activities and functions. Higher order functions can thus be found in cities that are lower-ranked in terms of size, and the other way around, a city may host a set of functions and activities that are of less significance than one would expect from its size. Together, these network characteristics lead to a diffused criss-cross pattern of spatial interactions. So, our question of whether a division of labour is developing is in part similar to the question of whether polycentric urban regions are characterised by a network model of spatial organisation, as has been assumed by Camagni and Salone (1993) and Van der Knaap (1994), who point to the Randstad as an example. Policy-makers also assume the presence of such a network model, as can be seen from the labelling of polycentric urban regions in strategic regional development policies, for instance in Belgium ('urban networks'), Estonia ('urban networks'), France ('réseaux de villes'), Germany ('Städtenetze'), Italy ('reti di città'), the Netherlands ('urban networks') and Switzerland ('vernetzte Städtesystem').

From a theoretical standpoint, however, a polycentric urban region is not necessarily an urban network. It makes sense to distinguish between both concepts. A polycentric urban region can be identified more or less by structural characteristics such as the location of its cities relative to each other and their size distribution (see Kloosterman and Lambregts, 2001; Parr, 2004). Urban networks could be considered an advanced sort of polycentric urban region. Polycentric urban regions also qualify for the label urban network when relational characteristics as described by the network model of spatial organisation have developed. So, to theoretically justify the label urban network, there should be a certain minimum extent of functional integration, of a relative disconnection between size and function as well as of complementarity.

Though some previous work on conceptualising 'complementarity' has been done (Ullmann, 1956; Lambooy, 1969; Camagni and Salone, 1993), it has remained a rather vague concept despite its increasingly frequent, but often casual appearance in both academic writings and policy documents. Here, we define complementarity as a result of supply and demand. For centres or cities to be complementary, they need to satisfy two important preconditions:

1. There must be differentiation between the centres or cities in terms of urban functions or activities taking place in the centre or city.[2]
2. The geographical markets of demand for these urban functions/activities or places must at least partly overlap. This means that mere differentiation does not suffice. The urban functions/activities in one centre or city should provide services to business or households also making use of functions/activities in other centres. Or, at the city level, activities in one city should provide their services also to businesses or citizens located in the other city.

To a certain extent both preconditions are linked, as interaction is likely to result from differentiation, which then leads to complementarity (Ullmann, 1956; Batten, 1995). However, not all differentiation leads to interaction because of intervening opportunities (intervening sources of supply) and the costs of interaction (Ullmann, 1956). Moreover, the scale on which the interaction takes place varies according to the multiple scales on which economic activities or urban functions operate.

The benefits of complementarity are linked to what Alonso (1973) referred to as 'borrowed size'. When two cities complement each other, then the citi-

2 Another source of differentiation that we do not elaborate on in this paper relates to differences in places, e.g. the working environment or living environment the centre or city provides (see also Musterd and Van Zelm, 2001).

zens and companies in one place can take advantage of the consumer and business services the other city has to offer. These functions can then be more specialised, as the demand market on which they build is larger given the overlapping of hinterlands. In other words, complementarity is linked to agglomeration economies, though, given the physical separation of the urban centres and of the firms involved, such advantages are more appropriately described as 'regional externalities' (Parr, 2004).

3.3 The analysis of complementarity

Our analysis of complementary relationships focuses on service sector activities of the main cities within three polycentric urban regions. This includes business services as well as public services. In 1999, 66% of all jobs were in the service sector in the RheinRuhr Area, while this number was 80.8% for the Randstad and 70.5% and 78.4% for the Antwerp and Brussels functional urban regions respectively (IAURIF, 2001). It could be hypothesised that such services, e.g. financial services, transportation and logistical services, education facilities etc., in one place may have a function for businesses and households in other places as well. This is less evident for the primary (agriculture, fishing etc.) and in particular secondary (manufacturing) sectors, as, in general, these are often relatively more connected to national or international markets rather than regional markets. Furthermore, our analysis focuses on the first criterion for cities to be complementary, namely differentiation on the supply side. Given the strong link between differentiation and interaction, this may also indirectly reveal more about the second criterion of overlapping demand markets, even though this second criterion is not further explored here. Data is also not available to establish the extent to which each and every service sector examined functions on a regional scale indeed. However, analyses for the producer services sector in one of our case study regions, the Randstad, revealed an intricate web of relationships spanning the whole Randstad area (Meijers, 1999) and beyond, as polycentric urban regions can by no means be defined as single, closed functional units. Rather they should be considered as open and multilayered complexes of nodes, networks, flows and interactions at global, regional and local scales (Albrechts, 2001). So, even when differentiation results in spatial interaction, this does not necessarily mean that this interaction takes place on the regional level of polycentric urban regions. However, our choice to focus on the service sector was also prompted by the assumption that these may operate relatively more on this regional scale than other sectors. Still, it may be more appropriate to speak of an analysis of *potential* complementarity, as we do not know the extent to which it has materialised in reality.

Figure 3.1 The Randstad, Flemish Diamond and RheinRuhr Area

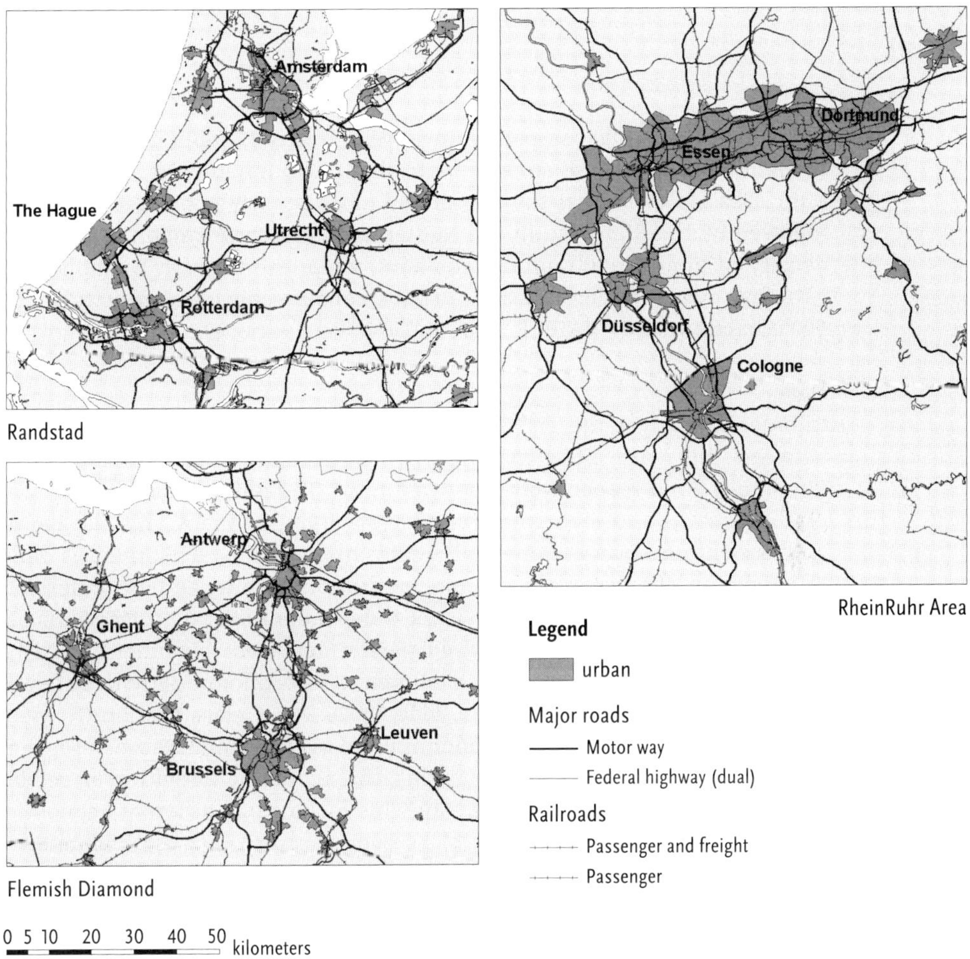

Case study regions

The Randstad, Flemish Diamond and RheinRuhr Area (see Figure 3.1) are all often cited as archetypical examples of polycentric urban regions and have therefore been selected as case study regions. They probably do not need much introduction given their currency in the literature.[3] It is exactly the comparison of these three regions that may put findings for individual regions into the right perspective.

The three regions have all been conceptualised as relevant functional entities by their respective governments, for strategic policies trying to enhance

3 The reader is referred to special issues of: *European Planning Studies* by Dieleman and Faludi, 1998b, 6 (4); *Urban Studies* by Kloosterman and Musterd, 2001b, 38 (4); *European Planning Studies* by Priemus, Zonneveld and Faludi, 2004, 12 (3), as well as a collection edited by Meijers *et al.*, 2003.

national and regional competitiveness. With nearly 12 million inhabitants and a population density of slightly more than 1000 inhabitants/km^2, the RheinRuhr Area in Germany is the largest and most densely populated conurbation, followed by the Randstad in the Netherlands (nearly 7 million inhabitants, a density of almost 1000 inhabitants/km^2), while the Flemish Diamond in Belgium has over 5 million inhabitants but a considerably lower density of nearly 600 inhabitants/km^2 (IAURIF, 2002, and own calculations).

Data

In order to analyse the division of labour in commercial and public services between the main cities making up the Randstad, Flemish Diamond and RheinRuhr Area respectively, use was made of databases registering all the establishments and the number of people working in them. This also includes government and non-commercial organisations. An establishment is defined as a location of a firm, organisation, institution or independent profession in or from which an economic activity or independent liberal profession is being practiced by at least one employed person. Multi-establishment firms have separate recordings for each establishment. The economic activities are coded according to the European Union wide NACE Rev. 1 classification (Nomenclature statistique des Activités économiques dans la Communauté Européenne). Use was made of datasets presenting the economic activities of establishments at the two-digit level of detail. This includes 29 different economic activities in the commercial and public services sector.[4] Each establishment was given a weighting based on the number of people employed in it.

For the Randstad, a dataset presenting data on the municipal level was derived from the National Information System on Employment (LISA) database for the years 1996 and 2002. The dataset for the Flemish Diamond was provided by the National Office for Social Security in Brussels (NOSS). This semi-governmental body is responsible for the financing of social security for employees. The data covers the municipal level for the years 1996 and 2002. The dataset for the RheinRuhr Area region was provided by an institution also involved in social security, the Institut für Arbeitsmarkt- und Berufsforschung and produced by its Regionaldirektion NRW der Bundesagentur für Arbeit. Data was available at the level of 'Kreisfreie Städte' for the five years 1998-2002. Due to divergent delimitations of functional urban areas, or the absence thereof (Flemish Diamond), our data concerns solely the central cities.

Method

Correspondence analysis was used to analyse the differentiation in the service

4 Code 22 'Publishing, printing and reproduction of recorded media', officially part of the manufacturing sector, is also included.

sector profiles of the cities within a polycentric urban region. Correspondence analysis is a technique to analyse the association between rows and columns of a table or matrix by representing the rows and columns as points in a low-dimensional Euclidean space (in practice often a two-dimensional plot). Categories with similar distributions are represented as points that are close in space, and categories that have very dissimilar distributions are positioned far apart. For an extensive discussion of correspondence analysis see Greenacre (1993) and Clausen (1998). Though often used as a tool to enable the graphic interpretation of complex data, correspondence analysis also provides a single statistic that describes the extent of differentiation in the service sector profiles of a group of cities. This statistic is called the total inertia. Total inertia is a measure of the extent to which the profile points are spread around a centroid, which represents the average profile. The larger the distance of the category points to the centroid, the higher the inertia. The highest attainable inertia is equal to the dimensionality of the problem (in our case the number of cities – 1). This maximum would be reached if all the cities host completely different service activities, whereas zero inertia is attained when they all have exactly the same commercial and public services within their boundaries. In reality, values will be far from the maximum, as reaching the maximum value would imply, for example, that all schools are located in one city, all supermarkets in another one, and all banks in yet another one. In other words, cities have a large component of employment in non-tradeable economic activities.

Provided that the contingency tables for the Randstad, Flemish Diamond and RheinRuhr Area have a similar format (the same number of cities in the rows and the same categories of service sector activities in the columns), the total inertia-statistic of the three regions provides for a comparable measure of differentiation. This implies that the same number of cities for these three regions had to be selected. Being the smallest region in terms of the number of cities included, the Flemish Diamond sets the maximum. Using a threshold value of 80,000 inhabitants in 2000, this region includes four cities, which also happen to be the corners of the 'diamond': Brussels, Ghent, Antwerp, Leuven. This also matches well with the Randstad region, where it is very common to identify four main cities (Amsterdam, Rotterdam, The Hague and Utrecht), which are distinctively larger than the others. We could have used a lower threshold for the Flemish Diamond to include two or three remaining smaller cities, but this would make the selection in the Randstad region quite arbitrary, as there is a much larger number of similar-sized cities in the league below the four main cities. Though identifying four main cities in the RheinRuhr Area is less obvious, for reasons of comparison a selection can also be made of four cities that have the most inhabitants and are characterised by the highest centrality: Cologne, Düsseldorf, Essen and Dortmund.

3.4 The division of labour in the Randstad, the Flemish Diamond and the RheinRuhr Area

A comparison in time of the total inertia statistic, presenting the extent to which the cities differ from each other in terms of service sector activities, leads to some remarkable conclusions.[5] Figure 3.2 presents the development of differentiation and thus the potential complementarity for the three regions.

The first conclusion is that the extent of existing and/or potential complementarity in the Randstad and Flemish Diamond is considerably higher than in the RheinRuhr Area. So, as regards service sector activities, the cities in the RheinRuhr Area are much more similar to each other than those in the Randstad and Flemish Diamond. The latter two seem to be characterised by cities that are more specialised in certain types of service activities. Perhaps this can be partly explained by the historical development of the three regions. The polycentric pattern in the Randstad and Flemish Diamond has basically been inherited from the past, as fragmented political and administrative structures prevailed for centuries in the Low Countries, thus preventing the rise of one powerful city that dominated the others (see also Dieleman and Faludi, 1998c). As a result all cities were able to develop specialised urban functions according to their competencies or local competitive advantages. Though this also holds for the RheinRuhr Area to a certain extent, this area later witnessed a rapid and overwhelming process of urbanisation and industrialisation linked to such natural resources as deposits of coal and iron ore. Consequently, the main economic base for each city turned out to be manufacturing, which dominated over other types of economic activities for a long time.[6]

However, at the same time, our second conclusion is that the overall extent of complementarity in the Randstad and Flemish Diamond has declined considerably in the period from 1996-2002. This decrease was 12.8% in the Randstad and even 18% in the Flemish Diamond. Interestingly, over the same period the cities in the RheinRuhr Area became more different from each other as regards their service sector activities. The sudden upward change between 2001 and 2002 in the RheinRuhr Area is largely due to Dortmund becoming relatively more specialised in adult education. The truth, however, is that

5 In order to test for the robustness of the analysis presented here, we ran the same correspondence analyses using more cities (fourteen) and a more detailed level of breakdown (3-digit) for the Randstad and RheinRuhr Area (similar data for the Flemish Diamond was not available), which repeatedly confirmed our main conclusions. A further analysis for all three regions, taking all 2-digit NACE-sectors into account confirms our main conclusions. Only the total inertia statistic for the RheinRuhr Area presents a somewhat more ambiguous picture, as in stead of being rather stable, the other analyses show a decline.

6 Note that manufacturing activities are not included in the analysis.

Figure 3.2 Development of the extent of (potential) complementarity in the Randstad, Flemish Diamond and RheinRuhr Area, 1996-2002

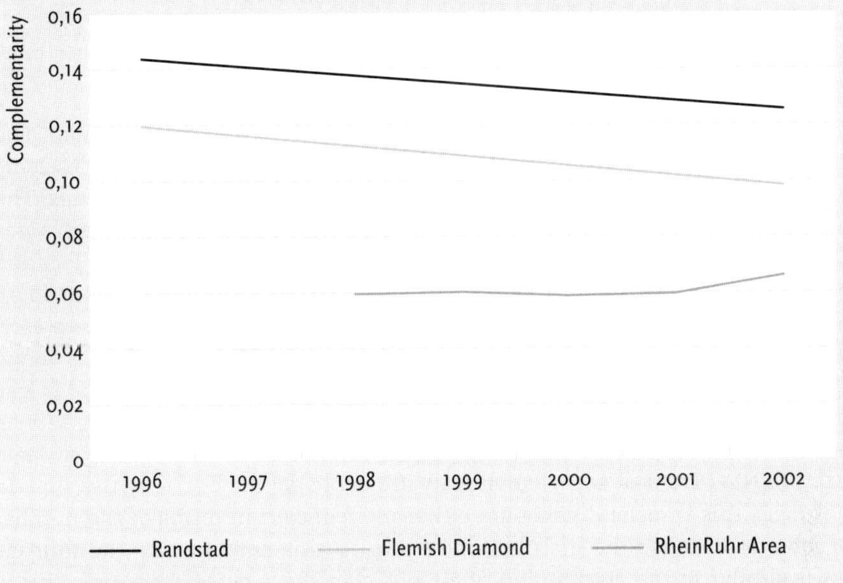

from 2002 on workers of mostly large firms who had become redundant were not simply dismissed but employed in a *Personalentwicklungs-Agentur*, a personal development centre where they are retrained for other jobs. So, they are not actually involved in teaching adults. Without this bias the extent of differentiation in the RheinRuhr Area would show a slight increase by some 3%.

Detailed regional analysis

In the remainder of this section, each polycentric urban region featuring as a case study will be presented individually. This allows a more detailed analysis of how the total inertia for each region has come about. It will tell us which cities and which service-sector activities contribute to the extent of complementarity (and which do not). One of the main advantages of correspondence analysis is that it graphically displays associations, thus enabling an easier interpretation of the associations between cities and service sector activities. These two-dimensional plots are analysed here (Figures 3.3, 3.4 and 3.5). However, they first require some guidance for correct interpretation.

The title of the Figures 3.3, 3.4 and 3.5 also presents the 'percentage of total inertia explained' by the plot. The method diminishes the number of dimensions (3 in our case) to just 2, in order to be able to present them in a two-dimensional plot. Though this is done in the most accurate way, it inevitably leads to a loss of information. This percentage of explained inertia indicates how accurate the two-dimensional plot still is. The percentages found for the three regions are all satisfying, even very high in the cases of RheinRuhr Area and Flemish Diamond.

In each plot, two axes together indicate the origin (0,0), which resembles the average profile of the four cities. The further a city is away from the origin, the more it contributes to the extent of complementarity. If two cities lie close together, then their economic profiles are more or less similar. The same condition applies to the economic activities. Economic activities lying close together are more or less similarly distributed between the cities. The distance between cities and economic activities is more complicated, since these are not defined as chi-square distances. All cities influence the location of an economic activity, and conversely, all economic activities contribute to the location of a city. In general, cities and activities will be close to each other when the observed value for this pair of points in the table is larger than expected, and the distance will be large when the observed value is less than the expected value. For reasons of clarity, out of the 29 economic service activities included in the analysis, only those activities contributing at least 0.001 to the extent of complementarity are depicted. Service activities that do not meet this threshold value are either insignificant in terms of the number of jobs, or because the distribution of jobs in this activity over the four cities is similar to the distribution of all jobs over these cities. Obviously, this is for instance the case with retail trade, where the expected number of jobs in the four cities is more or less equal to the observed number. In addition, the numbers in the figures that mark the location of a certain economic activity are displayed in three sizes. The largest size contributes at least 0.01 to the total inertia, the middle size between 0.005 and 0.01 and the smallest size between 0.001 and 0.005.

Randstad

In 2002, the three largest Randstad cities – Amsterdam, Rotterdam and The Hague – had relatively distinct profiles in commercial and public services. Utrecht had a more general and average profile and is, therefore, located closer to the origin (Figure 3.3). The Hague and Rotterdam contribute most to the total inertia (i.e. are most specialised) as they are located furthest from the origin. The Hague, which is the seat of the Dutch government, is very much associated with public administration and relatively more extra-territorial organisations and bodies are present there. Given the fact that Rotterdam's harbour is one of the largest in the world, it is not surprising to find that Rotterdam holds a strong position in water transport and supporting and auxiliary transport activities. Other specialisations include sewage and refuse disposal and construction. Amsterdam has a relatively dominant position in the commercial services sector, in particular in financial intermediation, computers and related activities and publishing and printing. Moreover, leisure seems to be more important for Amsterdam given the strong presence of the hotels and restaurants and recreation, culture and sports sectors. Utrecht's profile in service activities resembles Amsterdam's the most. Moreover, trade and business activities as well as education are activities strongly present in this city. In general, it seems that the three largest cities in the Randstad have different roles in providing services to companies and citizens, each of them specialis-

Figure 3.3 Differentiation in the spread of service sector activities over the main Randstad cities, 2002 (percentage of total inertia explained: 83,8%)

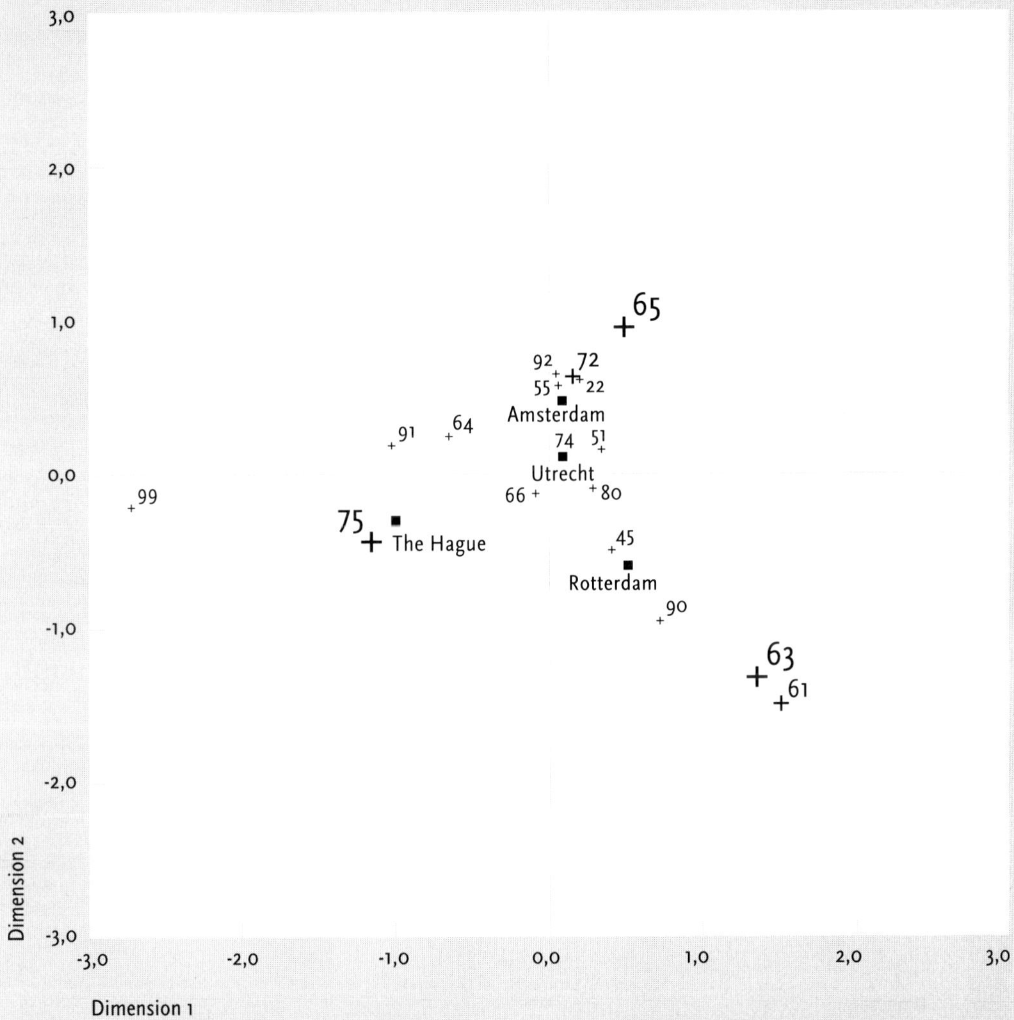

22 Publishing, printing and reproduction
45 Construction
51 Wholesale trade
55 Hotels and restaurants
61 Water transport
63 Supporting and auxiliary transport activities
64 Post and telecommunications
65 Financial intermediation
66 Insurance and pension funding
72 Computers and related activities
74 Other business activities
75 Public administration and defence
80 Education
90 Sewage and refuse disposal, sanitation
91 Activities of membership organisations
92 Recreational, cultural and sporting activities
99 Extra-territorial organisations and bodies

ing in either commercial services (Amsterdam), transportation (Rotterdam), or public administration (The Hague).

Figure 3.4 Differentiation in the spread of service sector activities over the main Flemish Diamond cities, 2002 (percentage of total inertia explained: 96,1%)

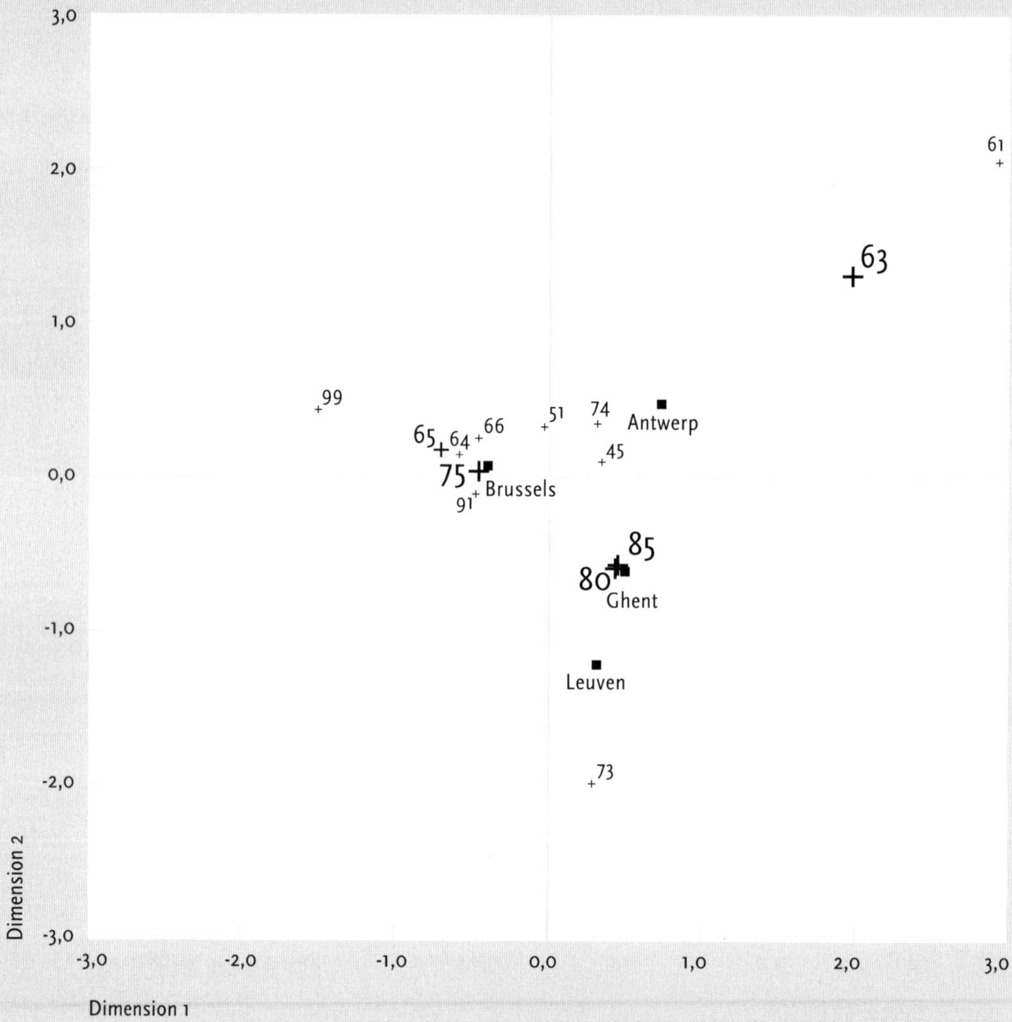

45 Construction
51 Wholesale trade
61 Water transport
63 Supporting and auxiliary transport activities
64 Post and telecommunications
65 Financial intermediation
66 Insurance and pension funding
73 Research and development
74 Other business activities
75 Public administration and defence
80 Education
85 Health and social work
91 Activities of membership organisations
99 Extra-territorial organisations and bodies

Flemish Diamond

As Figure 3.4 displays, out of the four main Flemish Diamond cities, the smallest one, Leuven, is the most specialised, namely in research and development. Together with Ghent, another old university town, it holds a strong position in

Figure 3.5 Differentiation in the spread of service sector activities over the main RheinRuhr Area cities, 2002 (percentage of total inertia explained: 92,2%)

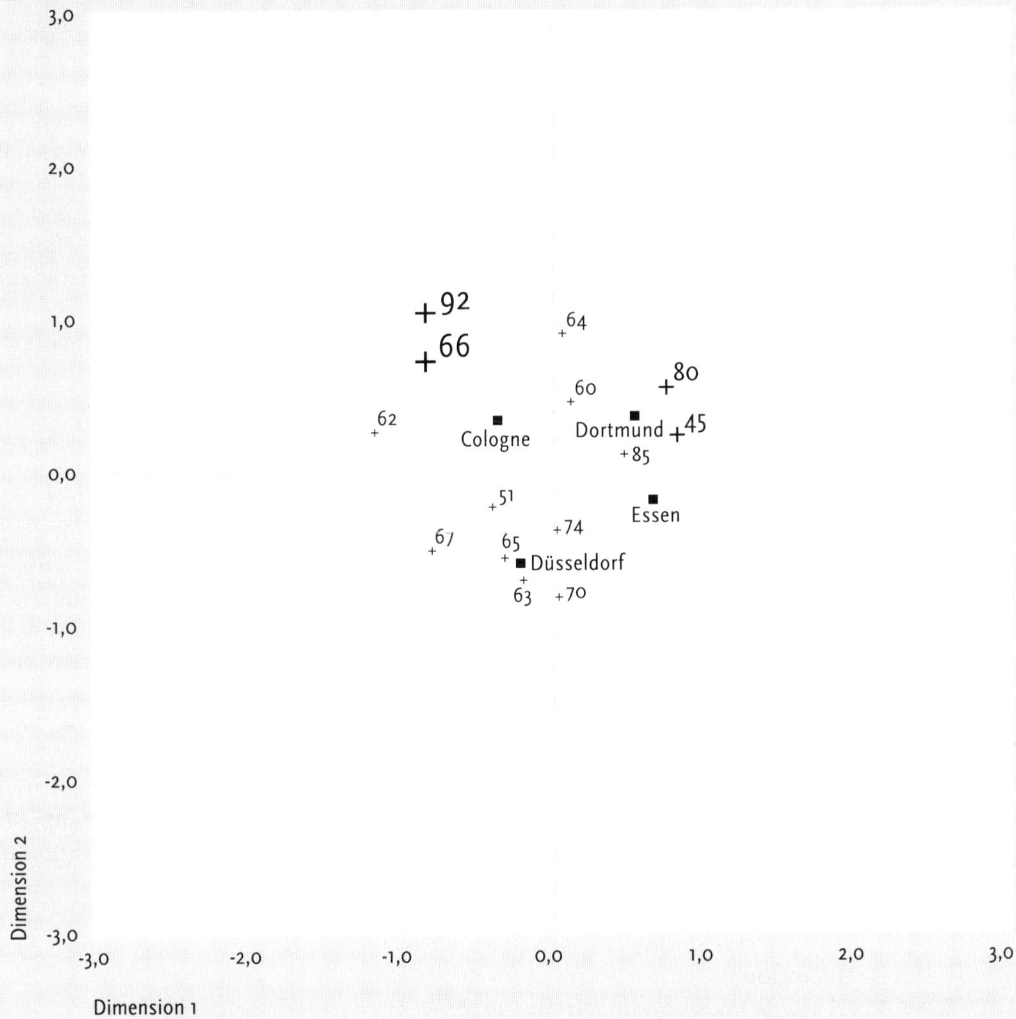

45 Construction
51 Wholesale trade
60 Land transport
62 Air transport
63 Supporting and auxiliary transport activities
64 Post and telecommunications
65 Financial intermediation
66 Insurance and pension funding
67 Activities auxiliary to financial intermediation
70 Real estate activities
74 Other business activities
80 Education
85 Health and social work
92 Recreational, cultural and sporting activities

education and healthcare and social work. Antwerp has – like Rotterdam – an important port within its boundaries, resulting in the strong presence of water transport and supporting and auxiliary transport activities. Also construction and business activities are relatively more common in Antwerp than in the other cities. Brussels, the main seat of government of the European Union, the Belgian state as well as the Flanders and Brussels Capital Region, is consequently strongly specialised in public administration and defence (for example NATO), and related activities of membership organisations and extra-territorial organisations and bodies. Moreover, it holds a strong position in commercial services activities, including financial intermediation, insurance and pension funding as well as in post and telecommunications. Like the Randstad, the Flemish Diamond seems to be characterised by a quite distinct division of labour between the cities.

RheinRuhr Area

Figure 3.5 presents Dortmund and Essen, the main cities of the Ruhr area, relatively close on the right of the plot, while Cologne and Düsseldorf, the main cities of the Rheinschiene are on the left, but more distant from each other. The activities most exclusively linked to one city (thus contributing most to the inertia), which are insurance and pension funding and recreation, culture and sports, are both linked to the city of Cologne. Air transport also has a strong presence, while Cologne's strong position in land transport and post and telecommunications is shared with Dortmund. Public services such as education, health and social work are relatively more common in Dortmund. The same holds for construction. Düsseldorf holds a strong position in a number of commercial services, such as financial intermediation, activities auxiliary to financial intermediation, real estate, activities that support transport activities and other business activities. It shares a strong position in wholesale trade with Cologne. At this level of analysis, Essen does not seem to offer anything the other cities do not already provide themselves. In general, the main groups of service activities seem to be more evenly spread over the region.

Closing remark

Looking at the three regions individually, it is apparent that main groups of economic service activities can be much more exclusively attributed to one city in the Randstad and Flemish Diamond than in the RheinRuhr Area. For instance, clusters of government-related activities can quite exclusively be found in The Hague and Brussels, commercial financial services in Amsterdam and Brussels, transport services in Rotterdam and Antwerp, leisure activities in Amsterdam, research and education in Ghent and Leuven. In the RheinRuhr Area, the activities making up these main groups of service activities are all much more spread over the whole region.

3.5 Conclusion

One could argue that polycentric urban regions are not necessarily urban networks. The first term primarily relates to the morphology of the regional urban system, 'the image on the map', the latter implies the presence of the characteristics of what is labelled the 'network model' of spatial organisation. According to the network model of spatial organisation, a key relationship between the centres is complementarity. In this paper, the analysis focused on the division of labour in service sector activities between the main cities of three prime examples of polycentric urban regions: the Randstad, the Flemish Diamond and the RheinRuhr Area. The objective was to examine whether or not these cities complement each other, or, to be exact, have the potential to do so, as for complementarity to develop not only a division of labour in service sector activities on the supply side is important, but also a geographical overlapping of demand markets for these activities. It has been assumed that a division of labour also implies strong spatial interaction, but this link requires further analysis. It was found that the division of labour between the main cities of the Randstad and Flemish Diamond is much stronger than in the RheinRuhr Area, thus indicating that the existing and potential complementarity is much higher in these regions. As far as the aspect of complementary relationships is concerned, the Randstad and Flemish Diamond seem to bear more features of the network model of spatial organisation than does the RheinRuhr Area nowadays. Comparatively, as far as the aspect of complementarity is concerned, the 'urban network' label is more applicable to the Randstad and the Flemish Diamond than to the RheinRuhr Area. Some explanation for this is likely to be found in the different urban development pathways of the regions. The polycentric layout in the Randstad and Flemish Diamond has been shaped over the past centuries as fragmented political and administrative structures and rivalry have prevented the rise of one continuously dominant city. Major urban development in the RheinRuhr area took place much later, when because of the presence of natural resources such as coal and iron ore the area witnessed rapid industrialisation and urbanisation.

The extent of existing and potential complementarity in the Randstad and Flemish Diamond is, however, declining at a relatively fast pace. This empirical evidence supports the idea that further polycentric development at the inter-urban scale eventually leads to a more homogeneous economic environment. This means either that the range of different business milieus and specialised clusters of service activities diminishes, or that local competitive advantages are becoming increasingly regionalised. Analysing business startups in the Randstad, Kloosterman and Lambregts (2001) found that cluster formation is indeed taking place at a supralocal level.

As regards the dimension of functional relationships, the meaning of polycentric development differs between the intra-urban and inter-urban scale.

Our explorative analysis at the macro-level suggests that opposing trends occur. A division of labour seems to develop at the intra-urban level, whereas at the inter-urban level this division of labour is diminishing. Perhaps an explanation can come from the differences in the genesis of polycentric urban patterns at both scales. Contrary to the intra-urban scale where new centres develop next to an existing main centre, polycentric urban patterns at the regional scale start from existing centres (cities) and derive their significance from the alleged development of functional relationships between them. Obviously, further research, for instance including the micro-level (individual sectors of activities), is needed to confirm these opposite trends.

Acknowledgement
The author would like to thank Hugo Priemus and Marjolein Spaans for their helpful comments. The author wishes to acknowledge the financial assistance of the Dutch government through the Habiforum Program Innovative Land Use and Delft University of Technology through the Delft Centre for Sustainable Urban Areas.

References

Albrechts, L. (2001) How to Proceed from Image and Discourse to Action: As Applied to the Flemish Diamond, *Urban Studies*, 38, pp. 733-745.

Alonso, W. (1973) Urban Zero Population Growth, *Daedalus*, 109, pp. 191-206.

Batten, D.F. (1995) Network Cities: Creative Urban Agglomerations for the 21st Century, *Urban Studies*, 32, pp. 313-327.

Bogaerts, A., F.M. Dieleman, M. Dijst and S. Geertman (2005) *Strengthening Polycentrism, or Edgeless Development? Employment Location and Growth in Randstad's North Wing, 1996-2002*. Unpublished paper based on research undertaken in the project Spatial Deconcentration of Economic Land Use and Quality of Life in European Metropolitan Areas (SELMA), Utrecht University, The Netherlands. Contact: Martin Dijst, m.dijst@geo.uu.nl.

Camagni, R. (1993) From city hierarchy to city networks: reflections about an emerging paradigm, in: T.R. Lakshmanan and P. Nijkamp (Eds) *Structure and change in the Space Economy: Festschrift in honour of Martin Beckmann*, pp. 66-87. Berlin: Springer Verlag.

Camagni, R. and C. Salone (1993) Network Urban Structures in Northern Italy: Elements for a Theoretical Framework, *Urban Studies*, 30, pp. 1053-1064.

Capello, R. (2000) The City Network Paradigm: Measuring Urban Network Externalities, *Urban Studies*, 37, pp. 1925-1945.

Clausen, S-E. (1998) *Applied correspondence analysis: an introduction*, Sage University Papers Series on Quantitative Applications in the Social Sciences, 07-121. Thousand Oaks, CA: Sage.

Davoudi, S. (2003) Polycentricity in European Spatial Planning: From an Analytical Tool to a Normative Agenda, *European Planning Studies*, 11, pp. 979-999.

Dieleman, F.M. and A. Faludi (1998a) Polynucleated Metropolitan Regions in Northwest Europe: Theme of the Special Issue, *European Planning Studies*, 6, pp. 365-377.

Dieleman, F.M. and A. Faludi (Eds) (1998b) *European Planning Studies: Special Issue: Polynucleated Metropolitan Regions in Northwest Europe*, 6 (4).

Dieleman, F.M. and A. Faludi (1998c) Randstad, RhineRuhr and Flemish Diamond as One Polynucleated Macro-region, *Tijdschrift voor Economische en Sociale Geografie*, 89, pp. 320-327.

Gordon, P. and H.W. Richardson (1996) Beyond polycentricity: the dispersed metropolis, *Journal of the American Planning Association*, 62, pp. 289-294.

Greenacre, M.J. (1993) *Correspondence analysis in practice*. London: Academic Press Limited.

Halbert, L. (2004) The Decentralization of Intrametropolitan Business Services in the Paris Region: Patterns, Interpretation, Consequences, *Economic Geography*, 80, pp. 381-404.

Hall, P. (2001) Global City-Regions in the Twenty-first Century, in: A.J. Scott (ed) *Global City Regions - Trends, Theory, Policy*, pp. 57-77. Oxford: Oxford University Press.

Institute d'Aménagement et d'Urbanisme de la Region d'Ile-de-France (IAURIF) (2001) *The Metropolises of North West Europe in Figures*. Paris: IAURIF.

Institute d'Aménagement et d'Urbanisme de la Region d'Ile-de-France (IAURIF) (2002) *Economic Performance of the European Regions*, Cahier No.135, Paris: IAURIF.

Kloosterman, R.C. and B. Lambregts (2001) Clustering of Economic Activities in Polycentric Urban Regions: The Case of the Randstad, *Urban Studies*, 38, pp. 717-732.

Kloosterman, R.C. and S. Musterd (2001a) The Polycentric Urban Region: Towards a Research Agenda, *Urban Studies*, 38, pp. 623-633.

Kloosterman, R.C. and S. Musterd (Eds) (2001b) *Urban Studies: Special Issue: Polycentric Urban Regions*, 38 (4).

Knaap, G.A. van der (1994) *Ruimtelijke complexen en schaalspanning op de stedenring*, EGI-onderzoekspublikatie 19, Rotterdam: Erasmus Universiteit Rotterdam.

Knaap, G.A. van der (2002) *Stedelijke bewegingsruimte, over veranderingen in stad en land*. The Hague: Sdu Uitgevers.

Lambooy, J.G. (1969) City and City Region in the Perspective of Hierarchy and Complementarity, *Tijdschrift voor Economische en Sociale Geografie*, 60, pp. 141-154.

Lang, R.E. and J. LeFurgy (2003) Edgeless Cities: Examining the Noncentered Metropolis, *Housing Policy Debate*, 14, pp. 427-460.

Meijers, L.D. (1999) *Ruimtelijke netwerken van zakelijke dienstverlening*. Rotterdam: Erasmus Universiteit Rotterdam.

Meijers, E.J., A. Romein and E.C. Hoppenbrouwer (Eds) (2003) *Planning polycentric urban regions in North West Europe: Value, feasibility and design*. Delft: Delft University Press.

Musterd, S. and I. van Zelm (2001) Polycentricity, Households and the Identity of Places, *Urban Studies*, 38, pp. 679-696.

Parr, J.B. (2004) The Polycentric Urban Region: A Closer Inspection, *Regional Studies*, 38, pp. 231-240.

Priemus, H., W. Zonneveld and A. Faludi (Eds) (2004) *European Planning Studies: Special Issue: Territorial Governance in Polynuclear Urban Regions in Northwest Europe*, 12 (3).

Roberts, M., T. Lloyd-Jones, B. Erickson and S. Nice (1999) Place and Space in the Networked City: Conceptualizing the Integrated Metropolis, *Journal of Urban Design*, 4, pp. 51-66.

Ullmann, E.L. (1956) The Role of Transportation and the Bases for Interaction, in: W.L. Thomas (ed) *Man's Role in Changing the Face of Earth*, pp. 862-880. Chicago: The University of Chicago Press.

Westin, L. and A. Östhol (1994) Functional Networks, Infrastructure and Regional Mobilization, in: L. Lundqvist and O. Persson (Eds) *Northern Perspectives on European Integration*, pp. 43-57. Stockholm: NordREFO.

4 From central place to network model:

Theory and evidence of a paradigm-change

Meijers, E. (2007) From Central Place to Network Model: Theory and Evidence of a Paradigm-change, in: *Tijdschrift voor Economische en Sociale Geografie*, 98 (2), pp. 245-259.

Abstract

While the deficiencies of the central place model have been often highlighted, no other paradigm has replaced it. However, recently some researchers have hinted at the development of a new model of spatial organisation, a network model. This model would hold most in polycentric urban regions. This paper discusses the features of this network model in comparison with the central place model. Moreover, it explores whether this model describes spatial reality better, thereby focusing on complementarity, a main feature of the model. The relationships within multi-location hospitals and universities of professional education (hogescholen), which spread their offer of care and study programmes over multiple, close-by cities, are analysed for this reason. Within the hospital care sector there is a clear trend towards complementarity, in line with the network model. The hogescholen sector provides a more ambiguous picture. The network model, however, still seems more appropriate than the central place model.

4.1 Intercity relationships: from hierarchy to network?

The study of the spatial structure of urban systems, and intercity relationships in particular, has occupied an important place in the fields of urban planning, regional science, urban and economic geography for a long time. Notably, the work of Christaller (1933) and Lösch (1941) on what has come to be known as central place theory has launched this strand of research. In the 1960s it became an important part of urban systems research. By defining sets of cities in terms of systems, explicit attention was drawn to the interdependency of cities and developments in other cities in a region or nation, and how such linkages affect growth and development. However, while this search for theories, rules and other regularities that describe patterns in sets of cities flourished in the 1970s and early 1980s, interest for urban systems research has been on the wane ever since, and central place theory has disappeared from policy discourse (Coffey, 1998).

One of the explanations for this is that the basic theoretical principles that are part of central place theory's conceptual core, such as the notion of hierarchy, have been challenged (Davies, 1998). Though in the heyday of urban systems research many enhancements and refinements of the initial work by Cristaller and Lösch were introduced by authors such as Berry, Dacey, Mulligan, Beckmann, Beguin, Parr and others (see Berry *et al.*, 1988, and Coffey *et al.*, 1998 for an overview), the central place model has had increasing difficulties explaining spatial reality. While the deficiencies of the central place model have been highlighted often, no other set of clearly defined hypotheses has replaced those of central place theory (Camagni, 1993).

However, from the early 1990s on, some researchers have hinted at the development of a new model of spatial organisation, which is generally referred to as a 'network model' (see Camagni, 1993; Batten, 1995; Van der Knaap, 2002). This model is essentially opposite to the central place model. Its basic principles can be dated back to the discussion on the concept of a 'Dispersed City' (Burton, 1963): a group of rather similar-sized politically discrete cities, separated by tracts of open land, functioning economically as a single urban unit. Not only is the central place model at odds with such a sudden clustering of relatively similar-sized cities, evidence suggested that such Dispersed Cities were also not arranged in a hierarchical pattern due to local specialisation. Instead of 'Dispersed City', the now common label for such regions is 'polycentric or polynuclear urban region' (see Kloosterman and Musterd, 2001; Davoudi, 2003; Parr, 2004), while also the terms 'polynucleated metropolitan regions' (Dieleman and Faludi, 1998), 'city network' (Camagni and Salone, 1993) and 'network city' (Batten, 1995) have been used. It is precisely in such a spatial setting of a group of relatively similar-sized close-by cities that it is most evident that the central place model does not hold true (Camagni, 1993;

Capello, 2000; Davies, 1998; Van der Knaap, 2002). Consequently, this network model would hold most for such polycentric urban regions. However, while the theoretical framework of the network model paradigm seems relatively well established, research demonstrating its empirical validity is largely non-existent (Capello, 2000).

The aim of this paper is to describe the features of this network model in comparison with the central place model as well as to assess whether this network model describes the spatial pattern in polycentric urban regions better than the central place model, at least for some of its features. As central place theory, in particular Christaller's approach, gradually developed into a descriptive and theoretical base of the geography of retail and consumer services (Von Böventer, 1963; Berry *et al.*, 1988), we will focus in our elaboration on consumer-oriented services as well: hospitals and universities of professional education in the Netherlands. Due to processes of scaling-up of supply and demand, hospitals and institutes for higher education have turned into regional rather than local facilities, which makes them an interesting case. Increased competition for patients/students and the introduction of 'the market' in both sectors has probably meant that their hinterland is becoming less connected to the definition of non-overlapping market areas. In addition, as a result of mergers, many multi-location institutions have developed in both sectors, spreading their activities over multiple cities in a region. According to Taylor (2003), who, similar to Pred's (1977) approach, argues that intercity relationships can well be empirically studied and understood by looking at the relationships between the locations of multi-location organisations, we will focus our attention on these multi-location organisations as well. Consequently, the research question is whether the spread of activities in the hospital and higher education sectors in polycentric regions obeys the rules of the central place model or whether it does justify the network model.

Section 4.2 describes the principal features of this network model in more detail. Section 4.3 presents our research approach. Our analysis of the higher education sector (universities of professional education) is presented in Section 4.4, the analysis of the hospital sector in Section 4.5. The final section compares the developments in both sectors and explores whether these underline the rise of a network model of spatial organisation.

4.2 A network model of spatial organisation

The ideas on a network model of spatial organisation have sprung up in response to the deficiencies of the central place model. While we intend to focus here on the features of this network model, we will first briefly discuss the basics of the central place model.

Christaller posited that each commodity has a given threshold of mini-

Table 4.1 Central place versus network systems

Central place system	Network system
Centrality	Nodality
Size dependency	Size neutrality
Tendency towards primacy and subservience	Tendency towards flexibility and complementarity
Homogeneous goods and services	Heterogeneous goods and services
Vertical accessibility	Horizontal accessibility
Mainly one-way flows	Two-way flows
Transport costs	Information costs
Perfect competition over space	Imperfect competition with price discrimination

Source: Batten (1995: 320)

mum demand as well as a fixed geographical domain beyond which people are unwilling to pay for it. Therefore, only a certain proportion of all settlements will offer higher-order goods and services. The variety of consumer goods and services offered by establishments in cities (or central places) of a certain class, or order, and of a given size is dependent upon the number of thresholds the combined population of the city and its hinterland can fulfil. If these thresholds do not meet the minimum demand necessary for certain goods and services, then a central place must obtain that class of goods and services from the nearest more populous central place which does meet the threshold requirement in question. The largest central place in a country or region is completely self-reliant. Central places of each class are distributed evenly across the region. Central place theory puts great emphasis on one-sided vertical relationships between different classes of hierarchically ordered central places. 'One-sided' means that the lower class of central places is dependent on the higher class of central places, not vice versa. Horizontal relationships between cities in the same class (thus of similar size) would be non-existent and also redundant, as these cities provide the same amenities and services. Although many enhancements and refinements have made the model less rigid (see Berry *et al.*, 1988, for an overview), its essence has remained. However, nowadays it is generally acknowledged that real city systems in advanced economies have departed in many respects from the Christallerian pattern of a nested hierarchy of centres and markets.

While the discourse on alternative models to the central place model began to take shape in the early 1990s, this discourse was informed by some early observations of alternative spatial patterns, particularly in polycentric urban regions. Next to Burton's work on the dispersed city, Gottmann's work on the Megalopolis is a case in point (Gottmann, 1961). In his analysis of the urbanised North-eastern Seaboard of the US Gottmann opposed the dominant view of hierarchical relationships, and instead suggested that complementarity existed in this polycentric region. In addition, Pred (1977) analysed the spatial structure of multi-locational business organisations, arguing that hierarchies are linked to functions rather than cities. Hierarchies in functions

Table 4.2 Changes resulting from the transition from hierarchies to networks

Hierarchy	Networks
Fixed number of spatial scales	Variable number of spatial scales
Economic functions rising with spatial scale, functions connected to spatial scale	Variable sets of economic functions on the same spatial scale
Urban population evenly distributed across territory	Uneven distribution of urban population across territory
Only vertical relationships between cities (on different spatial scales)	Both horizontal and vertical relationships between cities

Source: Van der Knaap (2002: 168), translation by author

are often not symmetrical to the hierarchy in cities, which implies that relationships between cities may not only be vertical but also of a horizontal nature. This also implies that complementarity between cities follows from hierarchies in functions that are asymmetric to the hierarchy in cities.

More recently, the spatial organisation of polycentric urban regions has been described by drawing analogies with economic linkages, or networks, among firms (Camagni and Salone, 1993; Batten, 1995), although this analogy is not undisputed, given the much stronger stability of urban systems over time (Pumain, 1992). However, Camagni and Salone (1993) argue that if the shape of the urban hierarchy is determined by the interplay of forces like economies of scale, minimum efficient production size, demand density and market size, as is the case in the Christallerian model, than it could well be that other production forces working at the micro-economic and micro-territorial scale of the firm may be considered as the driving forces of the new 'network' paradigm (Camagni and Salone, 1993). Based on the resemblance with networks among firms, they define networks among cities as 'systems of relationships and flows, of a mainly horizontal and non-hierarchical nature, among specialised centres, providing externalities or economies respectively of specialisation/complementarity/spatial division of labour and of synergy/ co-operation/ innovation' (Camagni and Salone, 1993:1059). Such non-hierarchical relationships are also emphasised by Batten (1995:313): 'A network city evolves when two or more previously independent cities, potentially complementary in function, strive to co-operate and achieve significant scope economies aided by fast and reliable corridors of transport and communications infrastructure.'

As both authors stress, the idea of horizontal and non-hierarchical relationships of complementarity and co-operation between cities in a polycentric urban region contrasts with the hierarchical, gravity-type relationships predicted by the central place model (see Table 4.1). Van der Knaap (2002) presents a comparable overview of the differences between both models (Table 4.2). However, rather than replacing the central place model with a network model, these authors suggest a sequential link between both models. Whereas the central place model seems most typical for industrial economies, the network model seems more applicable to economies that have become more service-sector dominated (Camagni and Salone, 1993; Batten, 1995; Van der Knaap, 2002).

A number of the features attributed to the network model (as in Tables 4.1 and 4.2) have for a long time been accepted as better describing spatial reality than the corresponding features of the central place model. This holds, for instance, for the idea of imperfect competition, a more flexible and variable number of spatial scales and the uneven distribution of urban population. A more innovative feature of the network model describing a non-hierarchical relationship between cities is the idea of 'complementarity'. This refers to the situation in which different cities fulfil different and mutually beneficial roles (Hague and Kirk, 2003), for instance through providing different sets of economic functions and services. So, complementarity results from the differentiation between centres or cities in terms of urban functions, while these urban functions should be provided, at least partly, for the same geographical demand market (Meijers, 2005; Ullman, 1956). Complementarity can be considered a main feature of the network model as it positively enhances the presence of other characteristics of the network model. Complementarity results in two-way flows between both different and similar-sized cities, thus emphasising also horizontal accessibility. Moreover, it may explain the aspect of size neutrality, which refers to a relative disconnection between size and function of a city. Higher-order functions may be found in smaller cities operating in a network because of complementarity, thereby drawing on the regional support base rather than the local. Consequently, complementarity is also linked to nodality, the position of a city in a network, rather than centrality.

Given these links between the features of the network model of spatial organisation, it seems that the feature of complementarity provides an excellent starting point for the comprehensive research agenda to test the empirical validity of the network model of spatial organisation. In the next sections we will focus our research question on whether the spread of activities in the hospital and higher education sectors in polycentric regions obeys the rules of the central place model or the network model on the feature of complementarity. Given the definition of complementarity above, the analysis should focus on aspects of differentiation between locations of hogescholen and hospitals as well as on the origins of students and patients.

4.3 Research approach

Hogescholen - The Netherlands has a binary system of higher education, which means that there are two types of programmes: research-oriented education *(wetenschappelijk onderwijs, WO)*, traditionally offered by research universities and leading to bachelor, master's and PhD degrees, and professional higher education (hoger beroepsonderwijs, HBO), traditionally offered by universities of professional education, or hogescholen (we will refer to them by this Dutch name), generally leading to bachelor's degrees. Research universities tend to operate on a supraregional or national level, less relevant to polycentric urban regions, while hogescholen function on a regional level, in theory more congruent with the scale of polycentric urban regions. Therefore, our analysis focuses on these hogescholen, using a dataset provided by the Informatie Beheer Groep in which all fulltime study programmes offered by these hogescholen are registered (CROHO-database). We define the relationship between locations of a hogeschool as complementary when they offer different study programmes while recruiting their students from more or less the same region. The dataset allows a quantitative analysis of the extent of differentiation in the offer of study programmes by using correspondence analysis techniques from which a complementarity ratio can be inferred. In addition, we carried out some interviews with public sector officials and managers of large multi-location hogescholen to learn more about their locational strategies as well as their institutional context. We further completed our analysis with a literature review.

Hospitals - In the Dutch hospital care system, general hospital care is provided by academic hospitals and general hospitals. Next to general care, academic hospitals, of which there are eight in the Netherlands, also deliver very specialised treatment for complicated disorders, for which they often have a 'last resort' function. The largest group of hospitals are the general hospitals, which provide a large variety of medical specialist care for their region. In our analysis we focus on the general hospitals as these provide the overwhelming majority of general hospital care, also functioning on a supralocal level, potentially that of a polycentric urban region, whereas academic hospitals function on a much higher and thus less relevant level. Locations of a multi-location hospital are considered as complementary when they provide for different medical specialisations, or specialise in different kinds of treatment whilst serving more or less the same region. No general datasets displaying aspects of complementarity are available in the Netherlands, which means that no quantitative analysis could be undertaken. Therefore, we gathered information during a series of interviews with managers of hospitals in our case study regions. In addition, we conducted a literature review.

Multi-location organisations - Following Taylor (2003), who, similar to Pred's (1977) approach, argues that intercity relationships can be empirically studied and understood by looking at the relationships between the locations of multi-location organisations, we will also focus our attention on multi-location organisations. By multi-location we mean that these organisations have locations in multiple cities.

Study region - The multi-location model has become increasingly dominant in both the hospital and higher education sector. Both hospitals and hogescholen spread their activities over multiple cities. Consequently, these facilities now have regional significance and are potentially, though not necessarily, functioning on the scale of a polycentric urban region.[1] Such polycentric regions are spread all over the Netherlands, which may not be surprising given it's high extent of urbanisation and high population density. In the Dutch spatial planning strategy polycentric urban regions are labelled 'urban networks', and the strategy distinguishes six of them being of national and international importance (see Van der Burg and Dieleman, 2004). Though we basically included all Dutch multi-location hogescholen for which data was available, these happen to be all located in these six urban networks distinguished in the national planning strategy. For the analyses of multi-location hospitals we selected hospitals from two of these urban networks, namely the South Wing of the Randstad and Brabantstad, for which the province of North Brabant is a good proxy. Camagni and Salone (1993) suggest that the Randstad is a prime example of a region in which complementary relationships have been developed.

4.4 Hogescholen

Macro-level context - Compared to neighbouring countries, institutions for higher education in the Netherlands are fairly autonomous (OECD, 2004; Onderwijsraad, 2005). This autonomy particularly concerns financial matters, but also spatially relevant decisions such as the closing, or opening of different locations of an institution in other places and co-operation or mergers with other institutions. In the past, central government has fostered a tremendous scaling-up in the hogescholen sector. In 1980 there were 353 hogescholen with an average size of 370 students, whereas in 2000 there were only 56 left with an average size of 4460 students (Onderwijsraad, 2004). According to the CROHO database, in 2005 there were 44 publicly funded hogescholen remaining, offering fulltime education at 114 locations (on average 2.5 locations per organisation). It follows that many hogescholen have multiple locations. In fact, this holds for 24 of these 44 hogescholen. This set of 44 hogescholen includes many locations offering just 1 fulltime bachelor, which often happens to be teacher training for primary schools. Art degrees are also often given at very specialised locations or organisations. If we exclude these small unidimensional organisations and locations, that is, those offering just two

1 Note that PURs as identified in the literature and by policy-makers differ substantially in scale, from large metropolitan regions as the Randstad or the RheinRuhr Area to a clustering of small cities and towns. Here, we argue that these supralocal facilities potentially operate on a scale that includes at least two cities of a PUR.

or less fulltime bachelor study programmes, then 35 organisations remain, spreading their offer of education over 67 locations. Nearly half of them have locations in a multitude of often close-by cities.

Although the Dutch government has in general advocated deregulation since about 1985, it still accredits new and existing study programmes. It approves a proposal submitted by a hogeschool for a new study programme leading to an academic degree, irrespective of whether this concerns an entirely new study programme, the addition of a study programme at a particular hogeschool that is already given at another hogeschool, or, most relevant for multi-location hogescholen, offering a study programme already given at one location also at another location of the same hogeschool (the latter only since 2002). In the process of accreditation, central government is assisted by a special agency that tests whether the programme satisfies certain quality standards. If a study programme is also to be funded by the government, the Ministry of Education tests for what is called 'macro-efficiency' using criteria such as innovativeness, demand by employers for graduates and also the existing dispersal of similar study programmes across the country as they try to avoid harmful effects for the existing hogescholen. Whether or not they do test for macro-efficiency depends very much on the minister in office. The number of accredited study programmes remained limited to about 80 in the period from 1993 up to 1998. After that, with a more liberal Minister of Education (Hermans) in office, some 250 new study programmes were registered (Adviescommissie Onderwijsaanbod, 2003). Recently, central government retraced their steps towards a more reserved approach, testing more rigorously for quality and macro-efficiency. Existing study programmes are nowadays also examined using criteria related to quality, but not of 'macro-efficiency'.

Trends in the differentiation in study programmes - We analysed the offer of study programmes of multi-location hogescholen using correspondence analysis. This is a method to analyse the association between two or more variables. These variables are the locations of multi-location hogescholen and the study programmes they offer. Correspondence analysis presents a statistic called the 'total inertia' expressing the extent of, in this case, the differentiation in study programmes between locations of multi-location hogescholen. The inertia is the weighted average of the squared χ^2 distances between the scores on both variables and the average scores. If all these locations provided exactly the same study programmes, the total inertia-statistic would be 0, thus representing maximum duplication. If all locations provided study programmes not given at any other location, then the total inertia would be equal to the dimensionality of the problem (in practice the number of locations of the organisation –1). For an extensive discussion of correspondence analysis see Greenacre (1993). In order to enable comparisons between hogescholen that differ in terms of the number of locations, we normalised the

Figure 4.1 Trends in the extent of differentiation in study programmes within multi-location hogescholen, 1993-2005

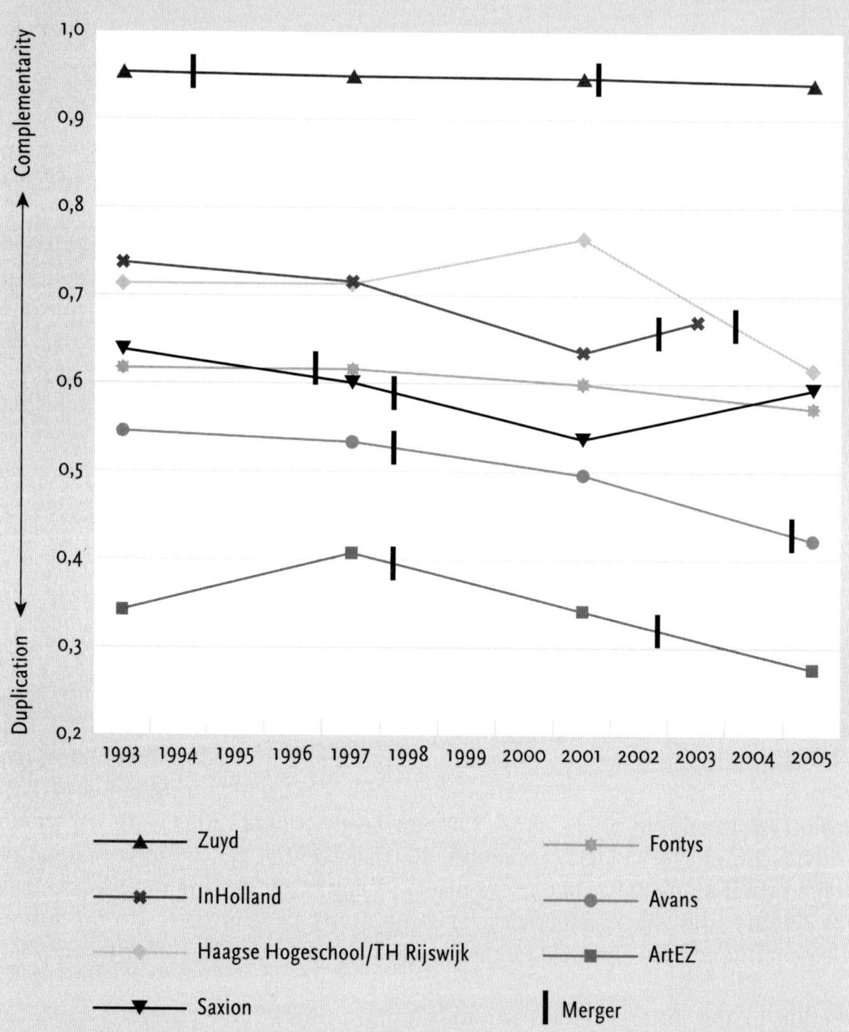

total inertia statistic by dividing it by the maximum total inertia that could have been achieved. This then results in what we call a complementarity ratio, with values between 0 (no differentiation, thus maximum duplication) and 1 (maximum differentiation, and hence complementarity). For the analysis we used a dataset in which accredited full-time bachelor study programmes of hogescholen are listed. This CROHO registration was provided for the academic years 1993-1994, 1997-1998, 2001-2002 and 2005. We selected all publicly-funded multi-location organisations and included all locations offering three or more fulltime study programmes. However, data was not available in the database for each organisation, as it is only since 2005 that the database has included separate recordings for different locations rather than organisations. This meant that we were only able to retrieve information for multi-location organisations resulting from a merger since 1993. The development

Table 4.3 Hogeschool Zuyd: high extent of complementarity among locations (2005)

Sectors	Total N of study programmes in sector	Location: Sittard-Geleen N of study programmes in sector	... that are not offered elsewhere	Location: Heerlen N of study programmes in sector	... that are not offered elsewhere	Location: Maastricht N of study programmes in sector	... that are not offered elsewhere
Economics	15	8	8	1	1	6	6
Social Sciences	6	6	5	0	0	1	0
Health Care	5	0	0	5	5	0	0
Education	4	0	0	1	0	4	3
Languages and Arts	5	0	0	0	0	5	5
Technology	17	0	0	17	17	0	0
Total	**52**	**14**	**13**	**24**	**23**	**16**	**14**

Table 4.4 Hogeschool Avans: limited extent of complementarity among locations (2005)

Sectors	Total N of study programmes in sector	Location: Breda N of study programmes in sector	... that are not offered elsewhere	Location: Tilburg N of study programmes in sector	... that are not offered elsewhere	Location: Den Bosch N of study programmes in sector	... that are not offered elsewhere
Economics	13	8	2	4	1	10	3
Social Sciences	4	4	0	0	0	4	0
Health Care	3	2	2	1	0	1	0
Education	2	2	2	0	0	0	0
Languages and Arts	2	2	0	0	0	0	0
Technology	18	11	5	8	2	11	2
Total	**42**	**29**	**11**	**13**	**3**	**26**	**5**

in the differentiation in study programmes offered by the locations of these seven organisations is presented in Figure 4.1.

Figure 4.1 shows that there are huge varieties in scores on the complementarity ratio. We find both multi-location hogescholen with a strong division of tasks between them, while others are characterised by strong duplication. In terms of trends, it seems that after the merger the locations duplicate rather than complement each other more. The average decrease in the extent of differentiation between 1993 and 2005 is 11.5%. Though two hogescholen show an upward trend following a strong decline, none of the hogescholen scored above their 1993 and pre-merger value.

Of the seven multi-location hogescholen in Figure 4.1 the locations of the Hogeschool Zuyd complement each other most. Conversely, there is a high extent of duplication between the locations of the ArteZ hogeschool and Avans hogeschool. Tables 4.3 and 4.4 provide a more detailed look at the Hogeschool Zuyd and Avans, as these are quite comparable regarding the number of locations (three) and the sectors in which they provide study programmes.

As Table 4.3 shows, the high score on complementarity for the Hogeschool Zuyd is because there is hardly any duplication of study programmes, even when its locations offer study programmes in the same sectors. This holds much less for the Avans hogeschool (Table 4.4), where each location offers study programmes that hardly makes them distinct from other locations. Interestingly, however, it is not the case that the largest location offers all study programmes also offered by smaller locations, as we would expect in the case of a hierarchical central place model. How can these findings be explained?

Micro-level behaviour - Competition for students is an important factor in explaining the behaviour of the managers of hogescholen as the number of students successfully finishing their studies determines a hogeschool's share of the public budget for education. A certain amount of competition has been eliminated through mergers, although there continue to be a couple of hogescholen competing in each region for students, so absolute monopolies are also avoided. An important aspect in this regard is the willingness of prospective students to travel for education. Some 53% of the students of hogescholen prefer to stay at home with their parents rather than move to the city where they study (IB-groep, 2005). One can imagine that this percentage is even higher for first-year students. Using a division of the Netherlands in 25 regions, Gordijn and Janssen (1997) found that 80% of the students of hogescholen studied in their own or an adjacent region in 1996. This means that, in general, students tend to choose the nearest hogeschool that offers their preferred study programme, even though Dutch students have free travel permits. For managers of such hogescholen it is not really possible to intervene in the spread of study programmes over their locations, as relocating study programmes from one place to another often means a loss of students. So, even after mergers, study programmes that are similar but given in different locations are not concentrated for the sake of scale economies. On the contrary, they often try to expand the offer of individual locations with study programmes already given at other locations of the same hogeschool. This is a relatively inexpensive way to attract more students as it does not involve development costs, though one can argue that this may lower the number of students of the same programme at the other locations. This also holds for the development of new study programmes that often, despite their fashionable labelling, do not differ much from existing study programmes. Conversely, when a truly new study programme is developed and appears successful in attracting students, other hogescholen tend to copy it soon (*Adviescommissie onderwijsaanbod*, 2003). It is clear, therefore, that competition between the hogescholen leads to duplication rather than complementarity. With complementarity being such an important feature of the network model of spatial organisation, this does not match the network model.

4.5 Hospitals

Macro-level context - Traditionally, the role of government in hospital care is to facilitate and to set conditions for the hospital care sector that is for the rest privately organised. These conditions relate to the quality and accessibility of hospital care and in particular to the control of the costs of hospital care. The latter was the main rationale for a policy to increase the scale of the hospitals and simultaneously decrease the overall capacity, in terms of the number of beds, in the past decades. The scaling-up, coupled with concentration, led to a diminishing of the number of hospitals from 221 in 1954 to 197 in 1970 (Boot, 1998); 86 were still left in 2005. Moreover, these hospitals have scaled-up considerably in terms of the number of beds provided: from around 330 in 1980 to over 500 in 2002. The process of scaling-up seems to have come to a halt recently now that, for reasons of accessibility of hospital care, the role of small hospitals received renewed recognition and their funding was increased. In addition, from the viewpoint of introducing more free-market competition in the hospital care sector, a further merging and concentration of hospital care is unwanted, as this may lead to regional monopolies (NMa, 2004). Government involvement has, however, since the 1990s been more reserved, and more issues are now left to the market.

Decisions relating to the spatial dispersal of regular hospital care, and hence whether or not complementarity develops, have been taken by the hospitals themselves for a long time. It was private incentives that determined the spatial dispersal of hospitals in the first place, and this is still practically the same today as the hospital institutions themselves decide to close down hospital locations, engage in co-operative partnerships or mergers, concentrate or deconcentrate hospital functions, or relocate hospital functions over several locations of the same organisation (College Bouw Ziekenhuisvoorzieningen, 2000).

Micro-level behaviour - The behaviour of hospital managers can be explained by various rationales, including the maximising of quality in health care, the realisation of a certain volume in health care as well as maximising the turnover (Den Hartog, 2004). In addition, Boot (1998) explains their behaviour as a pursuit of maximising the number of medical specialisations provided by the hospitals. In the Netherlands there are about 30 acknowledged medical specialisations and providing them all would mean that a hospital has reached its maximum possible size, as the number of beds they are allowed to have is linked to the medical specialisations provided. To realise this growth, the hospital needs a larger hinterland, for which they compete with other hospitals. Hinterlands widen through mergers, which is one of the explanations for the many mergers that took place in the sector. The relevance of all these mergers is that many multi-location hospitals result. While in 1990 only 41 of the 128

Figure 4.2 Hospital locations in the Netherlands, September 2004

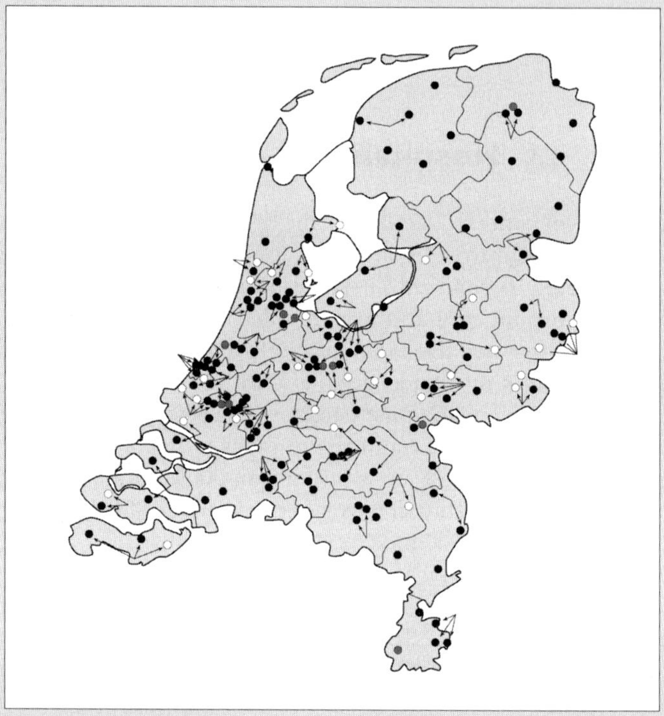

- Academic hospitals
- General hospitals
- Buitenpoli's
- Organisationally-linked locations
- WZV-regions

Source: RIVM, Volksgezondheid Toekomst Verkenning, Nationale Atlas Volksgezondheid (2004)

general hospital organisations had more than one location (Nienoord-Buré and Damen, 1992), the 86 hospital organisations that existed in 2005 had spread their activities over 168 locations. Nowadays, more than half of all the organisations have two or more locations, though some of them do not provide clinical care, but ambulatory care during office hours (a so-called 'buitenpoli'). If we leave these 'buitenpoli's' aside, we still find 24 hospital organisations with two locations, seven with three locations, while two hospital organisations have even spread their activities over four locations (see Figure 4.2).

Grosso modo, multi-location hospital organisations have a choice between three future location models: a.) having two or more locations offering the same care and cure; b.) concentrating their activities in one location; and c.) relocating the care and cure functions, resulting in locations developing a functionally specialised profile, so that they complement one another. Options a. and b. obviously conform to central place theories, while option c. would be a clear manifestation of a network model.

Which location model an organisation chooses depends on a number of factors and hence, is not necessarily the ideal model envisaged beforehand. These factors include the physical possibilities of the current locations: is there room for expansion? Financial matters play an important role as well. Developing a new building is costly, while often the existing locations have not depreciated fully in economic and technical terms. Also, government regulations with respect to building permits sometimes make the development of a new building (often involving a concentration of functions) impossible. One can also imagine that for reasons of efficient operational management concentration might be the most favourable situation, for instance because the facilities for laboratories and diagnostics, radiology etc. can be used more efficiently. However, it may also prove to be very efficient to concentrate for instance plan-able care in one location, so that specialists and staff become more practised and specialised and hence more people can be treated in a shorter period of time. Furthermore, the opinion of the medical specialists should not be overlooked. For them, having multiple locations and in particular specialised locations brings certain opportunities such as more tailor-made treatment for specific groups of patients. However, profiling locations also brings some practical difficulties, for instance the necessity to travel between the locations. Finally, competition with other hospital organisations plays a major role. If closing down one location means a loss of hinterland to another hospital organisation, then closing down is not seriously considered. In the situation where the organisation has more or less a monopoly in the region, concentration on one location may be more feasible.

The outcome of the balancing of all these factors is increasingly often the specialisation of different locations in certain hospital care functions. This is particularly true in strongly urbanised city-regions, where multiple hospital organisations co-exist close to each other and competition for the hinterland is fierce, so closing down locations is becoming uncommon. In these regions, for instance in the Randstad, we even see the opening of a number of buitenpoli's, which should be considered as outposts safeguarding or extending the hospital's hinterland. When competition is fierce and the multi-location model is seen as a necessity, a hospital's board of directors often decides to give distinct, complementary profiles to the locations so that the organisation benefits from the potential advantages of the merger. Table 4.5 summarises our findings from interviews, strategic policy documents and hospitals' annual reports for all multi-location hospitals in the South Wing of the Randstad and the province of North Brabant that resulted from a merger since 1990. No multi-location hospitals developed before that year, nor have any of the mergers in these regions since 1990 resulted in a concentration.

Table 4.5 shows that the majority of multi-location hospitals in both polycentric urban regions is implementing a functional specialisation of locations based on the type of care a patient needs: often one location specialising in

Table 4.5 Multi-location hospitals in the South Wing and Brabantstad and their desired future location model

Multi-location hospital organisation	Year merger	Locations	Desired location model	Implementation
Rijnland ziekenhuis	1990	Leiderdorp; Alphen aan den Rijn	Multi-location, locations having focused profiles (Leiderdorp: C; Alphen aan den Rijn: P)	Advanced
Reinier de Graaf Groep	1996	Delft; Voorburg	Multi-location, locations having focused profiles (Delft: C; Voorburg: P)	Advanced
TweeSteden ziekenhuis	1997	Tilburg; Waalwijk	Multi-location, locations having focused profiles (Tilburg: C; Waalwijk: P)	Advanced
Medisch Centrum Haaglanden	1998	The Hague; Leidschendam	Multi-location, locations having focused profiles (The Hague: C; Leidschendam: P)	Start/plan phase
Vlietland ziekenhuis	1999	Schiedam; Vlaardingen	Concentration	Concentration per 2007
Albert Schweitzer ziekenhuis	1999	Dordrecht (2); Zwijndrecht; Sliedrecht	Multi-location, locations having focused profiles (Dordrecht 1: C; Dordrecht 2: P; Zwijndrecht: C; Sliedrecht: P)	Advanced
ziekenhuis Bernhoven	2000	Veghel; Oss	Concentration	Start/plan phase
Amphia ziekenhuis	2001	Breda (2); Oosterhout	Multi-location, locations having focused profiles (Breda 1: W+CH+CHR; Breda 2: C; Oosterhout: P)	Intermediate
Jeroen Bosch ziekenhuis	2002	Den Bosch (3); Boxtel	Concentration (Den Bosch: C; Boxtel: PR)	Concentration per 2009
Máxima Medisch Centrum	2002	Eindhoven; Veldhoven	Multi-location, relative similar profiles	Continuation of pre-merger situation

C	Complex and emergency care	P	Plan-able, elective care
CH	Children	PR	Privately funded care
CHR	Chronic patients	W	Women

emergency and complex care, another one in plan-able or elective care and sometimes we find locations specialised in high-frequent care for chronic patients or focusing on women or children. The extent to which they have implemented their desired location model varies. In general they will continue to offer plan-able care also at the location for complex and emergency care, however only for patients with a high risk for complications. Three out of the ten multi-location hospitals will concentrate their activities on one location in the near future. One of them will continue to have two locations, but one will be for experiments with offering care on a private basis.

Given our definition, for hospitals to be complementary they should not only provide for different specialisations, but they should also serve more or less the same region. In the Netherlands, the hinterland of a hospital is termed its 'clinical adherency', that is the number of potential patients in the surrounding region, which is based on the share the hospital had previously in each municipality. Practically all mergers take place between hospital care organisations located in municipalities in which already a certain share of the population visits the other hospital. This means that the condition for complementarity, that the demand should come from more or less the same region, is met. As a result of profiling, for some types of hospital care patients can no longer get help from the nearest hospital location. It appears that, in general, there is a slight fall in the number of patients following the profiling of locations, but this tends to be adjusted within a couple of years. Moreover, it seems to be more due to a lack of clarity than to an unwillingness of some patients to travel further. A recent survey (Ecorys-NEI, 2003) showed that, alongside the expertise of the medical staff, travel time is the most determining factor in the patient's choice of a hospital. Also, some 40% of the respondents would prefer to get treatment in a considerably more distant hospital if they were treated much sooner than in the nearest hospital. Of course, for elective, plan-able care the willingness to travel is much larger than for emergency care or chronic care. Moreover, it appears that in general young people are more willing to travel than older people, who account for the largest demand.

4.6 Conclusion

According to Kuhn (1962), a crisis over the tenability of a paradigm may end with the emergence of a new candidate for paradigm and with the ensuing battle over its acceptance. In this paper we explored whether the network model of spatial organisation could be such a new paradigm replacing the criticised central place model, at least in polycentric urban regions. An important feature of this network model is that functions such as urban facilities are spread over the different cities in such a way that they complement each other. This paper explored the development of this complementarity, thereby focusing on two urban facilities, hospitals and hogescholen, as these are increasingly organised on a regional level, which takes shape through the development of multi-location organisations. They spread their locations over a number of close-by cities, more or less comparable to the notion of a polycentric urban region. Therefore, relationships between the locations of these multi-location organisations may be considered exemplary for intercity-relationships.

Can these relationships better be described by central place theory or is the network model more appropriate? Empirical evidence for the hospital sector supports the latter. A large number of the multi-location hospitals choose to give a more distinct profile to their locations leading to complementarity. The old situation of each city having its own hospital providing as much as possible specialisations as allowed by the size of their hinterland was very much in line with the central place model. However, the development of institutional ties between hospitals brings along a trend that hospital managers seek for scale economies through imposing a division of labour. Many of these multi-location hospitals are therefore characterised by a high extent of complementarity, thus supporting the network model. This specialisation is also forced by a strong need for efficiency given the high costs of hospitals and care.

Although the macro-context for the hogescholen sector is quite similar, the actual micro-level behaviour of managers of multi-location hogescholen diverges from those of hospitals. Multi-location hogescholen tend to copy study programmes rather than profiling their locations, a trend that contradicts the network model. Part of the explanation is that the costs of duplication are small for hogescholen, while also many prospective students are reluctant to travel far. On the other hand, it was possible that even in a situation with few complementarities between locations, the largest location did not offer all the study programmes offered by smaller locations, as we would expect in the case of a hierarchical central place model. This supports the idea of size neutrality, another feature of the network model. Even while our analysis of the hogescholen sector does not unambiguously support the network model of spatial organisation, as does the hospital sector, our findings do not support the central place model either.

While our exploration was necessarily limited in terms of scope, its results emphasise the necessity and value of further exploration of the comprehensive research agenda of whether a network model of spatial organisation is developing. Urban networks research could then become the contemporary pendant of what urban systems research used to be.

Acknowledgement
The author is grateful to Hugo Priemus and Marjolein Spaans for their helpful comments on earlier versions of this paper. The paper also benefited from comments by two anonymous referees. The author wishes to acknowledge the financial assistance of the Dutch government through the Habiforum Program Innovative Land Use and Delft University of Technology through the Delft Centre for Sustainable Urban Areas.

References

Adviescommissie Onderwijsaanbod (2003) *Eindrapport 1993-2003*. The Hague: Adviescommissie onderwijsaanbod.

Batten, D.F. (1995) Network Cities: Creative Urban Agglomerations for the 21st Century, *Urban Studies*, 32, pp. 313-327.

Berry, B.J.L., J.B. Parr, B.J. Epstein, A. Ghosh and R.H.T. Smith (1988) *Market Centers and Retail Location. Theory and Applications*. Englewood Cliffs: Prentice Hall.

Boot, J.M. (1998) Schaalvergroting en concentratie in het Nederlandse Ziekenhuiswezen, *Bestuurskunde*, 7, pp. 28-37.

Böventer, E. von (1963) Towards a Unified Theory of Spatial Economic Structure, *Papers of the Regional Science Association*, 10, pp. 163-187.

Burg, A.J. van der and F.M. Dieleman (2004) Dutch urbanisation policies: From 'compact city' to 'urban network', *Tijdschrift voor Economische en Sociale Geografie*, 95, pp. 108-116.

Burton, I. (1963) A restatement of the dispersed city hypothesis, *Annals of the Association of American Geographers*, 63, pp. 285-289.

Camagni, R. (1993) From city hierarchy to city networks: reflections about an emerging paradigm, in: T.R. Lakshmanan and P. Nijkamp (Eds) *Structure and Change in the Space Economy: Festschrift in honour of Martin Beckmann*, pp. 66-87. Berlin: Springer Verlag.

Camagni, R. and C. Salone (1993) Network Urban Structures in Northern Italy: Elements for a Theoretical Framework, *Urban Studies*, 30, pp. 1053-1064.

Capello, R. (2000) The city network paradigm: measuring urban network externalities, *Urban Studies*, 37, pp. 1925-1945.

Christaller, W. (1933) *Die zentralen Orte in Süddeutschland*. Jena: Fischer.

Coffey, W.J. (1998) Urban Systems Research: an Overview, *Canadian Journal of Regional Science*, XXI, pp. 327-364.

Coffey, W.J., L.S. Bourne, J.E. Randall, W.K.D. Davies and R. White (1998) Urban systems research: past, present, and future. A panel discussion, *Canadian Journal of Regional Science*, XXI, pp. 327-364.

College Bouw Ziekenhuisvoorzieningen (2000) *Uitvoeringstoets op hoofdlijnen inzake gewenste ziekenhuispreiding*. Utrecht: College Bouw Ziekenhuisvoorzieningen.

Davies, W.K.D. (1998) Urban Systems Research: Unfulfilled Promises?, *Canadian Journal of Regional Science*, XXI, pp. 349-356.

Davoudi, S. (2003) Polycentricity in European Spatial Planning: From an Analytical Tool to a Normative Agenda, *European Planning Studies*, 11, pp. 979-999.

Dieleman, F.M. and A. Faludi (1998) Polynucleated metropolitan regions in northwest Europe: theme of the special issue, *European Planning Studies*, 6, pp. 365-377.

Ecorys-NEI (2003) *Vraagfactoren ziekenhuizen*. Rotterdam: Ecorys-NEI.

Gordijn, C.M.N. and G.F.M. Janssen (1997) Hoger onderwijs regionaal bezien, 1996/'96, *Kwartaalschrift Onderwijsstatistieken*, 1997-III, pp. 21-28.

Gottmann, J. (1961) *Megalopolis, The urbanized Northeastern Seaboard of the United States*. New York: The Twentieth Century Fund.

Greenacre, M.J. (1993) *Correspondence Analysis in Practice*. London: Academic Press Ltd.

Hague, C. and K. Kirk (2003) *Polycentricity Scoping Study*. London: Office of the Deputy Prime Minister.

Hartog, den M. (2004) *Effecten van marktstructuur en gedrag op het resultaat van algemene ziekenhuizen* (PhD. thesis, University of Tilburg).

IB-Groep (2005) http://www.ib-groep.nl/ (Accessed June 3, 2005).

Kloosterman, R.C. and S. Musterd (2001) The Polycentric Urban Region: Towards a Research Agenda, *Urban Studies*, 38, pp. 623-633.

Knaap, G.A. van der (2002) *Stedelijke bewegingsruimte, over veranderingen in stad en land*. The Hague: Sdu uitgevers.

Kuhn, T.S. (1962) *The Structure of Scientific Revolutions*. Chicago: The University of Chicago Press.

Lösch, A. (1941) *Die räumliche Ordnung der Wirtschaft*. Jena: Fischer.

Meijers, E. (2005) Polycentric Urban Regions and the Quest for Synergy: Is a Network of Cities More than the Sum of the Parts?, *Urban Studies*, 42, pp. 765-781.

Nederlandse Mededingingsautoriteit (NMa) (2004) *Concurrentie in de ziekenhuissector, visiedocument*. The Hague: NMa.

Nienoord-Buré, C.D. and K.A.M. Damen (1992) *Functieprofilering bij meerlocatie-ziekenhuizen*. Utrecht: Nationaal Ziekenhuisinstituut.

Onderwijsraad (2004) *Bureaucratisering in het onderwijs*. The Hague: Onderwijsraad.

Onderwijsraad (2005) *De stand van educatief Nederland*. The Hague: Onderwijsraad.

Organisation for Economic Co-operation and Development (OECD) (2004) *Education at a Glance*. Paris: OECD.

Parr, J.B. (2004) The Polycentric Urban Region: A Closer Inspection, *Regional Studies*, 38, pp. 231-240.

Pred, A. (1977) *City-Systems in Advanced Economies*. London: Hutchinson.

Pumain, D. (1992) Urban networks versus urban hierarchies?, *Environment and Planning A*, 24, pp. 1377-1380.

Rijksinstituut voor Volksgezondheid en Milieu (RIVM) (2004) *Volksgezondheid Toekomst Verkenning, Nationale Atlas Volksgezondheid*. Bilthoven: RIVM. <http://www.zorgatlas.nl> (Accessed February 2004)

Taylor, P.J. (2003) *World City Network: a Global Urban analysis*. London: Routledge.

Ullman, E.L. (1956) The Role of Transportation and the Bases for Interaction, in: W.L. Thomas (ed.) *Man's Role in Changing the Face of Earth*, pp. 862-880. Chicago: The University of Chicago Press.

5 Realising potential:

Building regional organising capacity in polycentric urban regions

Meijers, E., and A. Romein (2003) Realizing potential: building regional organizing capacity in Polycentric Urban Regions, in: *European Urban and Regional Studies*, 10 (2), pp. 173-186.

Abstract

Regional planning for and in polycentric urban regions may entail certain competitive potentialities over a stand-alone development of their individual cities or city-regions. These potentialities relate to the pooling of resources, complementarities and spatial diversity. It seems that planners are increasingly aware of these potentialities as in several European countries attempts are made to identify such polycentric regional systems of formerly independent and distinct cities that are located close to each other, often building on increasing functional relationships between them. This article argues, however, that in order to actually exploit the theoretical potential planning for polycentric urban regions has, one needs to do more than just identify a polycentric system on the map. Rather, an active building of regional organising capacity is needed – that is, the ability to regionally co-ordinate developments through a more or less institutionalised framework of co-operation, debate, negotiation and decision-making in pursuit of interests at the regional scale – to shape a polycentric urban region's competitive advantages. This need for regional organising capacity may sound obvious, but in practice successful examples of proclaimed polycentric urban regions developing networks for regional co-ordination and action are rather thin on the ground. Basing our argument on evidence from four polycentric urban regions in North West Europe, it was found that the building of regional organising capacity is conditioned by a number of spatial-functional, political-institutional and cultural factors. Major constraints in the examined regions include institutional fragmentation, an internal orientation of key persons and the lack of identification with the region at large.

5.1 Polycentricity and regional development

The concept of polycentricity is becoming increasingly popular in spatial policies on a variety of spatial scales, ranging from the European to the local. Although the meaning of the concept, as well as the purposes of the policies, differ between these various scales, polycentricity in general is chiefly considered a means to achieve both a more balanced spatial pattern of development and a higher level of international territorial competitiveness by the area at stake. This article deals with the application of this concept to the regional scale, the so-called 'polycentric urban regions'.

At the regional level, polycentricity is the result of a rather general contemporary tendency in the urban geography of advanced post-industrial societies: the emergence of polycentric cities. In Europe, a transition can be observed since the 1960s[1] from urban patterns that were dominated by the self-contained functional entities of a central city with its immediate hinterland, towards networking urban systems of multiple centres of residence, employment and services. Due to predominant tendencies of spatial de-concentration and scaling-up, most urban functions, i.e. residence, manufacturing, office-based sectors, retail, wholesale, warehousing and leisure services, have extended over increasing territories to new suburban centres or to places that are strategically located from a transport point of view. Generally speaking, the traditional functional hierarchy and duality between the city centres and the multitude of suburban places is eroding in many city-regions.

Polycentric urban regions deserve special attention as they are the result of this spatial reorganising process in the specific case of a region where historically distinct and both administratively and politically independent cities are located in more or less close proximity – say within commuting distance – and are well connected through infrastructure. These cities have coalesced both functionally and morphologically into larger and more dispersed regional urban systems (e.g. Ghent Urban Studies Team, 1999; Bontje, 2001; Dieleman and Faludi, 1998a; Champion, 2001). The erstwhile dominant hierarchical patterns of functional relationships and mobility between central cities and their respective hinterlands have been supplemented with more horizontal patterns of relationships and flows between these formerly independent and separate city-regions. Often cited examples of polycentric urban regions are the Randstad in the Netherlands, the RheinRuhr in Germany and the Flemish Diamond in Belgium. Some examples can also be found in other parts of Europe, for example the Italian Padua-Treviso-Venice and Emilia Romagna regions and the Spanish Basque Country. Such regional polycentric systems are referred to by various concepts that are largely synonymous with the polycentric ur-

1 In the USA, such processes could be observed several decades earlier.

ban region-concept used here, for instance 'network cities' (Batten, 1995), 'city networks' (Camagni and Salone, 1993), 'polynucleated metropolitan regions' (Dieleman and Faludi, 1998b) or 'city clusters' (CEC, 1999).

Literature on the polycentric urban region is still limited and rather unconsolidated (Bailey and Turok, 2001). Consequently, a diversity of sometimes more or less implicit definitions, operationalisations and approaches to this type of urban configuration is still in circulation (Kloosterman and Musterd, 2001). The subject has, however, been attracting growing attention for more than a decade by professionals of various backgrounds, including (a) academics such as geographers, economists and social and political scientists, and (b) planners and policy-makers. The way academics and policy-makers deal with polycentric urban regions differs to some extent. In general, the concept has both an empirical/analytical and a strategic/conceptual component to it. So far, empirical-analytical research has strongly focussed on the tenability of the notion of the polycentric urban region as a functional spatial entity. Mostly, this question is being approached by research that focuses on spatial behaviour and mobility patterns of individuals and households (Clark and Kuijpers-Linde, 1994; Dieleman and Faludi, 1998; Van der Laan, 1998) or firms (Camagni and Salone, 1993; Batten, 1995; Lambooy, 1998). In addition, some analyses focus on the 'regional discourse' i.e. the process of institutionalising such polycentric systems in both policy and society (de Boer, 1996; Blotevogel, 1998; Knapp, 1998).

Planners and policy-makers put more emphasis on strategic motives and action: these professionals consider the region an 'actor' rather than just a 'space' (see Keating, 2001). Against the background of the growing belief that the region is becoming the most important spatial level of international territorial competition, planners, policy-makers and other stakeholders view the strengthening of its competitiveness as the predominant purpose of strategic actions. They usually refer to 'high road' competitiveness, i.e. the creation of an environment that lures investments in hi-tech production and high level services, highly qualified manpower, and visitors with great purchasing power. Often referring to the 'global city regions' debate (see Scott, 2001), some planners in major polycentric urban regions sometimes even voice the ambition that these should be able to compete successfully with the highest level metropolitan agglomerations such as New York, London or Paris as it provides economies of scale without incurring the costs or agglomeration diseconomies that these large metropolises entail. Bailey and Turok (2001:698) state that 'the PUR (*Polycentric Urban Region*) concept is alleged to offer a sound basis to promote regional economic competitiveness (...). It promotes the advantages of stronger interaction between neighbouring cities to develop specialised and complementary assets, while avoiding large-scale urban sprawl and destructive territorial competition'.

In this article we will establish a bridge between both the academic approaches to polycentric urban regions and the strategic approach of such regions adopted by many planners and policy-makers. We argue that for the optimal development and exploitation of the theoretical potentialities that a regional planning approach in polycentric urban regions holds over a stand-alone development strategy of its individual 'member' cities, efficient co-operation and joint policy-making on a regional scale, i.e. regional organising capacity, is an important condition. Although the benefits of a co-ordinated regional planning approach have been acknowledged by stakeholders in several polycentric urban regions (see Ipenburg and Lambregts, 2001), examples of the development of frameworks for regional co-ordination and action are rather thin on the ground. Perhaps, the development of regional organising capacity or even the further application of the concept of polycentric urban regions is not very appealing under certain circumstances. This article's main objective is to explore the question why such examples are the exception rather than the rule, in spite of the advantages of a co-ordinated regional approach. This question will be answered by analysing the institutional, political, cultural and spatial-functional contexts of polycentric urban regions in relation to the development of regional organising capacity. For this, we use empirical evidence from four polycentric urban regions (the Randstad, the RheinRuhr, the Flemish Diamond and Central Scotland, see Figure 5.1) that were studied in the research-project called EURBANET[2] on which this article builds. Our main 'benchmark' is the Randstad as this region is regarded as a prime or classic example of a polycentric urban region (Hohenberg and Lees, 1985; Batten, 1995) and, more importantly, is home to several past and recent attempts to build regional organising capacity. Prior to this analysis, we provide arguments to underpin the hypothesis that regional planning in and for polycentric urban regions benefits their competitiveness and that regional organising capacity is needed for an optimal and effective exploitation of the potentialities of regional planning in such regions. For this, we present an inventory of theoretical competitive potentialities of a regional planning approach in polycentric urban configurations. However, first a brief discussion of some interesting examples of applications of the polycentric urban region as a planning concept is presented.

5.2 The polycentric urban region in spatial planning policy

Spatial policy-makers apply the concept of polycentricity on a variety of spatial scales, most explicitly on the European and the regional scale. In their

2 The EURBANET-project was part of the Interreg IIC programme of the North Western Metropolitan Area and co-funded by the European Commission.

Figure 5.1 Major polycentric urban regions in North West Europe

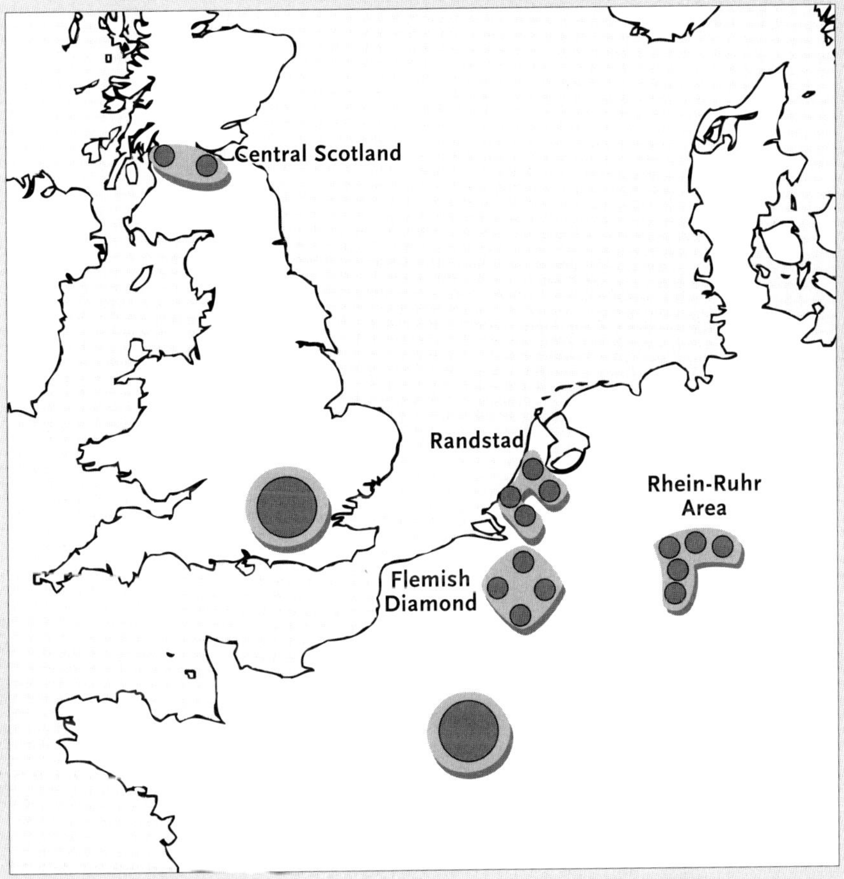

evaluation of the European Spatial Development Perspective (ESDP), Faludi and Waterhout (2001) state that polycentricity forms the (only) key substantive concept of this planning document at the European level. In addition to this transnational level, the ESDP also pays attention to polycentric development at the lower level of sub-national regions. The document refers to polycentric urban regions as 'city clusters' or 'city networks'. As policy options, it proposes to strengthen a polycentric and more balanced system of metropolitan regions, city clusters and city networks, as well as promoting integrated spatial development strategies for city clusters in individual member states or in trans-national and cross-border co-operations (CEC, 1999:21). Apparently, the European Commission favours the integrated development of polycentric urban regions.

The ESDP has strongly contributed to the debate on polycentric development within the EU member states and has in this way encouraged the application of polycentricity in national or sub-national spatial planning policies, though in some countries it was already under discussion before the ESDP was published. Polycentricity in these cases is often applied at a regional level, mostly for reasons of international competitiveness, the integrated devel-

Figure 5.2 Polycentric urban regions designated in the proposed Dutch national spatial planning policy

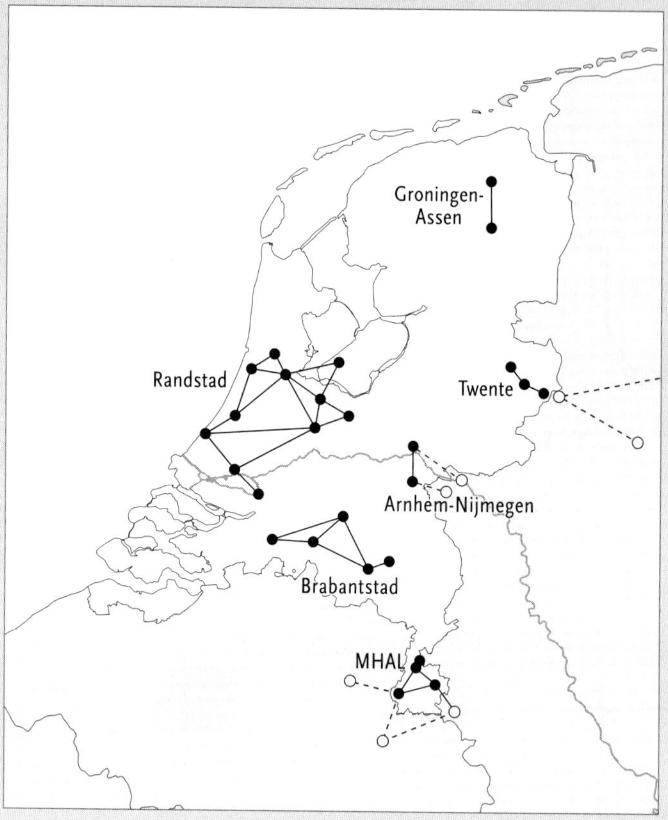

opment of polycentric urban regions is often initiated by national or sub-national state governments rather than by the regions itself. Examples of such a top down implementation of this concept are the Flemish Diamond (Brussels-Antwerp-Ghent-Leuven) (Albrechts, 1998) and the RheinRuhr (including cities such as Cologne, Bonn, Dortmund, Essen and Düsseldorf) (Knapp, 1998; Blotevogel, 1998).

The Dutch national government as well pays much attention to polycentric urban regions, but has been, in contrast, actually spurred into doing so by some of these regions, in particular the Randstad. The government's new spatial policy[3] refers to polycentric urban regions as *stedelijke netwerken* (urban networks). It has designated six urban networks of national importance (Figure 5.2). The Randstad[4] is one of these six polycentric regions and is composed of a ring of cities around a relatively open 'Green Heart', including the

3 *The Fifth Memorandum on Spatial Planning* still has to be considered by the Parliament. Its current status is that of a policy proposal. However, the concept of urban networks is well received.

4 *The Fifth Memorandum* refers to the Randstad as the Deltametropolis. We prefer to stick to the 'old' name for two reasons: the Memorandum has not yet passed Parliament and the public of foreign readers is more familiar with it.

Figure 5.3 The Randstad

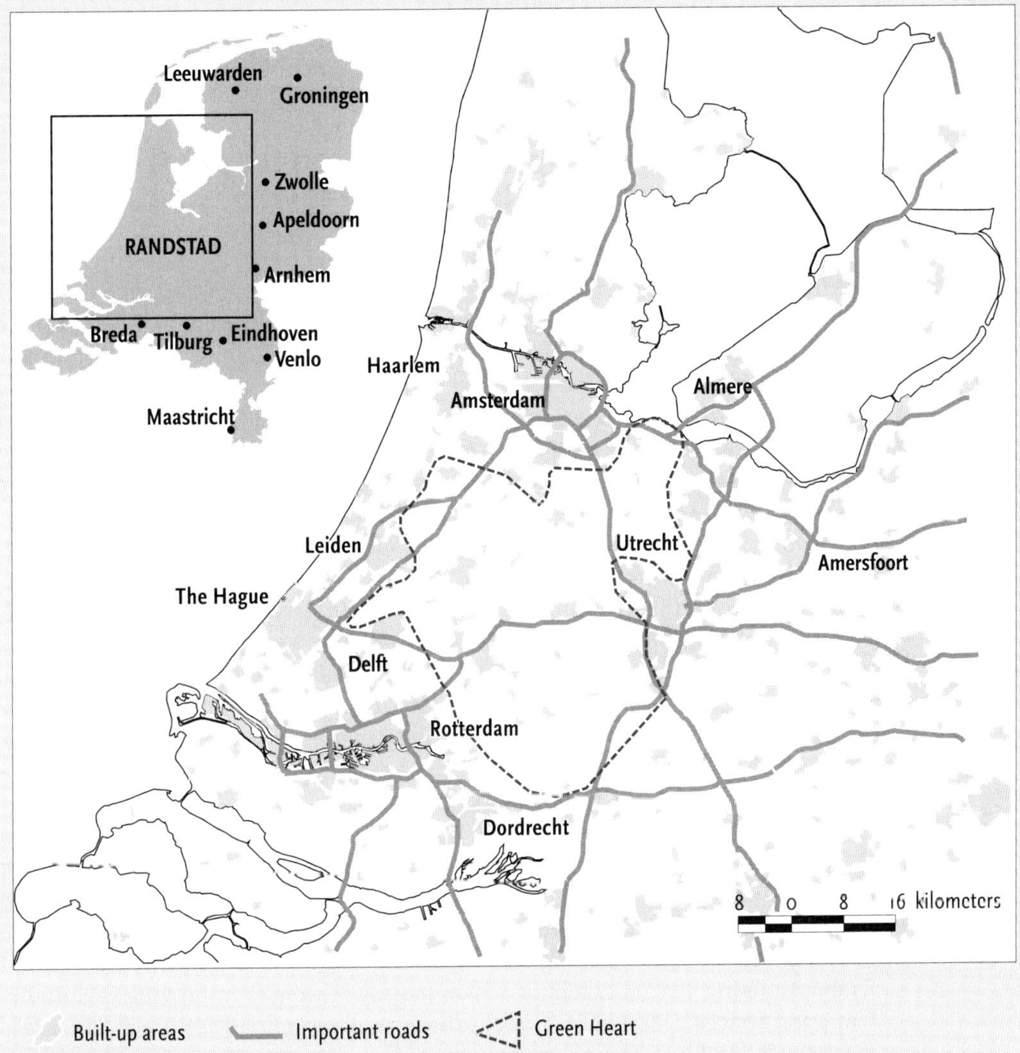

country's four largest cities – Amsterdam, Rotterdam, The Hague and Utrecht (see Figure 5.3). In the Dutch case, the policy is considerably far-reaching. The cities that make up the urban networks are required to draw up spatial programmes and plans in mutual consultation while they also have to see to it that there is an integrated system of both public and private transport (Ministry of VROM, 2001). The policy document puts great emphasis on regional co-operation and policy-making, but remains vague how that must be arranged. This holds true for the other policy documents mentioned here as well.

5.3 Potentialities of a regional approach in polycentric urban regions

In polycentric urban regions, many spatial decisions on location and mobility by the major decision-makers, firms and households, take into account wider sets of assets and broader spatial scopes than just individual cities. It seems plausible therefore that policies that aim at strengthening economic competitiveness at the strictly local level of individual cities make increasingly less sense now these cities are becoming part and parcel of a larger functional geographical entity. The emerging coherent polycentric configuration appears a more appropriate entity for policy and planning than the individual cities it is composed of for an increasing number of issues. Planning at the city or city-region level leaves much room for competition within polycentric urban regions for investments in high-level services and hi-tech industries, for professional workers, for tourists, and even for a marketable image. It leaves opportunities that are offered by the larger regional system unutilised and may even lead to waste through, for example, duplications. The observation by Scott *et al.* (2001:11) in their essay on the rise of global city regions that the 'individual city in the narrow sense is less an appropriate or viable unit of social organisation than this regional networks of cities'[5] is also applicable to the policy issue of territorial competitiveness.

Building on research findings of EURBANET, three potentialities of regional co-ordination and action in polycentric urban regions can be distinguished. Regional co-operation and co-ordination in these regions may open the road to (1) pooling resources in order to share facilities and services and to achieve 'critical mass', (2) developing and exploiting balanced complementarities and (3) optimising spatial diversity, which mainly relates to improving the quality of open spaces. Defined so broadly, these three potentialities are more or less acknowledged in all four regions examined in EURBANET.

The first potentiality of a regional approach in polycentric urban regions is the possibility to effectively pool assets that are spread across the region. This provides greater agglomeration or external economies for businesses. On the regional scale, businesses have access to larger and more varied pools of labour, suppliers, and customers than in any of its individual urban nodes or locations. A series of interviews with major stakeholders in the regions examined in EURBANET reveals that the pooling of highly qualified professional labour is considered a particularly important advantage (Ipenburg and Lambregts, 2001). In some cases, the pooling of local labour markets may solve a situation of unemployment in one area of the region and scarcity of workers in another. The surplus value of regional co-ordination and action may con-

5 Scott *et al.* mention the polynuclear Randstad Holland as an example of a global city region.

sist of policy measures to improve labour mobility at the regional level.

Besides the pooling of resources, the encouraging of interaction between neighbouring cities in a polycentric urban region may result in functional specialisations. Where such specialisations are complementary rather than competitive, the polycentric urban region as a whole may offer a broader package of higher quality, metropolitan services to businesses, households, consumers, workers and tourists. These services may be advanced producer services; educational and R&D institutes; specialised types of retail; recreation, leisure and cultural facilities; and last but not least residential environments (Ipenburg and Lambregts, 2001). A large variety of high quality and rapid accessible complementary services, universities, businesses and stakeholders in a polycentric urban region creates a favourable environment for innovations, which is definitely an advantage in the competition for investments. This is not to say that it is co-operation instead of competition that creates such a set of complementary local environments. Rather, it may be co-ordination and co-operation between public policy-makers, removing barriers against private competition (market imperfections) that are at the root of functional specialisation of places.

The third potentiality of regional planning, the improvement of the quality of open space, adds spatial diversity as a competitive quality to the above mentioned pooled economic resources and complementary facilities and amenities in polycentric urban regions. The current tendency towards dispersed and unbalanced patchworks of all kinds of 'constructions, topographies and spaces, with elements of urban as well as rural landscapes' (Schmitt *et al.*, 2001:18) that develop in the formerly unencumbered open landscapes of many polycentric configurations means a downgrading of their spatial diversity. This must be judged negatively from the competitive point of view because it harms the variety of urban scenery and rural landscapes across short distances, which is considered one of the basic competitive advantages of polycentric urban regions over single large metropolitan agglomerations. Avoiding such uncontrolled urban sprawl, and protecting the 'green (and blue) networks' for recreational functions requires co-ordinated policy-making from a regional rather than a local perspective.

One must be aware that, though these potentialities are promising on a regional scale, they may have drawbacks on a local scale. For instance, the co-ordinated development of complementary facilities and amenities may provide a larger variety and higher quality of these on the regional scale, but may also require that individual city-regions should make net sacrifices by subordinating their own interests to the greater regional good (e.g. Hospers and van Lochem, 2001). For instance, it may be decided on the regional level that a specific city may loose a highly appraised vocational training institute, theater, or medical specialism provided by the local hospital, to a neighbouring city without being sufficiently compensated for this loss in another sector. In our view, this still makes the case for developing an institutional framework for co-operation and co-ordination pressing, as this framework should allow exactly for these kind of trade-offs and a fair distribution of the regional good. Without such a framework, local interests will continue to prevail, so blocking the exploitation of regional potentialities.

5.4 Limited regional organising capacity in polycentric urban regions

Notwithstanding the importance of regional planning in polycentric urban regions and the strong contribution of regional organising capacity in exploiting its potentialities, the four polycentric urban regions considered in this study show that regional organising capacity has hardly been developed. Coupled with the eagerness of policy-makers to have their regions taken seriously by outsiders, it is striking that there is only limited interest in the development of this capacity. For instance, initiatives to develop regional organising capacity in the RheinRuhr – both morphologically and functionally a coherent entity (GEMACA, 1996) – are only limited so far. The same holds true for the Flemish Diamond. Although this polycentric urban region does appear in planning documents, one can hardly see the beginning of a developing regional organising capacity. Albrechts (1998) concludes that institutional coherence and co-operation within this region are rather weakly developed.

While the Randstad as a planning concept has occupied a central position in national planning strategies for at least the last fourty years, even there attempts to actually build regional organising capacity have not been successful. Most of the attempts have entailed the introduction of a formal (fourth) government tier in between the municipal and provincial tiers, but none of them have proven to be politically acceptable. The traditional Dutch three-tier system (national government, provinces, municipalities) has proved to be resistant to changes, making clear that regional organising capacity should be based on voluntary co-operation between the three tiers. Recent bottom-up attempts, some of them specifically aimed at improving the national and international competitiveness of the Randstad, have provided a new impulse for building regional organising capacity in the Randstad. Most notable are the *Bureau Regio Randstad* (Randstad Region Agency), an agency that supports the co-ordination of policies by the four provinces in the Randstad[6], and the Delta Metropolis Association, a rather informal body in which city authorities, district water boards, chambers of commerce and a variety of other semi-public and private institutions meet and discuss the way the Randstad can

6 These are the provinces of North Holland, South Holland, Utrecht and Flevoland.

develop into a competitive European metropolis. Now that the national government has published its proposals for a new spatial planning policy there is some discussion about building the organising capacity in the polycentric urban regions identified in the document. The four Randstad provinces and the mayors of the four largest cities have expressed their interest in designing a co-operative structure in which the provinces, the four largest cities and the four matching formal city regions are represented. Tasks could include putting Randstad-scale projects on the regional and national agenda and to define a way of elaborating and implementing them (BRR, 2001). However, the value of these more recent initiatives still has to be proven.

5.5 Context-bound constraints to the building of regional organising capacity

Apparently, applying the concept of polycentric urban regions and acknowledging the potentialities of regional planning in such regions do not consequently result in the development of regional institutional frameworks for co-operation and co-ordination. Here we identify the reasons for this in terms of constraints for building regional organising capacity in polycentric urban regions, which we base on our experience in the EURBANET project. A clear starting point lies in the analysis of the current political, institutional, cultural and spatial contexts of polycentric urban regions and the way these interfere with the building of regional organising capacity.

In building a more general framework to assess the possible constraints for the development of regional organising capacity in polycentric urban regions, we can partly build on previous research concerned with factors determining the potential for such developments. For instance, Van den Berg and Braun (1999) list seven factors contributing to urban organising capacity, which are: the formal institutional framework (the administrative organisation), strategic networks, leadership, vision and strategy, spatial-economic conditions, political support, and, finally, social support. Keating (2001:379) describes the concept of a development coalition; a place-based interclass coalition dedicated to economic development in a specific location. Keating claims that the context for building such a development coalition is determined by the current competitive situation of the region, but also by factors such as culture, institutions, leadership, social composition and external relations. With respect to regions constituting themselves as an actor he remarks that institutions, leadership and an ability to carry a definition of the interests of the region are required. While the focus here is on the regional rather than the urban level and is more broadly defined than just a development coalition, the factors named above provide clues to the components of the framework needed in order to analyse the context for building regional organising capacity. Irrespective of the precise categorisation used above, and basing ourselves on the EURBANET experiences, we are able to deduce three general dimensions that play a role in determining the feasibility of the building of regional organising capacity in a polycentric urban region: the spatial-functional dimension (which is quite specific for polycentric urban regions), the political-institutional dimension, and the cultural dimension.

Spatial-functional dimension

The further a polycentric urban region is functionally tied together and integrated, the greater the need for regional organising capacity. Clearly, there must be some spatial logic, or functional rationality behind the formation of regional organising capacity. This means that actors (enterprises, public and private institutions, households) have to maintain relations throughout the region to fulfil their needs for production, consumption and personal needs. Authors dealing with this spatial-functional dimension often centre on daily flows of people, translated into 'travel to work areas', 'daily urban systems' (Van der Laan, 1998) or 'functional urban regions' (Cheshire and Hay, 1989). But the functional dimension encompasses more. According to Pumain (1999:6) a functional urban unit presents 'a concentration of people, activity, capital and buildings, constituted by markets of, for example, labour, retail, services, culture or housing. It is structured on major roads, railroads and terminals and functions by flows of people, goods, energy, information and money'. Consequently, whether or not a polycentric urban region functions as a functional entity can be deduced from the spatial scopes of markets, infrastructure and flows.

The required functional rationality behind the development of regional organising capacity does not mean that a polycentric urban region needs to be one single, compact, functionally coherent and 'closed' system. Polycentric urban systems tend to be open and multi-layered complexes of nodes, networks, flows and interactions of global, regional and local scales (Albrechts, 2001). Consequently, the spatial scope and spatial orientation of interactions between places do not coincide exclusively with the polycentric system as a whole, but vary considerably between types of interactions and are dynamic. For some, the region has become one single polycentric 'urban field' but for others it is either too large or too small. In a recent analysis of the labour market of the Randstad, Van Ham *et al.* (2001) show that it has become one single labour market for some groups of highly qualified, high income and mobile professionals, but is subdivided into several sub-regional labour markets for other workers. The labour markets of lowly or unskilled and less mobile workers do not even surpass the level of individual cities and their immediate hinterlands. Similar conclusions can be drawn for other functions, like housing, leisure and recreational services: the urban system is one single market only for some selective groups of its population. Analysing the Rand-

Figure 5.4 Travel for social visits between Corop-regions in the Randstad, 1986 (left) and 1998 (right). Based on data CBS (OVG)

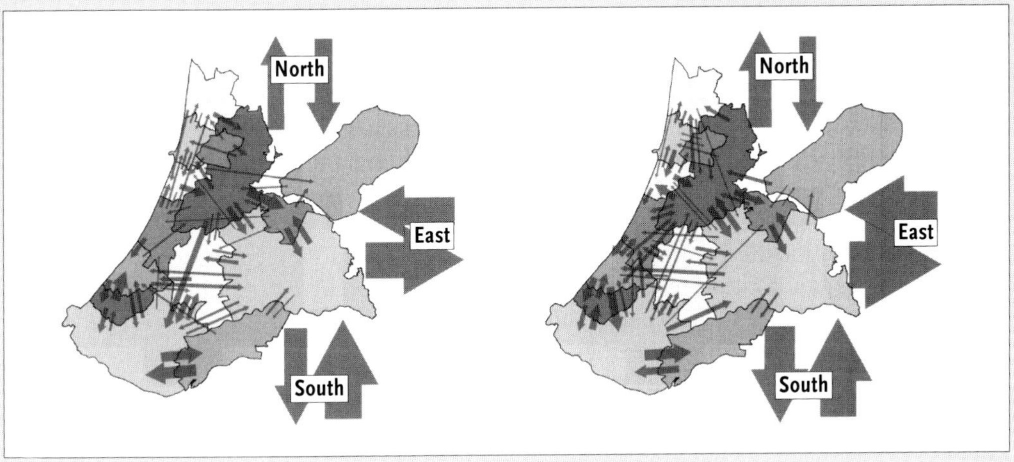

stad presents a clear picture: regional spatial relations increase, strengthen and get more dispersed, while the spatial scope of functional markets (in particular for labour, shopping, social activities, leisure and sports) is widening to a more regional scale, even though this is often not the scale of the entire Randstad (Hoppenbrouwer *et al.*, 2001). Similar tendencies can be found in the Flemish Diamond and the RheinRuhr. Figure 5.4 presents a view on the increase in travel for social visits between sub-regions in the Randstad. Social visits account for a large share (about 15% in 1999) of the total number of trips made.

The fact that polycentric urban regions cannot be defined as single, closed functional units is also reflected in the multitude of interactions that their cities maintain with cities in other regions. Some of their economic clusters, particularly those related to mainports (seaports, airports, or high-speed train stations), are connected more strongly within international rather than regional networks. Policies and planning regarding the competitiveness of these clusters are not primarily formulated on the level of the polycentric urban region. This means that the region is the appropriate platform to formulate and implement policies for only some of the spatial issues, while others can be better dealt with on other levels. Keeping these necessary differentiations in mind we nevertheless claim that, on the basis of the spatial-functional relations and their tendencies, there is reason for building regional organising capacity in the polycentric urban regions examined. The scope of the regional co-ordination, however, should be selective with regard to the spatial issue at stake.

Political-institutional dimension

The attitude and vision towards government, and in particular spatial planning by administrators in the polycentric urban region, are not factors to be neglected when it comes to the development of regional organising capacity. In general, many spatial issues these days call for an approach that is formulated and implemented at multiple scales and across administrative tiers rather than at only one. Additionally, an increasing number of spatial issues are, or preferably should be, addressed through a governance rather than a governmental mode. Regional co-ordination in polycentric urban regions requires the politicians and administrators to adopt a view on government and planning that puts emphasis on co-operation across administrative tiers and sectors and between public, private and organised interest groups, thereby taking into account that different issues call for different alliances with different spatial competencies and different life spans (see Boelens, 2000). Clearly, governing a polycentric urban region is an intricate affair. Putting such multi-level governance into practice is a complex task, even if politicians and administrators agree on its usefulness. There may be a lack of understanding on how multi-level governance works. Perhaps this partly explains the vagueness on the political-institutional dimension for polycentric urban regions in the national Dutch planning policy.

Besides the attitude and vision of administrators and politicians, the formal institutional framework is critical here as well. The question is whether or not this framework leaves room for regional co-ordination. Often, it needs to be adjusted to be able to cope with the interfering and multi-level nature of urban dynamics. The existing frameworks are often too static and hierarchical to recognise and deal with this complex, multi-scalar interplay of trends and forces. As mentioned above, attempts have been made in the Randstad to add a formal administrative tier for a long time, but the existing institutional and political structure has not allowed it. It has become slowly apparent that multi-level governance requires co-operation across scales and across actors, including private actors. The necessary adjustments (e.g. legislation, a formal redistribution of competencies) are only gradually being implemented.

Albrechts (2001:734) characterises polycentric urban regions as 'socio-spatial conflict zones for the articulation of multiple interests, identities and cultural differences'. While turning to identities and cultural differences below, here we deal with the different interests in a polycentric urban region. There appears to be a clear need to establish common and shared interests for the polycentric urban region. This is far from self-evident as there are many fields where the interests of places and stakeholders in a polycentric urban region are different or even opposite. Regional disparities (between central cities and between a central city and its suburban nodes) in, for instance, demographic and economic growth rates, social problems like poverty and unemployment, and in the attractiveness of residential environments, mean that the areas better off in these matters have no interest in adopting regional policies that may adjust this situation. Actors in the Randstad have shown that, to a certain extent, they are capable of defining regional interests. External incentives to do so have been important. These stimuli include the need to position the region externally as a metropolis and the way the national Dutch government funds programmes of projects (chances for investments increase if the region successfully co-operates and clearly defines a desired and prioritised investment programme).

Finally, leadership is important. The region's common and shared interests need to be picked up by leaders willing and able to build on them. Networks in particular need leadership as they lack a formal hierarchical structure. Such leadership can rely on the specific competencies of key figures and key institutions or on the charisma of public or private individuals (Van den Berg and Braun, 1999). The Delta Metropolis Association for instance was initiated by a professor who convinced the mayors of the largest cities to start a regional discourse on the future of the Randstad. Soon other stakeholders in the region followed and the scope expanded.

Cultural dimension

In recent thinking on urban and regional development, much emphasis has been placed on the cultural dimension. Here, the cultural dimension is concerned with the feeling of belonging together and the creation of cultural elements that help in perceiving the polycentric urban region as an entity. Social relationships, shared understandings, and norms of co-operation and reciprocity all ease regional networking. Sharp cultural divides on the other hand impose barriers to co-operation. Cultural discontinuities possibly reduce the opportunities for relationships and interaction. Again referring to the quote of Albrechts (2001:734) above, polycentric urban regions are regions in which potentially discordant multiple identities and cultural differences occur. Following the distinction between culture and identity we can distinguish two elements. The first one is a common culture and refers to the existence of a shared history and shared values, norms and beliefs in a region. Major sources of cultural differences are language, ethnicity, religion and political preferences. The second element is regional identity. This is a concept that is primarily a social construct and therefore a dynamic phenomenon. Moreover, it is a contextual and multi-layered concept. One belongs to many groups that together furnish one with a whole variety of discrete identities which vary in relative or contextual importance. Some of these are linked to a geographical entity, for instance the neighbourhood, city or country one lives in, but probably also the region. The existence of such a regional identity in the polycentric urban region helps to generate social support for regional co-ordination and action. According to Faludi (1999), a common identity helps to achieve common, functional or strategic goals.

Cultural divides can be present in polycentric urban regions even if their scale is relatively small. For instance, experiences in the polycentric urban regions of Central Scotland and the RheinRuhr show that cultural, if not psychological cleavages hamper the building of regional organising capacity. There are strong cultural cleavages between the Edinburgh and Glasgow urban areas and the Rhine and Ruhr areas respectively. In both regions, the most affluent areas, being the Rhine and Edinburgh, are not very enthusiastic about being identified with areas with a reputation for economic downturn, unemployment, and environmental and social problems. Moreover, the lack of a 'regional discourse' in the RheinRuhr adversely affects regional organising capacities. Lurking cultural divides can be found in the Flemish Diamond as well, as this polycentric urban region extends over an area consisting of two regions (Flanders and Brussels) that are not culturally homogeneous, for instance with respect to language. The Randstad performs comparatively better when it comes to the cultural dimension, at least in the sense that there are no major cultural cleavages present.

As polycentric urban regions are not seldom the result of strategic thinking by planners in a top-down manner, the regional identity in such regions is in general weak. Though the Dutch language has an official Dutch word for inhabitants of the Randstad ('*Randstedeling*') suggesting some homogeneity, this does not mean that the population and administrators have a regional 'Randstad' identity. This is because the Randstad lacks identifying power for various reasons:

- there is no undisputed official boundary of the region;
- there are no symbols (for instance special buildings, or a Randstad soccer team) connected to the Randstad-scale, except for one, its morphological form;
- institutions (public, private, social) do not take the Randstad as their territorial organising principle, thereby not reproducing the Randstad concept in daily life;
- the Randstad is not a political arena, which also means that the media do not operate on the Randstad-scale (no newspapers or regional television channels).

This lack of territorial, symbolic and institutional shape (see Paasi, 1996) and political space (see Keating, 1997) in the Randstad has not prevented the establishment of this region in people's consciousness, especially in the way they mentally structure their spatial environment. So, while cultural factors hamper the development of regional organising capacity in Central Scotland, the Flemish Diamond and the RheinRuhr, they play a rather neutral role in the case of the Randstad.

5.6 Conclusions

Like other interpretations of the principle of polycentricity, the concept of the polycentric urban region appeals very much to spatial policy-makers and for good reasons. In theory, the regional co-ordinated spatial development embodied by the concept entails certain potentialities over a stand-alone development strategy of the cities within such a region. These potentialities are:

- to pool resources in order to share facilities and services and to achieve critical mass;
- to develop and exploit balanced complementarities;
- to optimise spatial diversity and to better protect the quality of open spaces.

By arguing that all these potentialities require regional co-ordination and policy-making to make the best out of them, we have made plausible that the challenge for actors in polycentric urban regions is to generate the regional organising capacity to be able to seize and use these potentialities. Regional organising capacity involves regional co-ordination through regional policy networks, i.e. some kind of co-operative regional forum, in which all relevant stakeholders in a polycentric urban region (different public actors, but also private market parties and non-governmental organisations) meet, discuss and decide upon planning policies and their implementation.

Despite the seemingly apparent advantages of building regional organising capacity to make effectively and optimal use of the potentialities of polycentric urban regions, examples of such regions where this takes place are rather exceptional. This paper has explored the reasons for this. Basing our argument on evidence from four polycentric urban regions in North West Europe, and in particular the Randstad, we found that the building of regional organising capacity is conditioned by the spatial-functional, political-institutional and cultural context of the region. In general, the main constraints found in these regions can be categorised as institutional fragmentation combined with an internal orientation of key persons (such as politicians, policy-makers) and the lack of identification with the region at large.

Actors in both polycentric urban regions and other spatial scales (e.g. national) who feel attracted to applying the principle of polycentricity and its regional interpretation in the concept of the polycentric urban region in their spatial development policies, need to be aware that this involves new forms of regional co-ordination and the creation of regional organising capacity. Even this does not guarantee success – i.e. the realisation of the theoretical potentialities polycentric urban regions have – as success is also dependent on the functioning of such co-ordinating networks or partnerships. However, without regional organising capacity, there is danger of the concept of the polycentric urban region remaining a rather empty concept. Reviewing current policies introducing the concept of the polycentric urban region, it appears that the building of regional organising capacity to implement the concept is often simply forgotten.

Besides being aware of the need for regional organising capacity, these actors must also be mindful of the possible contextual constraints they may encounter in developing capacity and deal with them strategically. Lack of functional, cultural or political-institutional coherence does not mean that the building of regional organising capacity is impossible. It rather poses limits on what is achievable in the first stage. In the situation where large political-institutional and or cultural constraints exist, and where maybe also the functional coherence is relatively limited, the best start is a small start. In such a case, voluntary co-operation between a limited number of actors on simple, not too sensitive issues or well-defined projects with clear benefits to the individual actors is best. Mutual trust, understanding and stronger working relationships are likely to evolve, thus enabling the addressing of more complex policies and projects in a later stage. In cases such as the Randstad, where constraints are relatively limited, more structured co-operation yields more advantages. Here, regional organising capacity in the truest sense of the word must be developed to make possible ongoing deliberation, debate, negotiation and decision-making by all interested parties on a wide variety of more or less complex projects and policies that benefit the competitiveness of the region as a whole. This does, however, sometimes require concessions to the wider regional interest by individual actors. Some first attempts in this direction deserve our future attention.

Acknowledgement
The authors would like to thank Bart Lambregts for his valuable comments on an earlier version of the paper.

References

Albrechts, L. (1998) The Flemish Diamond: Precious Gem and Virgin Area, *European Planning Studies*, 6, pp. 411-424.

Albrechts, L. (2001) How to Proceed from Image and Discourse to Action: As Applied to the Flemish Diamond, *Urban Studies*, 38, pp. 733-745.

Bailey, N. and I. Turok (2001) Central Scotland as a polycentric urban region: Useful Planning Concept or Chimera?, *Urban Studies*, 38, pp. 697-715.

Batten, D.F. (1995) Network Cities: Creative Urban Agglomerations for the 21st Century, *Urban Studies*, 32, pp. 313-327.

Berg, L. van den and E. Braun (1999) Urban Competitiveness, Marketing and the Need for Organising Capacity, *Urban Studies*, 36, pp. 987-999.

Blotevogel, H.H. (1998) The Rhine-Ruhr Metropolitan Region: Reality and Discourse, *European Planning Studies*, 6, pp. 395-410.

Boelens, L. (2000) Inleiding, in: L. Boelens (ed) *Nederland Netwerkenland*, pp. 5-12. Rotterdam: NAi Uitgevers.

Boer, N. de (1996) *De Randstad bestaat niet, de onmacht tot grootstedelijk beleid*. Rotterdam: NAi Uitgevers.

Bontje, M. (2001) Dealing with Deconcentration: Population Deconcentration and Planning Response in Polynucleated Urban Regions in Northwest-Europe, *Urban Studies*, 38, pp. 769-785.

Bundesministerium für Raumordnung, Bauwesen und Städtebau (ed.) (1995) *Raumordnungspolitischer Handlungsrahmen*. Bonn: Selbstverlag der BfLR.

Bureau Regio Randstad (BRR) (2001) *NL/EU: from Randstad to Delta metropolis, A contribution to the discussion of the co-operation in the Delta Metropolis by the Queen's Commissioners of the provinces of South Holland, North Holland, Utrecht and Flevoland and the mayors of Amsterdam, Rotterdam, The Hague and Utrecht, Utrecht*. Utrecht: BRR.

Camagni, R. and C. Salone (1993) Network Urban Structures in Northern Italy: Elements for a Theoretical Framework, *Urban Studies*, 30, pp. 1053-1064.

CEC, Commission of the European Communities (1999) *European Spatial Development Perspective: Towards Balanced and Sustainable Development of the Territory of the EU*. Luxembourg: Office for Official Publications of the European Communities.

Champion, T. (2001) Urbanization, Suburbanization, Counterurbanization and Reurbanization, in: R. Paddison (ed) *Handbook of Urban Studies*, pp. 143-161. London: SAGE Publications.

Cheshire, P.C. and D.G. Hay (1989) *Urban Problems in Western Europe: An Economic Analysis*. London: Unwin Hyman.

Clark, W.A.V. and M. Kuijpers-Linde (1994) Commuting in Restructuring Urban Regions, *Urban Studies*, 31, pp. 465-483.

Dieleman, F.M. and A. Faludi (1998a) Randstad, Rhine-Ruhr and Flemish Diamond as one Polynucleated Macro-region, *Tijdschrift voor Economische en Sociale Geografie*, 89, pp. 320-327.

Dieleman, F.M. and A. Faludi (1998b) Polynucleated Metropolitan Regions in Northwest Europe: Theme of the Special Issue, *European Planning Studies*, 6, pp. 365-377.

Faludi, A. (1999) *De architectuur van de Europese ruimtelijke ontwikkelingspolitiek*. Nijmegen: Katholieke Universiteit Nijmegen.

Faludi, A. and B. Waterhout (2001) *Evaluation of the ESDP*, Report produced within the framework of the EURBANET project. Nijmegen: Katholieke Universiteit Nijmegen.

GEMACA (1996) *North-West European Metropolitan Regions*. Paris: IAURIF.

Ghent Urban Studies Team (1999) *The Urban Condition: Space, Community and Self in the Contemporary Metropolis*. Rotterdam: 010 Publishers.

Ham, van M., P. Hooimeijer and C.H. Mulder (2001) Urban Form and Job Access: Disparate Realities in the Randstad, *Tijdschrift voor Economische en Sociale Geografie*, 92, pp. 231-246.

Hohenberg, P. and L.H. Lees (1985) *The making of Urban Europe 1000-1950*. Cambridge, MA: Harvard University Press.

Hoppenbrouwer, E., E. Meijers, A. Romein and B. Lambregts (2000) *Regional Report on the Randstad*, Report produced within the framework of the EURBANET project. Delft: OTB Research Institute for Housing, Urban and Mobility Studies.

Hospers, G.-J. and R. van Lochem (2001) Stedelijk netwerk Twente: over economie, het spel en de spelers, in: F. Boekema and E. Kuijpers (Eds) *Stedelijke Netwerken; theoretische en empirische reflecties. Nieuwe ideeën in Nederlands ruimtelijk onderzoek*, pp. 65-76. Maastricht: Shaker Publishing.

Ipenburg, D. and B. Lambregts (Eds) (2001) *Polynuclear Urban Regions in North West Europe, a Survey of Key Actor Views*. Delft: Delft University Press.

Keating, M. (1997) The invention of regions: political restructuring and territorial government in Europe, *Environment and Planning C: Government and Policy*, 15 (4): 383-98.

Keating, M. (2001) Governing Cities and Regions: Territorial Restructuring in a Global Age, in: A.J. Scott (ed.) *Global City Regions, Trends, Theory, Policy*, pp. 371-90. Oxford: Oxford University Press.

Kloosterman, R.C. and S. Musterd (2001) The Polycentric Urban Region: Towards a Research Agenda, *Urban Studies*, 38 (4): 623-33.

Knapp, W. (1998) The Rhine-Ruhr Area in Transformation: Towards a European Metropolitan Region?, *European Planning Studies*, 6 (4): 379-93.

Laan, L. van der (1998) Changing Urban Systems: An Empirical Analysis at Two Spatial Levels, *Regional Studies*, 32 (3): 235-47.

Lambooy, J.G. (1998) Polynucleation and Economic Development: The Randstad, *European Planning Studies*, 6 (4): 457-66.

Ministerie van Volkshuisvesting, Ruimtelijke Ordening en Milieubeheer (VROM) (2001) *Ruimte maken, ruimte delen, Vijfde Nota over de Ruimtelijke Ordening (Fifth Memorandum on Spatial Planning)*, deel 3: kabinetsstandpunt. The Hague: SDU.

Paasi, A. (1996) *Territories, Boundaries and Consciousness: the Changing Geographies of the Finnish-Russian Border*. Chichester: John Wiley and Sons.

Pumain, D. (1999) *Summary Report on 2.2 Typology of cities and urban-rural relationships*, version 17/12/1999, Study Programme on European Spatial Planning 1998-1999, Reports from the Working Groups.

Schmitt, P., W. Knapp and K.R. Kunzmann (2001) *Regional Report on the Rhein-Ruhr Area*. Report produced within the framework of the EURBANET project. Dortmund: Institut für Landes- und Stadtentwicklungsforschung des Landes Nordrhein-Westfalen.

Scott, A.J. (ed) (2001) *Global City Regions, Trends, Theory, Policy*. Oxford: Oxford University Press.

Scott, A.J., J. Agnew, E.W. Soja and M. Storper (2001) Global City Regions, in: A.J. Scott (ed) *Global City Regions, Trends, Theory, Policy*, pp. 11-30. Oxford: Oxford University Press.

6 Summing small cities does not make a metropolis:

Polycentric urban regions and the provision of cultural, leisure and sports amenities

Meijers, E., Summing small cities does not make a metropolis: Polycentric urban regions and the provision of cultural, leisure and sports amenities. Paper submitted for publication.

Abstract

The paper explores whether a polycentric urban region can reap the advantages of its combined urban size to a similar extent as a similar-sized monocentric city region. This question is elaborated for the provision of cultural, leisure and sports amenities. Their presence in 42 Dutch regions is expressed in an index, which serves as the dependent variable in a multiple regression model. An explaining variable is the extent of polycentricity of a region. Correcting for differences between regions in terms of population size, the number of visitors and average income, it turns out that the more polycentric a region is, the less cultural, leisure and sports amenities are present. Conversely, the more monocentric a region, the more such amenities.

6.1 Introduction

In many European countries and regions, sets of distinct but proximally-located and well-connected cities have become the object of regional development policies and strategic spatial planning policies. Policy practice often refers to such sets of cities as 'city networks' or 'urban networks' (Meijers, 2005a), though in the literature, such regions are often referred to as polycentric or polynuclear urban regions (PURs). Policy-makers assume that taking a set of small or medium-sized cities together opens up possibilities for regional economic growth. Taken individually, these cities fear being overlooked, but taken together they would be able to 'play in the major leagues' (Priemus, 1994) of international competition. The latter ambition can be considered the prime reason for the policy interest in such clusters of cities, though occasionally this may be rooted in the objective to control urbanisation (Lambregts and Zonneveld, 2004). In addition, another reason is increasing functional integration, possibly making such regional networks of cities the next stage in the expansion of urban living space. However, the functional rationality or economic reality of these policy concepts is often not uncontested (see for instance Lambooy, 1998).

Although in the literature precursors of the concept of PURs were discussed as early as the 1960s (Gottmann, 1961; Burton, 1963) or even earlier, such as Stein's Regional City (see Larsen, 2005), it is in the past decade that it has gained substantial interest. Its inclusion in the European Spatial Development Perspective (CEC, 1999), albeit in different terms, can be considered one of the accelerators of its spread over Europe (Davoudi, 2003). Many of the recent contributions have been primarily focused on establishing the concept of PURs in the academic and policy debate, on its defining characteristics and on research agenda-setting (see for instance Batten 1995; Dieleman and Faludi, 1998; Kloosterman and Musterd, 2001; Parr, 2004), on its relevance for, or its potential application to specific PURs (Priemus, 1994; Albrechts, 1998; Bailey and Turok, 2001; Turok and Bailey, 2004), while also considerable attention has been paid to capacity building and governance in such regions (Albrechts, 2001; Mueller, 2001; Meijers and Romein, 2003; Lambregts and Zonneveld, 2004). As some of these authors argue, the focus in the discussion on PURs should now turn to empirically substantiating and validating the many claims that have been made for the PUR (Kloosterman and Musterd, 2001; Parr, 2004; Turok and Bailey, 2004).

Many assumptions circulate addressing the economic significance of PURs, often in connection to their spatial-functional layout. The broad idea is that, taken together, PURs are able to develop new sources of competitive advantage and better market their city-regions internationally. Due to their specific spatial structure, PURs would even have the potential for superior economic performance, as they allegedly enjoy economies of scale, scope and complexity similar to their monocentric counterparts, without, however, incurring the same costs or agglomeration diseconomies that the latter entail. The latter includes congestion, lack of space and high land prices, criminality and environmental pollution. Some validity may be hidden in the latter argument as many of the benefits of urban concentration can also be accessed from locations well outside the agglomeration. At the same time, agglomeration diseconomies remain largely confined to the agglomeration (Parr, 2002). However, this ignores the more fundamental question of whether agglomeration economies have developed at the scale of PURs in the first place.

This contribution aims to bring the discussion on PURs further by empirically exploring our research question of whether PURs, despite their polycentric spatial layout, are able to reap the advantages of urban size in a similar way to more monocentric urban regions. We elaborate this question for the provision of cultural, leisure and sports amenities, contrasting relatively monocentric regions with comparatively polycentric ones. Put simply, the question is whether in three close-by cities of, say, 100,000 inhabitants, a similar extent of support for such urban amenities can be organised as in a city of 300,000 inhabitants. The presence of these urban amenities is closely linked to the size of the population in a region, permanent or temporary (tourists, business travellers), which makes them a very useful object of analysis for our purpose. Does a polycentric spatial lay-out influence the support base in regions for cultural, leisure and sports amenities? In order to test for this, we calculated the extent of mono- or polycentricity - we consider both extremes of the same scale - for 42 Dutch regions. We also collected data on the presence of cultural, leisure and sports facilities in these regions, see Section 6.3. An index was developed stating the extent to which these amenities are present. The scores on this index will be linked to the extent of mono/polycentricity as well as some other independent variables in the multiple regression model presented in Section 6.4. Does the extent of mono/polycentricity explain the presence of cultural, leisure and sports amenities in regions? We will discuss this question in the final Section 6.5. First, we will theoretically elaborate on the research question in the next section.

6.2 Regional externalities in PURs

Many advanced or rare high-level urban amenities need a considerable minimum market size as regards both demand for the amenities offered and the supply for the necessary human capital. Therefore, a certain critical mass is deemed necessary for urban amenities to be able to diversify and function smoothly. Not surprisingly, the highest valued economic activities and the widest variety in economic and cultural functions are found within the largest agglomerations. As Capello (2000:1926) argues, 'the limit that the medium-sized cities come up against, and which often makes them succumb vis-à-vis the great metropolis, is the limit of critical mass and centrality'. It is a strategic issue whether such activities 'can also be realised in polynuclear urban structures, which lack the critical mass of large cities with agglomeration economies' (Lambooy, 1998:459). If this was possible, it would imply that external economies are equally present in PURs as in monocentric city regions, though in that case, given the physical spacing of cities, they could perhaps be better referred to as 'regional externalities' (Parr, 2002), or the more broad 'urban network externalities' (Capello, 2000) which possibly apply to networks of cities not necessarily within the same region. It corresponds with the concept of 'borrowed size' as introduced by Alonso (1973). This refers to the situation in which close-by and well-connected cities host urban functions normally found only in larger cities, such as top-level urban amenities, because the support base is larger given the proximity of more cities. This view is for instance supported by Burton (1963:287): 'the functions of the missing regional center have in part been taken over by the next lower group of centers', and Stein (1964:205): 'the total population of a regional group of towns and farms will be adequate to utilise and support central facilities equivalent to those provided by a great metropolis'. Also, it corresponds with the widely acknowledged perception that accessibility is becoming more important than proximity.

Not surprisingly, the idea of integrating formerly separate cities to form a larger entity able to reap the advantages of urban size is appealing to administrators and planners. However, the idea that the integration of separate cities results in agglomeration advantages comparable to similar-sized monocentric cities is 'rather simplistic' (Bailey and Turok, 2001). Parr (2004) points in this respect at the need for longer travel flows, longer commodity flows and less convenient flows of information in polycentric urban regions. Moreover, it should be reckoned that 'some of the advantages of urban size stem from the nature of the metropolitan environment, and are related to such factors as density, proximity, face-to-face contact, informal structures, unplanned interaction, etc.' (Parr, 2004:236), and consequently hold less for PURs. Moreover, in this respect historic development pathways do not favour the position of PURs either. Cultural, leisure and sports amenities tend to be strongly rooted in their urban context, and their presence in qualitative and quantitative terms is strongly based on the city and the size of its population, including that of its 'rural' hinterland. Simply pooling the urban amenities present in the different cities of a PUR together is likely to lead to duplication rather than to a higher level of the urban amenities at stake. For instance, having three medium-sized theaters in three medium-sized cities together constituting a PUR does not mean they can attract those top-end theater productions that demand more physical space as well as larger receipts and thus more attendants. Such productions tend to be reserved for larger theaters, generally found in larger cities.

In sum, many doubts can be raised concerning the support base of polycentric urban regions in comparison to similar-sized monocentric urban regions. Still, other research findings suggest that too much concentration is not good either. For instance, Henderson (2000), reports a strong relationship between the level of urban concentration and economic growth for countries. He finds that a very monocentric urban system is not favourable for economic growth, nor is too much dispersal. Perhaps this also holds for the regional scale, as on that scale too agglomeration economies are traded off with agglomeration diseconomies. When too much concentration as well as too much deconcentration is not favourable, then perhaps PURs, with their 'concentrated deconcentration'-shape provide the optimum compromise? Taking into account the shape of the urban system such as in Henderson (2000) is rather exceptional. Most of the time, the shape of the urban system is taken for granted (Scott, 2000; Kloosterman and Musterd, 2001). In this contribution we try to overcome this omission. In the next sections we will empirically explore whether a polycentric spatial lay-out does influence the provision of cultural, leisure and sports amenities in regions.

6.3 Research design

We analyse the relationship between the shape of the urban system in regions and how this influences the support base for cultural, leisure and sports amenities by developing a multiple regression model. In this model, the dependent variable is an index representing the extent to which selected cultural, leisure and sports amenities are present in regions. One of the explaining variables is an indicator that expresses the extent of mono- or polycentricity of a regional urban system.

Case study regions

Ideally, the case study regions would be delimited on the basis of functional relationships relating to the use of cultural, leisure and sports amenities. However, in the Netherlands, such detailed travel data is not sufficiently reliable. There exists a relatively objective demarcation of city-regions (*stadsgewesten*), but these depart from a 'nodal' perspective and an overwhelming majority is consequently monocentric by definition. Moreover, their scale is rather small – supralocal – in the light of most of the amenities studied here that function on a regional level. Therefore, we chose a regional delimitation that is relatively recent, that is not by definition confined to old provincial administrative borders such as the Corop-delimitation and that provides for a proxy of a functionally coherent region: the *WGR-samenwerkingsgebieden*. These regions have been delimited within the framework of the Intermunicipal Statutory Regulations Act (*Wet Gemeenschappelijke Regelingen*; WGR). This act enables municipalities to jointly work on issues that need to be addressed on a higher spatial scale than the municipal scale by means of issue-based common arrangements. The Act does not specify which issues should be jointly addressed, but in practice these often concern regional aspects of economic development, tourism, recreation, housing, employment, traffic and transport, spatial development, nature and environmental affairs, welfare and social affairs. Until recently, the act required that such common arrangements had to be clustered within the same regions in order to avoid a too territorially uncoordinated patchwork of common arrangements. As the delimitation of WGR-regions is based on municipal and provincial administrators' perceptions of the scale on which issues in need of a regionally co-ordinated approach rise, these regions provide for an indirect proxy of functionally coherent regions. Although most are located within one Dutch province, some cover the area of multiple provinces. Their average population size (2005) is 387,034 inhabitants, the minimum being 107,620 (Zeeuwsch-Vlaanderen) and the maximum 1,352,680 (Agglomeration Amsterdam). In general, the relatively small size of the WGR-regions makes it possible to go from one place to another in the same region within half an hour. Here we will refer to them as WGR-regions. We collected data for all 42 WGR-regions, which together cover the entire Netherlands (Figure 6.1).

Cultural, leisure and sports amenities

Cities are no longer seen as landscapes of production, but as landscapes of consumption (Zukin, 1998). Consumer-oriented amenities such as cultural, leisure and sports amenities are increasingly considered important assets in the inter-urban competition for attracting visitors, high-skilled workers and companies, not to mention the 'creative class' (Florida, 2002). Consequently, many urban governments have developed policies to improve the presence and quality of these urban amenities, often in connection with urban regeneration projects.

We made an inventory of the presence of certain cultural, leisure and sports amenities in the 42 WGR-regions. The data refers both to quantity and quality. We selected the types of amenities that have a potentially supralocal significance, thus needing the support or critical mass of a region rather than an average-sized city. This excludes both the amenities functioning at the level of small cities, as well as most of those operating on a larger, for instance national scale. Data for 20 variables were collected from a wide variety of sources. These variables can be grouped into six categories: cinema, theater, museum, concert, sports and a rest category comprising leisure activities not yet belonging to the other categories. Table 6.1 presents details on the variables.

In general, the list includes indicators related to the size of such amenities (e.g. largest cinema, large theaters, capacity largest pop/concert venue, capacity stadium), as a larger amenity generally will be able to attract larger,

Figure 6.1 WGR-regions

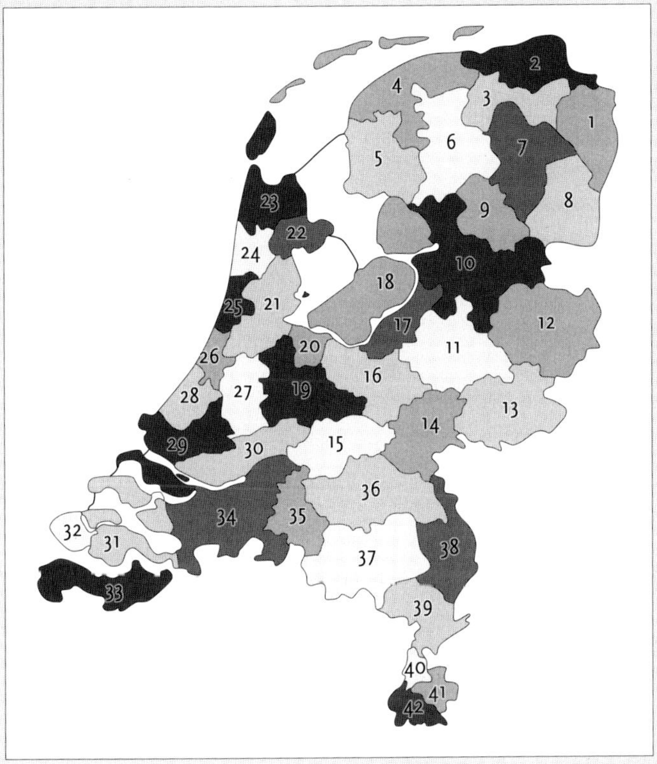

Source: CBS

1. Oost-Groningen
2. Noord Groningen & Eemsmond
3. Centraal & Westelijk Groningen
4. Friesland Noord
5. Zuidwest-Friesland
6. Friesland-Oost
7. Noord- & Midden-Drenthe
8. Zuidoost-Drenthe
9. Zuidwest-Drenthe
10. IJssel-Vecht
11. Stedendriehoek
12. Twente
13. Oost-Gelderland
14. Arnhem-Nijmegen
15. Rivierenland
16. Eem & Vallei
17. Noordwest-Veluwe
18. Flevoland
19. Utrecht
20. Gooi & Vechtstreek
21. Agglomeratie Amsterdam
22. Westfriesland
23. Kop van Noord-Holland
24. Noord-Kennemerland
25. West-Kennemerland
26. Zuid-Holland-Noord
27. Zuid-Holland-Oost
28. Haaglanden
29. Rijnmond
30. Zuid-Holland-Zuid
31. Oosterscheldereglo
32. Walcheren
33. Zeeuwsch-Vlaanderen
34. West-Brabant
35. Midden-Brabant
36. Noordoost-Brabant
37. Zuidoost-Brabant
38. Noord-Limburg
39. Midden-Limburg
40. Westelijke Mijnstreek
41. Oostelijk Zuid-Limburg
42. Maastricht & Mergelland

Table 6.1 List of variables: cultural, leisure and sports amenities

Category	Variable	Year	Source
Cinema	Number of screens in cinemas in WGR-region	2005	NVB Dutch Association of Film Exhibitors
	Number of seats in cinemas in WGR-region	2005	NVB Dutch Association of Film Exhibitors
	Number of screens in art house cinemas in WGR-region	2005	NVB Dutch Association of Film Exhibitors
	Number of seats in art house cinemas in WGR-region	2005	NVB Dutch Association of Film Exhibitors
	Number of screens in the largest cinema in WGR-region	2005	NVB Dutch Association of Film Exhibitors
Theater	Number of large theaters (>400 seats) in WGR-region	2005	Theater Instituut Nederland
	Number of medium-sized theaters (200-400 seats) in WGR-region	2005	Theater Instituut Nederland
	Number of small theaters (<200 seats) in WGR-region	2005	Theater Instituut Nederland
Museum	Number of museums in WGR-region	2006	Stichting Museumkaart
	Number of museums in WGR-region belonging to the 50 most visited in the Netherlands	2004	The Netherlands Museum Association
Concert	Number of concert halls in WGR-region	2006	Vereniging van Schouwburg- en concertgebouwdirecties
	Capacity of pop/concert venues (attendants) in WGR-region	2006	Vereniging van Nederlandse Poppodia en -Festivals
	Capacity of the largest pop/concert venue (attendants) in WGR-region	2006	Vereniging van Nederlandse Poppodia en -Festivals
Sports	Number of indoor-ski halls in WGR-region	2006	Own inventory
	Number of skating rinks in WGR-region	2006	Own inventory
	Number of karting tracks in WGR-region	2006	Own inventory
	Number of m^2 indoor climbing walls in WGR-region	2006	NKBV, ESAC
	Capacity sports stadiums (seats) in WGR-region	2006	World stadiums, Own inventory
Leisure	Number of casinos open to the public in WGR-region	2006	Holland Casino
	Number of Michelin-stars (restaurants) in WGR-region	2006	Michelin

more renowned productions, more well-known bands or sports events. Next, the list also includes variables on amenities that do not need a big audience, but that, given their specialised nature, require a larger support base (e.g. art house cinemas, concert halls, climbing walls, Michelin-star restaurants). Similarly, the number of museums belonging to the 50 most visited ones in the Netherlands may be considered an indicator of quality.

Indexes

We developed indexes summarising the scores on the six categories and a 'total index' summarising the scores on all six categories together. The scores of the 42 WGR-regions on these 20 variables were normalised and we used these z-scores to develop our index. Each variable within a category (cinema, theater etc.) was given the same weight, and each of the six categories was also given the same weight in the total index. Therefore, the total index is the average score on the six constituting categories. A z-score of 0 was given a score of

100, and 1 standard deviation 20. So, when a region scores a z-score of 1 on a certain variable, it got a score of 100+20=120 etc. Table 6.2 presents the scores of all 42 WGR-regions on the six categories as well as the total index.

Measuring the extent of mono- and polycentricity

Polycentricity is essentially a scale-less phenomenon. The term has been applied to a wide variety of spatial scales ranging from Europe, to many of its countries, to regions and to cities. Basically, polycentricity refers to the plurality of centres in a given area. However, there are important differences in interpretation between these scales. For instance, at lower spatial scales the concept is mainly analytical, while at the national or European scale it is also, or even predominantly a normative concept (Davoudi, 2003). But also in analytical terms there are differences. While on the national spatial scale a country's urban system is considered more polycentric when the main cities are evenly distributed across the territory, it is exactly the opposite – a clustering of cities – that leads to polycentricity on the regional scale. Here, we adopt Meijers' theoretical distinction between polycentric urban regions and urban networks (Meijers, 2005b). While the first term refers to particular morphological characteristics such as a clustering of relatively similar-sized cities in close proximity, in fact 'the image on the map', the latter term denotes an advanced sort of polycentric urban region, namely one in which relational aspects accord with a network logic (see Batten, 1995; Van der Knaap, 2002). A regional urban network is therefore a polycentric urban region characterised by functional integration, by a relative disconnection between size and function of its cities as well as by specialisation and interaction, leading to complementarity. It is the difference between a region with development potential, and one in which this potential has already been realised.

Consequently, we should consider the morphological characteristics of regions to determine to what extent they are polycentric. Parr (2004) points to the spatial and size distribution of cities in the region. In terms of spatial distribution, there should be a maximum and a minimum limit to centre separation. The spatial distribution of cities within WGR-regions does not seem to be a very distinguishing factor for measuring polycentricity as it is generally possible to get from one place to another within the same WGR-region within half an hour. In addition, strict Dutch planning policies have avoided the coalescence of separate cities into larger conurbations. Therefore, the size distribution of cities should be considered the most important indicator for establishing whether or not any region is polycentric or the opposite, monocentric at the regional scale. A dichotomous approach to the question, however, must be avoided. Rather than considering a given area polycentric or monocentric, it is more appropriate to score an area on a scale ranging from (very) polycentric to (very) monocentric. The size distribution is even more appropriate for this research as size is strongly related to the support base of regions. Here

Table 6.2 Presence of cultural, sports and leisure amenities in WGR-regions

WGR-region	Cinema	Theater	Musea	Concert	Leisure	Sports	Total index
1 Oost-Groningen	88.2	87.0	95.0	90.0	85.6	93.3	89.8
2 Noord-Groningen & Eemsmond	79.0	84.5	90.4	90.0	89.5	88.6	87.0
3 Centraal & Westelijk Groningen	106.0	93.1	95.0	120.1	115.8	107.4	106.3
4 Friesland Noord	96.9	92.9	107.8	90.0	85.6	94.1	94.5
5 Zuidwest-Friesland	89.2	90.4	95.5	92.6	85.6	84.9	89.7
6 Friesland-Oost	92.6	91.1	89.4	93.3	93.4	108.1	94.6
7 Noord- & Midden-Drenthe	84.9	85.7	95.0	90.0	85.6	104.8	91.0
8 Zuidoost-Drenthe	95.9	88.6	86.3	90.0	89.5	94.0	90.7
9 Zuidwest-Drenthe	89.7	89.4	86.8	90.0	85.6	88.6	88.4
10 IJssel-Vecht	96.7	103.1	105.2	94.6	116.7	93.8	101.7
11 Stedendriehoek	105.1	102.0	101.7	94.0	93.4	99.1	99.2
12 Twente	109.2	124.4	107.3	104.6	112.0	108.1	110.9
13 Oost-Gelderland	92.1	92.3	96.0	92.4	89.5	90.6	92.2
14 Arnhem-Nijmegen	132.5	120.8	127.9	118.9	112.0	112.8	120.8
15 Rivierenland	82.8	91.1	94.0	90.0	85.6	88.6	88.7
16 Eem & Vallei	107.2	103.1	107.3	91.0	89.5	85.6	97.3
17 Noordwest-Veluwe	84.6	87.4	89.4	90.0	97.3	88.6	89.6
18 Flevoland	102.9	93.2	83.7	92.1	85.6	102.7	93.4
19 Utrecht	109.9	124.0	106.8	113.3	131.4	115.8	116.9
20 Gooi & Vechtstreek	93.5	94.8	95.6	93.5	89.5	91.9	93.1
21 Agglomeratie Amsterdam	177.2	174.7	190.1	164.5	139.2	139.2	164.2

we will present a measure of mono/polycentricity for the urban system of the WGR-regions based on the rank-size order of cities. In doing so we partly draw on the work carried out within the framework of the ESPON 1.1.1 project on polycentricity (Nordregio *et al.*, 2004).

Rank-size distribution as indicator for mono- and polycentricity

Characteristic for a polycentric urban system is that no city dominates over other cities in economic, cultural and other respects. In other words, a polycentric urban system lacks strong hierarchy. The rank-size distribution of the regional urban system provides information on this hierarchy and is therefore an excellent indication of the extent of mono- or polycentricity. Figure 6.2 presents the rank-size distributions of three WGR-regions that are either among the most polycentric (Oostelijk Zuid-Limburg), not polycentric nor monocentric (Noord-Kennemerland) or among the most monocentric (Centraal & Westelijk Groningen). The population data presented in the figure is for the actual towns and villages, not the municipalities in which they are located. In the Netherlands, the average municipality contained just over five and the

Table 6.2 Continued

WGR-region	Cinema	Theater	Musea	Concert	Leisure	Sports	Total index
22 Westfriesland	79.0	88.1	97.6	92.8	85.6	88.6	88.6
23 Kop van Noord-Holland	92.2	89.9	93.5	90.0	85.6	96.2	91.2
24 Noord-Kennemerland	96.5	96.9	90.9	94.4	93.4	103.8	96.0
25 West-Kennemerland	98.1	102.7	104.8	105.9	127.5	109.7	108.1
26 Zuid-Holland-Noord	99.6	87.4	109.5	110.3	89.5	84.9	96.9
27 Zuid-Holland-Oost	92.3	98.2	90.4	94.4	85.6	84.9	91.0
28 Haaglanden	129.2	133.8	130.5	113.2	143.1	143.1	132.1
29 Rijnmond	136.3	127.7	132.5	172.3	127.5	114.2	135.1
30 Zuid-Holland-Zuid	90.0	101.9	94.5	94.3	89.5	102.5	95.4
31 Oosterschelderegio	79.0	85.7	89.4	93.4	101.2	88.6	89.5
32 Walcheren	95.8	84.5	88.9	90.0	85.6	88.6	88.9
33 Zeeuwsch-Vlaanderen	91.2	93.6	86.8	90.0	101.2	88.6	91.9
34 West-Brabant	107.1	112.7	101.1	94.6	115.8	118.7	108.3
35 Midden-Brabant	96.9	98.2	87.8	118.6	85.6	102.3	98.3
36 Noordoost-Brabant	107.2	116.3	111.9	95.6	97.3	108.8	106.2
37 Zuidoost-Brabant	115.4	119.3	106.3	108.5	127.5	122.9	116.6
38 Noord-Limburg	90.9	97.0	88.3	91.8	93.4	91.4	92.1
39 Midden-Limburg	93.6	89.9	89.4	91.8	89.5	92.3	91.1
40 Westelijke Mijnstreek	96.0	87.4	81.7	92.1	85.6	93.4	89.4
41 Oostelijk Zuid-Limburg	91.8	88.2	83.7	90.9	93.4	101.0	91.5
42 Maastricht & Mergelland	106.2	86.9	94.5	90.0	139.2	94.5	101.9

average WGR-region almost 60 such cities and villages in 2005.[1] The population data was collected for the year 2005. Given the strong stability of urban systems over time (Batty, 2001), data for one year presents a robust picture.

Figure 6.2 presents the five largest places in three regions and also the regression line that best fits the distribution of their sizes. The argument now is that in a polycentric region, with little hierarchy, this line will be more flat than in a monocentric region. Therefore, the slope of the regression line is a good indicator of the extent of mono- or polycentricity.

Obviously, the number of towns included in the regression analysis influences the outcome of these calculations. In general, sample size can be either a fixed number of towns, a fixed size threshold, or a size above which the sample accounts for some given proportion of a region's population (see also Cheshire, 1999). The latter has disadvantages for this research, as it will turn out that the number of towns included in the analysis is large for polycen-

1 Recognised by the Dutch postal services as official place names (i.e. names that you can write down on an envelope, which will subsequently be delivered).

Figure 6.2 Monocentric and polycentric rank-size distributions based on five towns per region

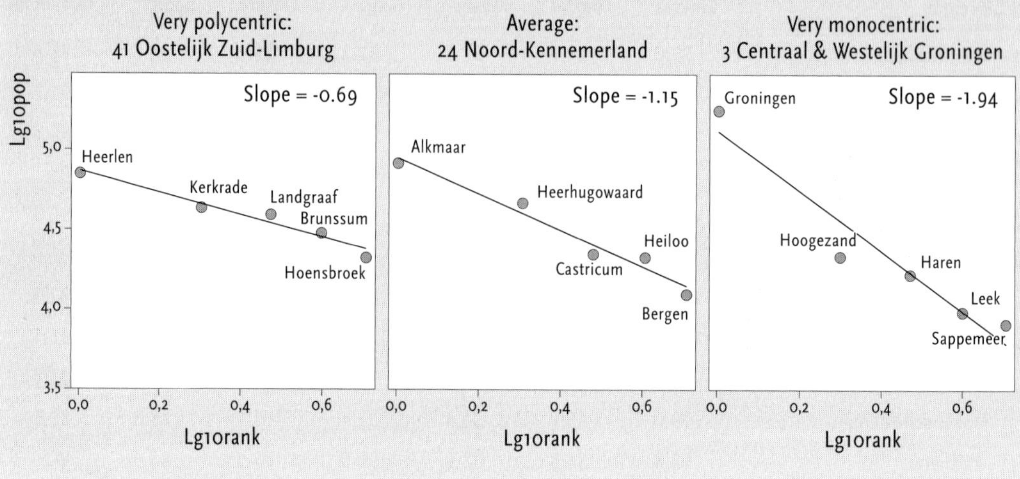

tric regions and small for monocentric regions. Hence, the number of towns comprising a given proportion of the population is in itself an indicator of mono- or polycentricity and applying such a measure twice would distort the picture. A fixed size threshold is equally inappropriate as in large and more densely populated regions a town of say 20,000 inhabitants may be insignificant, while it could be of great importance in small or less populated regions. It could be argued that a town ranked for instance third in a region is of importance in that region, despite its possible small size. Therefore, when measuring polycentricity, the sample size could best be based on a fixed number of towns. The question then is what this number should be. The answer seems arbitrary. Our tentative impression of the extent of polycentricity of a region is often based on just a mere handful of places. In this study we measured the extent of polycentricity by calculating the slope of the regression line that was based on either the five or three largest cities. The outcomes correspond strongly. Figure 6.3 maps the results for the calculations based on five cities in each region.

The scores presented on the extent of mono/polycentricity are normally distributed, with an average slope of the regression line of –1.15 and a Standard Deviation of 0.31 for the regression line based on five cities per WGR-region or an average slope of the regression line of –1.26 and an SD of 0.51 for three cities per WGR-region. It is important to emphasise that there is no relationship between the population size of regions and the score on this mono/polycentricity indicator. So, we have both populous and thinly populated polycentric regions and monocentric regions.

In the analysis that follows we use the indicator for mono/polycentricity based on the regression line through the five main cities in WGR-region. We will refer to this indicator as the 'polycentricity' indicator, because the higher the score on this indicator, the more polycentric a region is. However, in practice, a low score implies that it is in fact a monocentric region. In order to test for robustness, we will also check results with the scores for the slope of the regression line based on just three cities per region.

Figure 6.3 WGR-regions and their extent of mono- or polycentricity, measured for samples of five towns

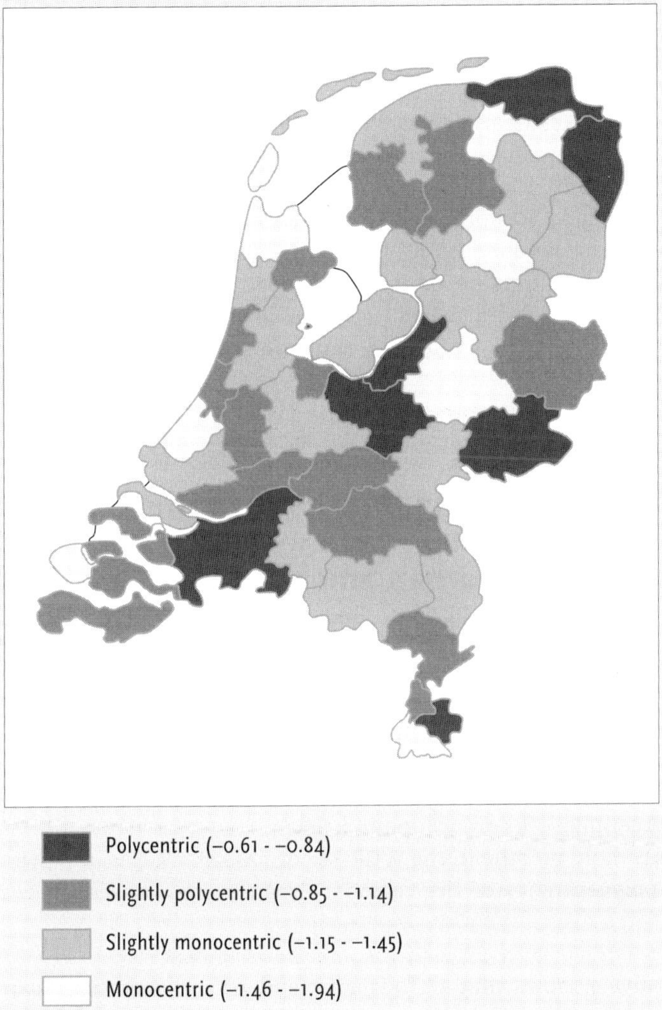

Other independent variables

We will use the scores on the indicator polycentricity, e.g. the slopes of the regression line, as explaining variable for the index of the presence of cultural, leisure and sports amenities in these regions. There are some other explaining variables that will be included in the multiple regression analysis. These include the population size of a region, the absolute number of beds in hotels in that region weighted by the region-specific average percentage of their occupation (as a proxy for the size of the non-permanent population such as tourists and business travellers), as well as the average household income in that region. We clearly expect these three indicators to positively affect the presence of cultural, leisure and sports amenities in our 42 case study regions. After all, when there are more people present in a region (residential or visiting population), then the support base for such amenities is larger. Moreover, as enjoying these amenities nearly always requires the paying of an entrance fee or subscription rate, it can be hypothesised that a more affluent residential population will lead to a larger demand for such amenities. Data on the population of WGR-regions was provided by Statistics Netherlands (CBS), and refers to the situation on January 1, 2005. Regional data on the number of hotel beds as well as regional data on their average occupation rate was provided for the year 2004 by the *Bedrijfsschap Horeca en Catering*, a knowledge and innovation centre for the hotel, restaurant and cafe sector. Finally, the data on household income per WGR-region is for 2002 and was also provided by Statistics Netherlands.

6.4 Analysis: linking the shape of the regional urban system with the presence of urban amenities

Table 6.3 summarises the results of our multiple regression analysis. The 42 WGR-regions serve as cases. The dependent variable is the total index of cultural, leisure and sports amenities (see Table 6.2, final column). Independent variables were entered simultaneously into the model and include:

1. the total population of the WGR-region on January 1, 2005;
2. the number of beds in hotels in WGR-regions, weighted by the region-specific average percentage of their occupation, 2004;
3. the average household income in the WGR-region, 2002;
4. the extent of polycentricity of the regional urban system based on n=5, 2005.

The regression analysis shows that all four independent variables significantly contribute to the presence of cultural, leisure and sports amenities. Given the perspective of the present paper, the most important finding obviously is that the shape of the urban system is of significance for explaining the presence of these amenities. This relation is negative, which means that the more polycentric a region is, the fewer such amenities are present. Or, the more monocentric, the more cultural, leisure and sports facilities it has. We will elaborate on this important finding in the final section.

The multivariate analysis clearly shows that the size of the population in a region is by far the most important explaining variable. In fact, the adjusted R^2 would amount to 0.874 solely based on the population variable. The number of non-resident population, for which we used the proxy of average number of occupied beds in hotels, has the second highest beta. The shape of the urban system then explains slightly more than the average household income. The four variables together explain 94.8% of the variance in the scores on the total index of cultural, leisure and sports amenities.

Table 6.3 Multiple regression analysis of total index of cultural, leisure and sports amenities in WGR-regions

	Unstandardised coefficients		Standardised coefficients	Level of significance (p values, two-tailed)
	B	Standard Error	Beta	
(Constant)	95.591	10.129		0.00**
N occupied hotel beds	0.001	0.000	0.264	0.00**
Household income	-0.642	0.314	-0.078	0.05*
Polycentricity	-5.381	1.871	-0.109	0.01**
Population size	3.991E-05	0.000	0.761	0.00**
N	42			
R^2	0.953			
Adjusted R^2	0.948			
F	187.764			
Sign F	0.000			

** Significant at the 0.01 level.
* Significant at the 0.05 level.

When we fill in the average values for population (387,034), the number of occupied hotel beds (1956.8) and household income (30,188), as well as the minimum value we found for polycentricity (thus, the most monocentric region: -1.94) in the regression equation, we are expected to find a total index value of 104.28. When we take again these averages but include the maximum, thus the most polycentric value for polycentricity, we expect a value of 97.12. A very polycentric WGR-region would remain more than 7 index points behind the most monocentric region because of the shape of its urban system. This equals nearly half the value of the standard deviation of the total index variable.

When we include the values found for the polycentricity indicator based on just three cities in each WGR-region instead of the values based on five towns in each region, we find that the extent of polycentricity is also a significant variable (p = 0.04) in explaining the presence of cultural, leisure and sports amenities. In this case, the Beta value is slightly less compared to the Beta presented for the indicator based on five cities as presented in Table 6.3.

Having established that the size of the residential population is by far the most explaining factor for the presence of cultural, leisure and sports amenities, we will now look at which variables correlate with the polycentricity indicator while correcting for the size of the population. We will do this by making all values of the variables expressing frequencies relative to the population number, resulting for instance in the number of seats in cinemas per 1000 inhabitants, see Table 6.4.

For eight types of amenities we found significant correlations with the extent of polycentricity. All of these significant correlations are negative, which means that the more polycentric a region is, the less these amenities are present. This means that polycentric regions have less seats in cinemas and art house cinemas. This is linked to the fact that there is also less choice in movies as the number of screens in both cinemas and art house cinemas is

Table 6.4 Correlations between the shape of the urban system and cultural, leisure and sports amenities

Variables in WGR-regions per 1.000 inhabitants	Polycentricity (n=5)
Number of seats in cinemas in WGR-region/1.000 inh.	-0.533(**)
Number of screens in cinemas in WGR-region/1.000 inh.	-0.473(**)
Number of seats in art house cinemas in WGR-region/1.000 inh.	-0.384(*)
Number of screens in art house cinemas in WGR-region/1.000 inh.	-0.427(**)
Number of large theaters (>400 seats) in WGR-region/1.000 inh.	-0.055
Number of medium-sized theaters (200-400 seats) in WGR-region/1.000 inh.	0.102
Number of small theaters (<200 seats) in WGR-region/1.000 inh.	-0.291
Number of museums in WGR-region/1.000 inh.	0.076
Number of museums in WGR-region belonging to the 50 most visited in the Netherlands/1.000 inh.	-0.186
Number of casinos open to the public in WGR-region/1.000 inh.	-0.431(**)
Number of Michelin-stars (restaurants) in WGR-region/1.000 inh.	-0.033
Number of concert halls in WGR-region/1.000 inh.	-0.343(*)
Number of possible attendants of pop/concert venues in WGR-region/1.000 inh.	-0.317(*)
Number of m^2 indoor climbing walls in WGR-region/1.000 inh.	-0.377(*)
Number of skating rinks in WGR-region/1.000 inh.	-0.161
Number of indoor-ski halls in WGR-region/1.000 inh.	0.078
Number of karting tracks in WGR-region/1.000 inh.	-0.074
Number of seats in sports stadiums in WGR-region/1.000 inh.	-0.148

** Correlation is significant at the 0.01 level (2-tailed).
* Correlation is significant at the 0.05 level (2-tailed).

less in polycentric regions. Apparently, entrepreneurs in this sector consider the support base of such regions weaker than of their monocentric counterparts. There are also less casinos, concert halls and pop/concert venues in polycentric regions. Indoor climbing halls are also less common, or smaller, in polycentric regions. However, the shape of the urban system does not matter for other sports amenities. Nor does it matter for the theater sector, although it seems that small theaters are less present. Medium-sized theaters appear more present in polycentric regions. This is one of the three positive correlations, albeit not significant, next to indoor-ski halls and museums. It seems that particularly those amenities that need a large support base because they provide specialised services are less present in polycentric regions.

6.5 Conclusion

The issue addressed in this paper is fundamental: is it possible that agglomeration advantages develop to a similar extent in a cluster of spatially separated cities as in a single city? We considered this question in terms of urban size. The research question was whether a PUR can reap the advantages of its combined urban size to a similar extent as a monocentric city region. In our research we focused on activities whose presence is closely linked to the size of the urban population: cultural, leisure and sports amenities. Their presence in regions was expressed in a total index of these amenities, which was then linked to an indicator of the extent of polycentricity of these regions. This indicator was based on the rank-size distribution of the major towns in each region. Next to this indicator, three other explaining variables were entered into a multiple regression model. 42 Dutch regions, so-called WGR-regions, were analysed.

The regression analysis resulted in the observation that, when correcting for differences between regions in terms of population, the number of visitors and the average income, PURs have a disadvantage compared to more monocentric city regions: the more polycentric a region is, the less cultural, leisure and sports amenities are present. Conversely, the more monocentric a region, the more these amenities are present.

The specific dispersed spatial layout of polycentric regions implies that they cannot reap the advantages of urban size in a similar way as more monocentric urban regions, at least, as far as our selection of cultural, leisure and sports amenities is concerned. These empirical findings support the view of Parr (2004) and Bailey and Turok (2004) who suggested that PURs are behind more monocentric regions in terms of agglomeration advantages, or, in the case of PURs, regional externalities. Parr provides part of the explanation: in polycentric urban regions there is a need for longer travel flows, commodity flows, less convenient flows of information and a lack of a metropolitan environment. In addition, duplication between the competing cities is likely to be high (see Malecki, 2004) and cultural, leisure and sports amenities tend to be strongly rooted in their urban context.

The analysis presented was necessarily limited in terms of scope and scale, but obviously the issue of regional externalities in polycentric urban systems calls for further exploration. First of all, this exploration should focus on recognising trends: are polycentric regions closing a gap with monocentric city regions, or is this gap widening? Arguments could be made for both. The gap could be closed through the slowly but steadily progressing functional integration in PURs. On the other hand, it may be that such integration is progressing too slowly to keep pace with the needs of both firms and consumers for increasingly specialised services. Additionally, next to exploring trends, it may be that polycentric regions perform better on other indicators than the presence of cultural, leisure and sports amenities presented here. Therefore, another research issue is whether PURs score better on other issues, typically those summarised under the label 'agglomeration diseconomies'. Also, empirical results from a larger variety of countries and regions could shed an interesting light on these matters. It would also be worthwhile to know whether polycentric regions that have progressed further on the path to being urban networks perform better than polycentric regions that have just started the development in that direction. In other words, do PURs with higher levels of interaction, complementarity, functional integration and internal accessibility perform better than PURs with fewer such characteristics?

Finally, what this research revealed is that the question raised in Meijers (2005a) of whether a network of cities is *more* than the sum of the parts is phrased rather optimistically. As far as the support for urban amenities is concerned, such networks of cities are not even the sum of the parts.

Acknowledgement

I am grateful to Hugo Priemus and Marjolein Spaans for their helpful comments on earlier versions of this paper. The author wishes to acknowledge the financial assistance of the Dutch government through the Habiforum Program Innovative Land Use and Delft University of Technology through the Delft Centre for Sustainable Urban Areas.

References

Albrechts, L. (1998) The Flemish Diamond: Precious Gem and Virgin Area, *European Planning Studies*, 6, pp. 411-424.

Albrechts, L. (2001) How to Proceed from Image and Discourse to Action: As Applied to the Flemish Diamond, *Urban Studies*, 38, pp. 733-745.

Alonso, W. (1973) Urban Zero Population Growth, *Daedalus*, 109, pp. 191-206.

Bailey, N. and I. Turok (2001) Central Scotland as a polycentric urban region: useful planning concept or chimera?, *Urban Studies*, 38, pp. 697-715.

Batten, D.F. (1995) Network Cities: Creative Urban Agglomerations for the 21st Century, *Urban Studies*, 32, pp. 313-327.

Batty, M. (2001) Polynucleated Urban Landscapes, *Urban Studies*, 38, pp. 635-655.

Burton, I. (1963) A restatement of the dispersed city hypothesis, *Annals of the Association of American Geographers*, 63, pp. 285-289.

Capello, R. (2000) The City Network Paradigm: Measuring Urban Network Externalities, *Urban Studies*, 37, pp. 1925-1945.

CEC, Commission of the European Communities (1999) *European Spatial Development Perspective: Towards Balanced and Sustainable Development of the Territory of the EU*. Luxembourg: Office for Official Publications of the European Communities.

Cheshire, P. (1999) Trends in Sizes and Structures of Urban Areas, in: P. Cheshire and E.S. Mills (Eds) *Handbook of Regional and Urban Economics, Volume 3*, pp. 1339-1372. Amsterdam: Elsevier Science.

Davoudi, S. (2003) Polycentricity in European Spatial Planning: From an Analytical Tool to a Normative Agenda. *European Planning Studies*, 11, pp. 979-999.

Dieleman, F.M. and A. Faludi (1998) Polynucleated Metropolitan Regions in Northwest Europe: Theme of the Special Issue, *European Planning Studies*, 6, pp. 365-377.

Florida, R. (2002) *The Rise of the Creative Class*. New York: Basic Books.

Gottmann, J. (1961) *Megalopolis, The urbanized Northeastern Seaboard of the United States*. New York: The Twentieth Century Fund.

Henderson, V. (2000) *The effects of urban concentration on economic growth*, working Paper 7503. Cambridge, MA: National Bureau of Economic Research.

Kloosterman, R.C. and S. Musterd (2001) The Polycentric Urban Region: Towards a Research Agenda, *Urban Studies*, 38, pp. 623-633.

Knaap, G.A. van der (2002) *Stedelijke bewegingsruimte, over veranderingen in stad en land*. The Hague: Sdu uitgevers.

Lambooy, J.G. (1998) Polynucleation and Economic Development: The Randstad, *European Planning Studies*, 6, pp. 457-466.

Lambregts, L. and W. Zonneveld (2004) From Randstad to Deltametropolis: Changing Attitudes Towards the Scattered Metropolis, *European Planning Studies*, 12, pp. 299-321.

Larsen, K. (2005) Cities to Come: Clarence Stein's Postwar Regionalism, *Journal of Planning History*, 4, pp. 33-51.

Malecki, E.J. (2004) Jockeying for Position: What It Means and Why It Matters to Regional Development Policy When Places Compete, *Regional Studies*, 38, pp. 1101-1120.

Meijers, E. (2005a) Polycentric Urban Regions and the Quest for Synergy: Is a Network of Cities More than the Sum of the Parts?, *Urban Studies*, 42, pp. 765-781.

Meijers, E. (2005b) Van polycentrische stedelijke regio naar stedelijk netwerk: Complementariteit in de Vlaamse Ruit en de Randstad, *Ruimte en Planning*, 2005, pp. 8-21.

Meijers, E. and A. Romein (2003) Realizing potential: Building Regional Organizing Capacity in Polycentric Urban Regions, *European Urban and Regional Studies*, 10, pp. 173-186.

Mueller, B. (2001) Urban Networks and Polycentric Spatial Development in Europe – the Case of Germany, *EUREG*, 9, pp. 40-46.

Nordregio *et alia* (2004) *ESPON 1.1.1: Potentials for polycentric development in Europe*, Project report. Stockholm/Luxembourg: Nordregio/ESPON Monitoring Committee.

Parr, J.B. (2002) Agglomeration economies: ambiguities and confusions, *Environment and Planning* A, 34, pp. 717-731.

Parr, J.B. (2004) The Polycentric Urban Region: A Closer Inspection, *Regional Studies*, 38, pp. 231-240.

Priemus, H. (1994) Planning the Randstad: Between Economic Growth and Sustainability, *Urban Studies*, 31, pp. 509-534.

Scott, A.J. (2000) Economic geography: the great half-century, *Cambridge Journal of Economics*, 24, pp. 483-504.

Stein, C.S. (1964) A regional pattern for dispersal, *Architectural Record*, pp. 205-206.

Turok, I. and N. Bailey (2004) The Theory of Polynuclear Urban Regions and its Application to Central Scotland, *European Planning Studies*, 12, pp. 371-389

Zukin, S. (1998) Urban Lifestyles: Diversity and Standardisation in Spaces of Consumption, *Urban Studies*, 35, pp. 825-839.

7 Synthesis

7.1 Introduction

In understanding and explaining the economic, social, cultural and spatial functioning of cities contemporary urban and regional studies attribute great significance to intercity relationships. These relationships are both external, between urban regions, and internal, within urban regions. While much of the recent research on intercity relationships has been focused on these external linkages, this thesis has focused on relationships within urban regions. More specifically, it has focused on Polycentric Urban Regions (PURs). PURs are collections of historically distinct and politically independent cities that are located close-by and which lack a strong dominance of one of them in economic, social and cultural terms. There are several reasons for this focus on PURs. In the first place, urban research has long been preoccupied with the study of single cities. A continuing process of extension of the scale on which spatial processes take place has, however, made this perspective less and less relevant. Examples are manifold, but include for instance the expansion of labour and housing markets that have become increasingly regional in nature. Complex and multifarious societal processes are the engines behind this scaling-up. The implication is that cities should be examined in their wider regional context. A focus on collections of cities rather than sole cities is therefore needed. In the second place, as a consequence of the decade-long strong dominance of the central place model, intercity relationships are primarily described in terms of hierarchy. Suggestions have been made that the spatial configuration of PURs – in particular the location of rather similar-sized cities close to each other – is at odds with the central place model (Camagni, 1993; Capello, 2000; Davies, 1998; Van der Knaap, 2002). This would particularly hold true for the intercity relationships within such a region. These relationships would conform to the logics of the network model of spatial organisation, which should be considered as essentially opposite to the central place model. The introduction to this thesis pointed out that while the theoretical framework of the network model paradigm is relatively well established, research demonstrating its empirical validity is largely non-existent (Capello, 2000). In order to fill this evidential deficit in the network model, the PUR constitutes the most appropriate geographical object of research. In the third place, this research is focused on PURs because many claims have been made for this concept building on their specific spatial configuration – which obviously includes intercity relationships. Due to their specific spatial structure, PURs would have the potential for enjoying economies of scale, scope and complexity similar to their monocentric counterparts without, however, incurring the same costs or agglomeration diseconomies that the latter entail. As has been argued by several authors (Kloosterman and Musterd, 2001; Parr, 2004; Turok and Bailey, 2004) these claims lack empirical validation.

The aim of this thesis was to fill parts of the lacunas in our understanding of PURs and intercity relationships identified above. In the first place, this implies that the research aims to provide a further theoretical clarification and empirical assessment of the PUR concept and in particular the claims and assumptions that have been made with regard to their spatial-functional structure, with an emphasis on regional intercity relationships. Secondly, the research aims to theoretically explicate the features of the network model further and to provide an empirical assessment of its validity as a description of the spatial-functional structure of PURs. Both aims appeared to be strongly linked as the claims and assumptions made with respect to the spatial-functional structure of PURs are largely in concordance with the basic ideas of the network model of spatial organisation. The overarching research theme that frames this research is the extent to which cities constituting a PUR relate to each other in a synergetic way. In other words, to what extent are they more than the sum of the parts?

This overarching research theme was broken down into three research questions relating to three dominant issues that arise on both research agendas:
1. complementarity
2. organising capacity
3. critical mass.

Each of these issues was addressed by a separate research question:
1. *To what extent is the complementary development of cities within polycentric urban regions happening and worthwhile pursuing?*
2. *What is the potential of a regional co-ordinated planning approach in PURs and what factors foster or hamper the development of regional organising capacity in such regions?*
3. *To what extent does the polycentric spatial layout of PURs influence their support base for urban functions?*

This chapter summarises our research findings and formulates answers to the research questions. This is done for the three research questions separately in subsequent subsections of Section 7.2. In addition, Section 7.2 ends with a discussion of synergetic relationships in PURs, which considers the three issues in an integral way. Section 7.3 presents some reflections on the research. Section 7.4 presents some of the implications of the findings in this thesis for regional development strategies in PURs. Finally, Section 7.5 presents an outlook to further research on PURs.

7.2 Summary of results

Complementarity

Research question 1: *To what extent is the complementary development of cities within polycentric urban regions happening and worthwhile pursuing?*

This question is about the value that should be attributed to complementarity as well as about spatial trends with respect to complementarity in practice. Attention has also been paid to the conceptualisation of complementarity. Chapters 2, 3 and 4 address this research issue of complementarity.

Though some previous work on conceptualising complementarity has been done (Ullmann, 1956; Lambooy, 1969), it has remained a rather vague concept despite its increasingly frequent, but often casual appearance in both academic writings and policy documents. This lack of conceptual clarity partly explains why the concept of complementarity has so far not been empirically analysed. Complementarity refers to the situation in which different cities fulfil different and mutually beneficial roles (Hague and Kirk, 2003). In this thesis it has been conceptualised as resulting from differentiation and integration. In the context of PURs, such a multi-faceted concept as complementarity can refer to differentiation in terms of economic activities or urban functions, but also to differences in residential or working environments. Research in this thesis has focused on activities or urban functions. In Chapter 2 the focus was on all economic activities and thereby the economic role of cities in PURs, in Chapter 3 attention was paid to complementarities in service sector activities and in Chapter 4 to two specific types of urban amenities: universities of professional education (hogescholen) and hospitals. So, complementarity results from the differentiation between centres or cities in terms of activities or urban functions, while the demand for these activities and functions should come from more or less the same region. Notwithstanding the fact that mere differentiation does not suffice for complementarity to occur, as it also needs integration, the analyses in Chapters 2, 3 and 4 have predominantly focused on the differentiation facet. The differentiation facet is obviously the main starting point for complementarity, because, for instance, it has been argued that differentiation between cities is the main explanation of the development of spatial interaction (Ullmann, 1956; Batten, 1995), hence resulting in integration.

Complementarity should be valued positively. When two cities complement each other, then the citizens and companies in one place can take advantage of the various functions the other city has to offer. These functions can then be more specialised, as the support base on which they build is larger given the overlapping hinterlands. In this way, companies, citizens and tourists can choose from a larger, more specialised and diverse collection of urban functions. Complementarity is therefore strongly linked to agglomeration economies, though, given the physical separation of the cities and of the activities involved, such advantages are perhaps more appropriately described as 'regional externalities' (Parr, 2004). The worthiness, or value of complementarity was more theoretically explored in Chapter 2, in which the idea of synergy in economic networks was analysed. Complementarity came out as a major synergy-generating mechanism in web type networks, leading to vertical synergy through a specialisation process, redistributing resources and activities over the participating actors according to their competence. This allows for an improvement of the individual performance of actors as they can focus their efforts on their core activities. PURs resemble such web type networks when the individual cities perform different economic roles, and host complementary urban facilities and amenities, activities and residential and business environments from which larger parts of the region benefit.

This thesis presents correspondence analysis techniques as an appropriate technique to examine the relative differentiation in terms of activities between cities, both in a quantitative and visual way.

As outlined in the introduction, a macro-micro scheme was applied as an analytical model to answer the question of whether there is a trend towards complementarity in PURs in practice. Both Chapters 2 and 3 analyse trends in the spatial-functional structure of PURs on a macro-level. In a first analysis in Chapter 2 all economic activities present in the 14 largest cities in the Randstad region were included. General accounts of complementarity, for instance in policy documents, tend to refer to this division of labour in sectoral economic activities. Differentiation in economic roles, or profiles of cities also indicates to some extent the differentiation in business environments. A dataset derived from the Dutch National Information System on Employment (LISA) database was used, which contained data on the number of jobs classified according to the two-digit NACE Rev. 1 classification of economic activities for fourteen urbanised municipalities in the Dutch Randstad region. Three subsets of cities were made: the four main cities Amsterdam, Rotterdam, The Hague and Utrecht, and, following the common divide of the Randstad, a subset for the North Wing of this region and one for the South Wing of this region. The analysis confirmed the widespread idea that the main cities in the Randstad, in particular the three largest ones, perform distinct roles, each of them specialising in, grossly speaking, either commercial services (Amsterdam), manufacturing and transport (Rotterdam), public administration (The Hague) or trade and education (Utrecht). At the same time, the extent of differentiation in economic profiles diminished during the 1996-2002 period by almost 13%. Differentiation in economic roles of the cities was substantially higher in the North Wing than in the South Wing.

Using the same correspondence analysis techniques, Chapter 3 presents an international comparison of the differentiation in service sector activities between the four largest cities of three archetypal examples of PURs: the Randstad, the RheinRuhr Area and the Flemish Diamond. In Chapter 3 the focus was on service sector activities because it could be hypothesised that such services in one place may have a function for businesses and households in other places in the PUR as well. This is less evident for the primary and in particular secondary sectors that were also included in Chapter 2 as, in general, these are often relatively more connected to national or international markets rather than regional markets. The analysis of service sector activities therefore comes closer to meeting the precondition of integration, next to differentiation, for complementarity to occur. The comparison in time between the three PURs revealed that the division of labour between the main cities of the Randstad and of the Flemish Diamond is much stronger than in the RheinRuhr Area, thus indicating that complementarity is likely to be much higher, even twice as high, in these two regions. Some explanation for this is to be found in the different urban development pathways of the regions. The polycentric layout in the Randstad and the Flemish Diamond has been shaped over the past centuries as fragmented political and administrative structures and rivalry have prevented the rise of one continuously dominant city. Major urban development in the RheinRuhr Area took place much later when, because of the presence of natural resources such as coal and iron ore, the area witnessed rapid industrialisation and urbanisation. The extent to which there is a division of labour in the Randstad and Flemish Diamond is, however, declining at a relatively fast pace, contrary to the RheinRuhr Area which exhibits a more stable pattern. This means that the range of different business milieus and specialised clusters of service activities diminishes, and that cluster formation takes place on a supralocal, perhaps even regional scale. It appears that local competitive advantages are becoming increasingly regionalised. This decline also fits in with a more general trend that the sectoral specialisation of cities of all sizes has already been declining for a long time (Duranton and Puga, 2003), probably giving way to a more functional specialisation. Chapter 3 furthermore raised the question of whether the common distinction between polycentric development at the intra-urban scale (polycentric cities) qualitatively differs from polycentric development at the inter-urban scale (PURs) in terms of trends in the division of labour. This certainly is the case as, contrary to the intra-urban scale, there is no further unfolding of a sectoral division of labour in PURs.

Chapter 4 analysed the micro-aspects of trends towards complementarity, thereby focusing on two types of urban facilities: universities of professional education (hogescholen) and hospitals. Micro-level behavioural and locational decisions with regard to the spatial dispersal of these facilities across space were analysed within the macro-context, providing opportunities and constraints for these decisions. Chapter 4 analyses this choice-set, the resulting locational behaviour and the underlying rationales with respect to the dispersal of study programmes and health care over locations of hogescholen and hospital organisations. The analysis focused on multi-location hospitals and hogescholen, thus having locations in multiple, generally close-by cities. As a result of mergers, the multi-location model has become increasingly dominant in both the hospital and higher education sectors, leading to organisations operating on the scale of regions and potentially, but not necessarily, functioning on the scale of a PUR. Therefore, relationships between the locations of these multi-location organisations may be considered exemplary for intercity relationships. All multi-location hogescholen for which data was available happen to be located in the six urban networks (PURs) distinguished in the Dutch national spatial strategy (Ministerie van VROM, 2005). The multi-location hospitals studied were all located in the South Wing of the Randstad and in 'Brabantstad', for which the Dutch province of Noord-Brabant is a good proxy. A dataset in which all fulltime study programmes offered by hogescholen are registered, was provided by the Informatie Beheer Groep and allowed for a quantitative analysis of the differentiation in study programmes between the locations of a multi-location hogeschool, again using correspondence analysis techniques. Additional information was collected in some interviews with directors of these hogescholen (see Appendix A). The information on multi-location hospitals was gathered during a series of interviews with managers of such hospitals (see Appendix A) as well as from hospitals' annual reports and policy documents.

A large number of the multi-location hospitals choose to give a more distinct profile to their locations leading to complementarity. In the old situation each city had its own hospital providing as many specialisations as possible, as allowed by the size of their hinterlands. The development of institutional ties between hospitals in different cities brings with it a trend that hospital managers seek for scale economies through imposing a division of labour. Such specialisation of locations is also enforced by the strong need for efficiency given the high costs of hospitals and care. This trend towards complementarity particularly holds in strongly urbanised city-regions, where multiple hospital organisations co-exist close to each other and competition for the hinterland is fierce. Such a functional specialisation of locations is generally based on the type of care a patient needs. It is common for one location to specialise in emergency and complex care, another one in planable or elective care. As mergers between hospitals nearly always take place between hospitals in cities that are, to a greater or lesser extent, located in each other's hinterland, both the preconditions for complementarity to occur – differentiation and integration – are met.

Although the macro-context for the hogescholen is quite similar, the actual micro-level behaviour of managers of multi-location hogescholen diverges from those of hospitals. Multi-location hogescholen tend to copy study programmes rather than profiling their locations. This diminishes existing complementarities and enhances duplication. Part of the explanation is that the costs of duplication are small, while many prospective students are reluctant to travel far. So both trends towards complementarity and duplication were found in both sectors. Which one prevails depends on sector-specific efficiency needs, the willingness of consumers to travel and the extent of regional competition.

Being a multi-faceted concept, we explored selective facets of complementarity. While complementarities were found between cities in terms of the economic profile, as well as between locations of hogescholen and hospitals, trends generally point to a diminishing of complementarities, the hospital sector being the exception to the rule.

Organising capacity

Research question 2: *What is the potential of a regional co-ordinated planning approach in PURs and what factors foster or hamper the development of regional organising capacity in such regions?*

Chapters 2 and in particular 5 present the research findings with regard to the research issue of organising capacity. Regarding the potential of a regional co-ordinated planning approach in PURs, it was argued in Chapter 2 that co-operation is a main synergy-generating mechanism, in particular in the case of the so-called 'club' type networks in which actors share a common objective, activity or service and have parallel interests. Co-operation then leads to horizontal synergy through economies of scale and so-called positive network externalities. Co-operation issues include both the addressing of similar urban problems as well as challenges. In Chapter 5, three such co-operation issues of particular significance for PURs are identified and further explored: 1) the pooling of resources in order to share facilities and services and to achieve 'critical mass'; 2) developing and exploiting balanced complementarities; 3) optimising spatial diversity, in particular the quality of open spaces. Regional planning and co-ordination for these issues may entail competitive potentialities over a stand-alone development of individual cities in PURs.

Public administration tends to be organised in a territorial hierarchy. However, co-operation in PURs involves multiple scales and cuts across several administrative tiers. Additionally, multi-level governance requires the involvement of multiple public, private and organised interest groups, thereby taking into account that different issues call for different alliances with different spatial competencies and life spans. Therefore, the exploitation of the theoretical potential that regional co-operation for PURs not only concerns co-operation between cities, but rather, the development of what was coined 'regional organising capacity'. The concept of regional organising capacity was introduced in Chapter 5 and refers to the ability to regionally co-ordinate developments through a more or less institutionalised framework of co-operation, debate, negotiation and decision-making in pursuit of regional interests in which a multitude of public and private stakeholders participate. To what extent positive externalities arise from co-operation obviously depends on the utilisation and functioning of such frameworks, for instance with respect to the level of interaction, the willingness and ability of participating actors to set aside local interests for the greater regional good and the avoidance of free-rider behaviour.

While the functioning of such frameworks is of great importance for the development of externalities (see Capello, 2000), the analysis in Chapter 5 focused on the development of regional organising capacity in the first place. Despite the seemingly apparent advantages of building regional organising capacity to make effectively and optimal use of the potentialities of PURs, examples of PURs in which this capacity has actually been developed are rather thin on the ground. Basing our argument on evidence from four PURs in North West Europe – the Randstad, the RheinRuhr Area, the Flemish Diamond and Central Scotland – it was found that the building of regional organising capacity is conditioned by the spatial-functional, political- institutional and cultural context of the region. The spatial-functional dimension refers to the functional rationality behind the identification of a region as a PUR, as becomes apparent in the spatial scopes of markets, infrastructure and flows. Even though PURs should by no means be considered 'single' or 'closed' functional systems, the lack of strong and evident functional interactions within PURs, or these being under discussion, continuously hampers the development of regional organising capacity. The political-institutional dimension is about the attitude, vision and leadership of administrators and politicians and the flexibility of the formal institutional framework to respond to the need for multi-level governance. The cultural dimension is concerned with the feeling of belonging together and the creation of cultural elements that help in perceiving the PUR as an entity. The extent to which the region has a common culture refers to the existence of a shared history and shared values, norms and beliefs. Major sources of cultural differences such as language, ethnicity, religion and political preferences may exist within PURs. In addition, there is the issue of the contextual, multi-layered social construct 'regional identity'. Whether or not a PUR has 'identifying power' depends on how clear its delimitation is, the extent to which symbols are connected to it, the extent to which institutions (public, private, social) take the PUR as their territorial organising principle, thereby reproducing the PUR concept in daily life, and the extent to which the PUR is a political arena, which includes media. It was found that the main constraints hampering the development in the four PURs considered can be categorised as institutional fragmentation combined with an internal orientation of key persons (such as politicians, policy-makers) and the lack of identification with the region at large. Compared to the other case study regions, the context in the Randstad fosters the development of regional organising capacity relatively better. Interesting examples of regional organising capacity, e.g. the Deltametropolis Association and the Bureau Regio Randstad, have developed in this region.

Critical mass

Research question 3: *To what extent does the polycentric spatial layout of PURs influence their support base for urban functions?*

Chapter 6 explored whether a PUR can reap the advantages of urban size to the same extent as a monocentric city region. One of the main advantages of a larger urban size is that the support base, an important manifestation of critical mass, becomes larger. Critical mass was made operational as the extent to which supralocal or regional cultural, leisure and sports amenities were supported in a region. The presence of these amenities is closely linked to the size of the urban population. Data on the presence of cultural, leisure and sports amenities was collected and indexed for 42 Dutch regions, the so-called WGR-regions. These regions have been delimited according to local administrators' perceptions of what regions constitute the right scale for jointly addressing regional issues for co-operation. Contrary to other delimitations of regions in the Netherlands, the WGR-delimitation has advantages in that regional borders are not confined to relatively outdated administrative borders – at least in functional terms – like those of the Dutch provinces, the delimitation is relatively recent and can be considered a proxy for functional urban regions, albeit indirectly. The scores on the total index of amenities in a region served as the dependent variable in a multiple regression analysis. Explaining variables included the population size of a region, the number of visitors to a region (as indicated by the number of averagely occupied hotel beds), the average household income and a measure for the extent of mono- or polycentricity. For the latter, an innovative measuring method was developed that enabled each region to be scored on a scale ranging from very monocentric to very polycentric, drawing on the log linear rank-size distribution of the main cities or towns in each region. The regression analysis resulted in the observation that, when correcting for differences between regions in terms of population, the number of visitors and the average income, PURs have a disadvantage compared to more monocentric city regions: the more polycentric a region is, the less cultural, leisure and sports amenities are present. Conversely, the more monocentric a region, the more these amenities are present. The dispersed spatial layout of polycentric regions implies that they cannot reap the advantages of urban size in the same way as more monocentric urban regions, at least as far as our selection of cultural, leisure and sports amenities is concerned. It seems that agglomeration advantages have not yet turned into regional externalities. These empirical findings support the view of Parr (2004) and Bailey and Turok (2004), who suggested that PURs are behind more monocentric regions in terms of agglomeration advantages, or, in the case of PURs, regional externalities. Parr provides part of the explanation: in polycentric urban regions there is a need for longer travel flows, commodity flows, less convenient flows of information and a lack of a metropolitan environment. In addition, duplication between the competing cities is likely to be high (see Malecki, 2004) and cultural, leisure and sports amenities tend to be strongly rooted in their urban context. This leads to the interesting observation that the research theme of this thesis of whether cities in a PUR relate to each other in such a way that the collection of cities is more than the sum of the parts needs to be qualified. As far as the support for urban amenities is concerned, PURs are even less than the sum of the parts.

Synergetic relationships in PURs

All three research issues addressed in this thesis refer to synergetic relationships between cities. Firstly, the value of complementarity was outlined above: complementarity leads to certain regional externalities, that is agglomeration advantages following from specialisation on a regional level. Secondly, the same holds for the issue of critical mass. If the collection of cities in a PUR is able to organise a regional support base rather than separate local demand markets, it will profit from the larger regional critical mass present in such regions. This means that higher-order functions that, according to Christallerian central place theory would only be found in increasingly larger cities, could be present in PURs as well. Finally, organising capacity and therewith actual co-operation may lead to synergy following from economies of scale in addressing common issues, and, moreover, may foster the presence of complementarity and an enhancement of regional critical mass through the pooling of resources. Obviously, the enhancement of complementarity, regional organising capacity and critical mass all implies the increase in performance of the entire system of cities in a PUR although at the same time establishing new types of dependency relationships between the cities.

This brings us to the relationships between the three issues. Although addressed separately so far, the research issues are linked to each other. Complementarity implies that cities, or the actors within them, become more dependent on each other, which increases the need for interaction to make up for the uncertainties rising from dependency. Complementarity therefore makes regional organising capacity more urgent. A similar reasoning holds for the link between critical mass and organising capacity. The other way around appears obvious. Organising capacity allows for co-operation, discussion, debate, and negotiations on a regional scale. Issues addressed within such regional co-operative frameworks may be linked to the enhancement of complementarity and critical mass. For instance, complementarity may be fostered and duplication diminished through a better co-ordination of investment strategies in the cities. This could prevent cities from working in competition with each other in cases where this would lead to suboptimal developments. In addition, regional actors could use regional organising capacity to pool their resources together in order to enhance their critical mass in trying to develop, for instance, large-scale regional infrastructure, or in influencing the policy and investment strategies of central or European governments. Complementarity and critical mass seem to mutually enforce one another. When cities complement one another, it requires actors in the shared hinterland to develop a regional orientation in order to fullfil their demand for more specialised services or products. This regional orientation then fosters a larger critical mass. A larger, regional support base also allows for further specialisation. When these specialisations develop in different cities, it follows that complementarity rises. Given these linkages, it seems probable that complementarity, critical mass and organising capacity mutually enforce each other, thus creating synergy between the cities of a PUR.

Whether or not PURs have entered this upward spiral was questioned in this research. In doing so, a theoretically founded distinction was made between the concept of PURs and the concept of city networks or urban networks. From a theoretical standpoint, a polycentric urban region is not necessarily an urban network. A polycentric urban region can be identified more or less by structural characteristics such as the location of distinct, historically rather independent cities relatively close to each other and their quite even size distribution (see Kloosterman and Lambregts, 2001; Parr, 2004). Urban networks, on the other hand, could be considered an advanced sort of polycentric urban region. Polycentric urban regions also qualify for the label urban network when relational characteristics as described by the network model of spatial organisation have developed. These features of the network model were presented in the introduction. To theoretically justify the label urban network, these features should be present. This means that there should be, amongst others, a certain minimum extent of functional integration, a relative disconnection between size and function, complementarity and a critical mass that is relatively regionally based and allows for specialisation. All polycentric urban regions could thus be scored on a scale ranging between these two rather hypothetical extremes: on the one side the PUR as a loose collection of cities, on the other side the urban network strongly characterised by the features of the network model and the resulting synergy.

The question then becomes where our case study regions should be positioned on this scale, or alternatively phrased, have these developed from PURs into urban networks in the true sense of the word? Although answering this broad question requires much more research than present in this volume, our results on some of the aspects of this transition to urban networks do shed some light on probable answers. The set of case study regions used in this thesis can be compared in only a limited way as the analysis of the three research issues has focused on different sets of case study regions. The overall impression, however, is that there is still much to gain for PURs on their path towards true urban networks. The regional organising capacity that may foster this trend was relatively well established in the Dutch case study regions (Randstad, North Wing, South Wing, Brabantstad), although not really present in the two foreign case study regions (Flemish Diamond and RheinRuhr Area). The results of the actual co-operation within the co-operative frameworks are unknown. The extent of complementarity in the RheinRuhr was only half of the extent in the Randstad and Flemish Diamond regions. However, trends with respect to this sectoral divsion of labour were diminishing. On the other hand, in the Dutch hospital sector a clear upward trend in complementarity can be witnessed (see also Meijers, 2005). This, however, was not the case with respect to multi-location hogescholen in the Netherlands, although a certain rise in complementarity was caused by the development of new privately funded hogescholen looking for niches in the education market (see Meijers, 2006). The previous chapter made clear that the critical mass, in terms of the support base for cultural, leisure and sports amenities is less compared to more monocentric regions with an equal number of inhabitants, visitors and average household income. Taking this all into account, it seems that PURs have made only some initial steps on their way to becoming urban networks. However, once again it should be stressed that the question of to what extent PURs are transforming into urban networks requires further analysis for definite answers.

The more general background to this question is provided by the academic debate into whether the network model of spatial organisation is replacing the traditional hierarchical spatial organisation, owned by the central place model. This theoretical debate was extensively documented in Chapter 4. An empirical assessment of this trend was provided by an analysis of spatial-functional trends within the Dutch hospital and higher education sectors. This analysis was focused on a single, but important feature of this network model, namely complementarity. The relationships between the locations of multi-location hogescholen and hospitals were considered exemplary for intercity relationships. Empirical evidence for the hospital sector confirms the rise of a network model of spatial organisation as complementarity relationships are developing. However, this trend was not confirmed in the analysis of multi-location hogescholen. However, even in a situation with few complementarities between locations of a hogeschool, evidence was found for size neutrality, another feature of the network model. So even when our analysis of the hogescholen sector did not unambiguously support the development of a network model of spatial organisation, our findings did not support the central place model either. A recent study by the Netherlands Institute for Spatial Research (RPB; Van Oort, 2006) focusing on inter-firm networks arrives at the conclusion that both the network model and central place model hold for the regional structure of inter-firm relationships. In absolute terms, the hierarchical model still persists as central places dominate these inter-firm networks. Criss-cross inter-firm relationships between non-central places are, however, more present than expected. However, as has been explained in Chapter 4, the network model encompasses more features than complementarity or criss-cross relationships. With these explorations being limited in scope, a further exploration of the comprehensive research agenda of whether a network model of spatial organisation is developing is needed.

7.3 Reflections

Synergy versus agglomeration economies
As the title makes clear, this thesis takes the notion of synergy as its point of departure. In the process of writing this thesis, there has been some hesitance to do so, most particularly because of the 'buzz word' association encircling this notion. An alternative for synergy could have been 'agglomeration economies', which is rather similar to the notion of synergy and a much more common concept in urban studies. However, there were several reasons to hold to the notion of synergy. In the first place, calling a group of close-by cities a network brings along a huge intellectual baggage. A parallel can perhaps be drawn between the network metaphor and the 'system' metaphor that was used in a similar way to enhance our understanding of social phenomena a couple of decades ago. The network metaphor emphasises relationships between - in our case - cities. The notion of synergy is strongly linked to the concept of networks, as it is about how two or more nodes of a network relate to each other (Kamann, 1989). In the second place, explicit claims for synergy are made in relation to PURs in policy documents, examples of which were given in Chapter 2. In the third place, the notion of agglomeration economies seems less applicable to PURs, as it departs from a single agglomeration, while the essence of PURs is that they are made up by a number of such agglomerations. Given this, Parr (2004) has coined the term 'regional externalities', as he considers the term 'agglomeration economies' inappropriate given the physical distance between the cities constituting a PUR. While this thesis focused on synergy for the reasons given above, it also fosters our understanding of this new concept of regional externalities in PURs.

Integration in PURs
An issue on which insufficient light has been shed so far, is the issue of integration within PURs in connection to complementarity. Basically, complementarity was defined as resulting from differentiation and integration. While the importance of integration was acknowledged in this thesis, our analyses have been predominantly focused on the aspect of differentiation. This has led to some cautiousness with respect to our findings on complementarity, for instance by stating that, actually, the potential complementarity was measured, not knowing the extent to which it had materialised in practice as the aspect of integration was less touched upon in Chapters 2 and 3. One of the reasons for this limited attention being paid to the aspect of integration, or the extent to which different specialised activities serve the same hinterland, was simply because data on interactions or flows is elusive. However, two recent studies that focused entirely or in part on the Dutch Randstad region may improve our understanding of integration. These studies were conducted by the Netherlands Institute for Spatial Research (RPB; Van Oort *et al.*, 2006) and

within the framework of the Polynet project (see Hall and Pain, 2006; Lambregts *et al.*, 2006). Both studies examined the spatial pattern in input/output relationships of companies, the RPB for the industrial, services and wholesale trade sectors and Polynet for knowledge-intensive advanced producer services. Van Oort *et al.* (2006) collected data on the location of the most important purchasing/sales relationships of companies, gathering data for the four main city-regions in the Netherlands, the regions of Amsterdam, Rotterdam, The Hague and Utrecht on the level of municipalities. As larger cities will automatically attract a greater number of absolute relationships simply because there are more companies and hence the number of potential relationships is larger, they correct for the magnitude of all origin and destination municipalities. It follows that relationships between the four central cities in the Randstad, though significant in absolute numbers, are fewer than would be expected on the basis of their magnitude. They conclude that the Randstad, its North and South Wing all comprise sub-systems that are linked to each other, but these links are less strong than would be expected given their size. Note that the analysis does not correct for distance between municipalities.

The Polynet project also set out to understand how cities and regions are knitted together through business practices. An estimation of network connectivity in terms of intra-firm networks of offices of 176 services firms located in the Randstad, showed that, out of twelve main cities in the Randstad, Amsterdam is the most connected city in office networks, closely followed by Rotterdam (91% connectivity compared to Amsterdam) and at some distance by Utrecht (72%) and The Hague (71%). These percentages relate to the connectivity in comparison to Amsterdam. In the RheinRuhr Area, an analysis of 297 firms resulted in Düsseldorf (100%) and Cologne (99%) competing for being the most connected cities in terms of intra-regional office networks, followed by Dortmund (90%) and Essen (89%). The study defined a Central Belgium region that is larger in scale than the Flemish Diamond, but here Brussels scores highest (100%), seconded by Antwerp (94%), and at some distance Ghent (66%), while Mechelen is the fourth most connected (25%). 324 firms in the Central Belgium region were analysed (Taylor *et al.*, 2006). These figures require careful interpretation. As Lambregts *et al.* (2006) argue, the fact that many firms find it necessary to have a simultaneous presence in multiple Randstad cities may also indicate that the Randstad is not functioning as a single market, but is rather split up into several (at least four) separate business markets. A strong network connectivity of offices is not equivalent to strong functional linkages in these PURs. According to a series of interviews with senior business practitioners in the Polynet project there seems to be a dividing line between on the one hand services firms with a client orientation towards small and medium sized enterprises for whom the Randstad is split up into several business markets, and on the other hand those firms servicing multi-national companies often operating from just one office in the Randstad and who consider the Randstad the 'centre court' of a market that is made up by the entire Netherlands (Lambregts *et al.*, 2006). Another interesting finding is that the Randstad seems more polycentric in its regional context than in its international context. Advanced producer services are largely clustered in Amsterdam, also leading to Amsterdam being the most incorporated into European and global firm networks, while the interviewed managers indicate that Amsterdam also has the most 'global city milieu'. Consequently, from an international perspective, the Randstad seems rather monocentric, with Amsterdam being the central core, and the remainder of the Randstad, and even large parts of the Netherlands, acting as its hinterland. Another indication of this apparently growing dominance of Amsterdam is that investments to improve the accessibility of the Amsterdam region pay the most in terms of economic growth for the entire Netherlands (Thissen *et al.*, 2006).

The findings from these studies will undoubtedly fuel the discussion on the functional rationality behind the Randstad concept as well as the long debate about the scale at which regional co-operation needs to take place. Finding definite answers in this discussion seems very hard if not impossible given that the right delimitation of regions on the basis of interaction is strongly dependent on the issue or activity in question. For each issue or activity a different scale can be identified. For one issue or activity the Randstad will be too large, for the other issue too small. This also has consequences for the implications of these studies for our question of complementarity. On the basis of Van Oort *et al.* (2006) and the Polynet findings, it seems that the extent of differentiation found in the Randstad region cannot be equated with a similar extent of complementarity. This is because spatial interaction in terms of purchasing/sales relationships in business practise is less than what would be expected on the scale of the entire Randstad, which is partly due to the fact that the Randstad is split up into several smaller business markets. This, however, holds less for our analysis of differentiation for the North and South Wings. Being more functionally linked, it appears that actual complementarities come closer to the potential complementarities found.

Co-operation versus competition

The value of a regionally co-ordinated development has been emphasised in this thesis, thereby indicating the importance of regional organising capacity to enable such co-operation and co-ordination. It was also stated that competition is likely to lead to duplication rather than complementarity as cities tend to copy each other's successes. This may have given the impression that the point of departure was perhaps a simple scheme in which co-operation is placed against competition. However, in practice this dichotomy needs to be qualified in several respects. In the first place, competition is not negatively linked with complementarity or critical mass. Cities tend to compete with each other to attract investments in high-level services and hi-tech industries, for professional workers, for tourists, and even for a marketable image. Therefore, any extent of potential or actual complementarity found in our analyses has come about in a competitive context. From the outset, different local competitive advantages have played an important role in the shaping of the division of labour between a set of cities. It may also be that co-operation between public policy-makers is about removing barriers against private competition (market imperfections). In the second place, co-operation and competition are just two types of network behaviour out of a much wider range of possible behaviour. In general, none of the actors in a network is normally keen to give up autonomy unless it is considered a necessity, so it would appear that a delicate balance between rivalry and competition can be found in networks. Therefore, whether competition or co-operation prevails depends on the issue concerned. Actors in networks therefore maintain competitive and co-operative relationships simultaneously (Wassenberg, 1980). In addition, it is also quite possible that there are issues where there is neither a co-operative nor a competitive relationship: actors can also ignore each other.

As regards co-operation, some aspects need to be stressed once more. Firstly, this concerns the fact that the focus in this thesis was on the development of regional organising capacity (Chapter 5). While this should be considered a *conditio sine qua non* for effective regional co-ordination and co-operation, the latter is furthermore dependent on the network behaviour of the participating actors. For instance, Capello (2000) demonstrates that the achievement of important advantages from the network locally also requires commitment to participation and an open mentality to network behaviour. In this thesis it was concluded that in the Netherlands, in particular the Randstad, regional organising capacity is comparatively better developed than in the RheinRuhr, Flemish Diamond and Central Scotland. This has contributed to a better positioning of the Randstad region on the national policy agenda and as a consequence, a strong clustering of investments in this region. At the same time, this apparent lead is also fragile, being possibly dependent on the politicians and business leaders in charge and their personal networks and preferences. Regional co-ordination in the Randstad often seems 'management by speech'.

Complementarity ratio

There is a slight inconsistency in the way the complementarity ratio was calculated. In Chapter 2 and 4, the total inertia indicator was normalised by dividing the total inertia score by the maximum possible score. In Chapter 2 this ratio was multiplied by 100, resulting in a value between 0 and 100. In Chapter 4, this ratio was not multiplied, thus leading to values between 0 and 1. The principle is the same, and none of these options is better than the other.

Related to this is the issue of what score of the complementarity ratio would be desirable. It has already been stated in this thesis that cities have a large component of employment in non-tradeable economic activities. While this thesis supports the idea that a higher extent of complementarity is beneficial for regions, it should be acknowledged that there are maximum limits on complementarity too. While on the one hand complementarity in terms of business services or cultural, leisure and sports amenities with a supralocal significance is desirable, it would on the other hand be highly undesirable if typical local assets such as schools, bakeries, supermarkets etc. were no longer available locally. For social and sustainability reasons, complementarity should not be promoted for urban amenities and facilities that are used by households and companies on a daily basis and that involve the physical movement of persons. A reasonable access to services needs to be maintained, particulary for those whose mobility is limited, the elderly, children, non-car users and those that are not serviced by a decent collective transportation system. This should also prevent the rise of mobility resulting from complementarity to levels that are considered unsustainable.

Scale-issues

Polycentricity is essentially a scale-less phenomenon, as it refers to the existence of multiple centres in a given region. As a consequence, polycentric patterns have been identified at a variety of spatial scales. This thesis features the polycentric urban region (PUR). Its definition leaves room for the identification of PURs of varying size. The PUR was defined as 'a collection of historically distinct and both administratively and politically independent cities located in close proximity, well connected through infrastructure and lacking one dominating city in political, economic, cultural and other aspects' (see Kloosterman and Lambregts, 2001). 'Close proximity' is often equated with 'within commuting distance' and for this, an upper limit of one-hour travel time is often considered the rule of thumb. As the size of these cities is not specified, the term PUR can be applied to any sudden clustering of close-by cities located within one-hour travel time from each other. In this thesis several PURs acted as case studies that comply with these rules. This included PURs that have also been identified as such ('urban networks') in policy strategies, for instance the Randstad, its North Wing and South Wing, Brabantstad, the Flemish Diamond and the RheinRuhr Area. Our definition leaves room for a broader interpretation of PURs than present in policy strategies. On the basis of morphological aspects, attention was paid to Central Scotland as well. In addition, Chapter 4 featured multi-location hospitals and universities of professional education spreading their offer over multiple cities. Often their spatial scope resembled PURs, or parts of PURs, also identified in policy strategies. This was less self-evident for the Dutch so-called WGR-regions employed as case studies in Chapter 6. While some of these regions also resemble PURs as identified in policy practice, e.g. Twente, the Knooppunt Arnhem-Nijmegen and the city triangle Apeldoorn-Deventer-Zutphen, most of them do not, even though quite a number of them came out as polycentric according to the lack of hierarchy between the cities of their regional urban system. Each WGR-region in the Netherlands resembles a PUR in that each city or town in the region can be accessed normally within half an hour maximum from any other city or town in that region. Even though in each region the major cities or towns are easily recognisable, it must be admitted that the WGR-region delimitation conforms generally less to the general impression of what PURs are according to policy practise. This is probably related to the fact that the extent to which cities in a WGR-region are actually clustered in comparison to cities in surrounding WGR-regions is unknown. However, in terms of intercity relationships and spatial-functional structure, the principles are the same, irrespective of the size of the PUR concerned.

However, there are differences in this respect between the PUR and other spatial scales on which polycentric patterns have been identified. In the introduction emphasis was already placed on the differences between polycentricity in PURs, thus at the inter-urban scale, and polycentricity at the intra-urban scale. Chapter 3 provided empirical evidence that supports this. Contrary to the intra-urban scale where new centres develop next to an existing main centre thereby initiating a new and increased division of labour between the centres, the division of labour in PURs is diminishing. In addition, an important difference between polycentricity at the scale of PURs and the higher level, thus at the national and European scales, is that on the latter scales a country or Europe is considered more polycentric when cities are more evenly dispersed across the territory (see Meijers *et al.*, 2005), while at the scale of PURs it is exactly the opposite, a clustering together of cities, that leads to polycentricity.

Network model

Finally, in Chapter 2, reference is made to the network model that includes both a spatial-functional dimension and a co-operative dimension. In the introduction, Chapter 4 and this synthesis, a narrower interpretation of this network model, in the sense that it solely refers to a spatial-functional dimension, was adhered to, as both dimensions are part of different academic debates. This thesis aims to contribute to the debate on the spatial-functional configuration of urban regions.

7.4 Implications for regional development strategies in PURs

While the issues addressed in this thesis – further theoretical clarification and empirical justification of the development towards a network model in PURs and the related claims made for PURs – are obviously theoretical challenges, the findings are also relevant for designing regional development strategies.

In the first place, this relates to the underpinning of existing policies. Their possible effectiveness is also determined by the accuracy of the assumptions on which the policy builds. PURs feature in many strategic policy documents in many European countries, as was indicated in the introduction to this thesis. In policies, the term city networks or urban networks is often used to refer to PURs. However, in this thesis it has been stated that, from a theoretical perspective, PURs need to be distinguished from urban networks, the latter being an advanced sort of a PUR characterised by a spatial-functional structure that is in concordance with the network model of spatial organisation. What has become apparent is that PURs have only moved some initial steps towards such urban networks, as was just outlined. This raises questions about the validity of the premises on which policies for PURs are built. As Zonneveld and Verwest (2005) also argue, the presence of urban networks has so far not been sufficiently empirically validated. This is in particular not the case for the metropolitan character of the Randstad region. Therefore, coining the concept of city networks or urban networks in PURs often seems a manifestation of wishful thinking. This makes Van Oort *et al.* (2006) wonder whether the concept of 'urban networks' reflects an existing situation or, if not, whether it is capable of anticipating further spatial developments in the fields of housing, working, infrastructure and leisure in the Netherlands, thus providing a policy framework to cope with them. This reflects the uncertainty about the scale on which spatial developments should be best addressed. Pinning down such developments solely to the scale of PURs as in several Dutch policies seems paradoxically opposite to the essence of the 'new geography' (see Asbreek Brusse *et al.*, 2002) with its emphasis on apprehending the world in a dynamic, processed-based manner. There is a need to address the issue of scale not in a generic way, but rather more differentiated: function-dependent and case specific. For certain issues, the wider regional scale of the PUR will be more accurate, while for others the scale of the city-regions that together constitute the PUR may be more appropriate. The most important message, however, is that policy-makers and other local and regional stakeholders do not take the existence of urban networks in PURs for granted, thus avoiding a possible mismatch between the scale on which policies are targeted or from which they depart and the actual scale on which the issues addressed function.

In the second place, given the positive effects of higher degrees of complementarity, regional organising capacity and a regional support base for PURs, it seems that fostering these may well be part of regional development strategies that aim for increased synergy in PURs. In fact, when one reads strategic development perspectives for PURs, one will often find that the fostering of complementarity, critical mass and regional organising capacity are major policy objectives. However, it is not self-evident that the enhancement of these three issues solely belongs to the public domain. This thesis sheds some light on how in particular complementarity and to a lesser extent regional organising capacity come about, with an emphasis on the issue of complementarity. Chapter 4 gives a detailed account of the development of complementarity in the hospital and higher education sectors. It led to the observation that whether or not complementarity develops is dependent on a complex balancing of macro-level conditions such as laws, rules, central government funding schemes and the micro-level behaviour of organisations, individuals or households, that is their behavioural rationales following from the pursuit of their interests (see also Figure 1.1 in Chapter 1). These interests generally follow a market-principle: private actors aim to optimise their own interests within the market conditions set at the macro-level. Public actors influence only part of these macro-level conditions, but may still have a significant impact. To take the hospital sector as example, the trend towards complementarity that was found for privately organised multi-location hospitals was due to the strong need for efficiency, which was formulated at the macro-level. One step back in time, the emergence of multi-location hospitals resulted from both a condition set by the public government, which aimed to scale up, combined with the strong competition between hospitals for patients that are in general reluctant to travel far for health care. This example shows that the rise of complementarity in multi-location hospitals resulted mainly from the market behaviour of privately run hospitals, although complementarity was also an indirect side effect of public incentives at the macro-level. For multi-location hogescholen, the result of this balancing between macro-level public incentives and micro-level market competition was predominantly a trend towards the opposite, increased duplication. Therefore, whether or not complementarity develops seems the result of a series of coincidences and is highly dependent on the complex interplay between macro-level conditions and micro-level rationales. As regards the latter, actors on this micro-level are often not within the realm of public administration, have different agendas and are not committed to planning objectives such as to enhance complementarity.

The best possibilities for purposefully encouraging complementarity in PURS are likely to occur when new publicly funded supra-local amenities, facilities and business locations are developed simultaneously and when there is regional organising capacity to jointly co-ordinate their development from a regional perspective. However, even in such cases, the elaboration of development plans has proven to be very difficult. A case in point is the '*Nadere Uitwerking Randstad Internationaal*' (NURI), a programme drawn up in the early 1990s under the guidance of the administrators of the Randstad provinces and major cities. The ambition of this programme was to arrive at a certain functional division of labour between the main city regions in the Randstad in order to enhance its metropolitan nature, amongst others through developing high-order international-class amenities and avoiding duplication and an impending surplus of business locations and office space. During the process of developing this programme, it became obvious very quickly that such an enhancement of complementarity at this scale and at that time was unmentionable and appeared impossible (Zonneveld, 1992; Zonneveld and Verwest, 2005). A complicating factor with respect to the spatial allocation of facilities and amenities is also that their attractiveness varies: for instance, some will have a NIMBY character, while there is strong competition for others. This further nuances the role of public interventions when it comes to enhancing complementarity.

This does not mean, however, that there is no role for public policy-making in regional development strategies for PURs. It should be clear, however, what the main challenge is for PURs. This challenge is to raise the extent of specialisation, which can relate to urban facilities, amenities, business services, residential environments, business locations etc. Thus, the idea is that a 'top'-level should be added, reflecting the support base present in the PUR rather than at the local level of its constituent cities. Such specialised activities or environments can be distributed rather evenly across the cities in a PUR, which implies a situation of complementarity. Alternatively, however, these can also be more or less clustered in one and the same city. In both cases, the region profits from increased specialisation, but the spatial pattern is highly different. It seems that the first option – complementarity – is more probable in a PUR, as cities of relatively similar magnitude are well matched and none of them wants to be inferior. The second option implies the development of a hierarchy in a PUR, which seems contradictory to the historical development pathways such regions have generally followed. While all cities that make up a PUR will acknowledge the need to develop these specialised activities and environments, in practice they generally tend to opt for a concentration of specialised activities and environments in their own cities. A good illustration of this practice is the silly competition between Rotterdam and Amsterdam for the establishment of a national photography museum (see Nuchelmans, 2005). Instead of the envisaged national centre for visual culture, a trimmed down version was established in Rotterdam, and a smaller local photo museum was founded in Amsterdam. In another Dutch PUR (Drechtsteden) with one comparatively large city (Dordrecht), all cities contribute, according to their number of inhabitants, to a regional theater, the capacity of which is larger than would be possible if the cities did not co-operate. From these examples it appears that the extent of polycentricity has a strong influence on intercity-competition and therewith on the way increased specialisation can take shape spatially. The recent indications presented in the previous section that Amsterdam appears to become increasingly dominant may well mean that increased specialisation in the Randstad region will spatially take place in this city rather than through the mode of complementarity.

7.5 Directions for further research

As is often the case after finalising a research project, one ends up with more questions than one started with. Here, three directions for further research that are worth exploring can be identified. The first remains close to the issues addressed in this thesis, continuing the research where it ends now. The second direction takes a broader perspective and addresses the spatial organisation of city regions. The third direction discerned reflects my opinion on what the main challenge for research on the subject of PURs is: the empirical substantiation and validation of the many claims that have been made for such regions.

The first direction for research builds on this thesis. Being a multi-faceted concept, many facets of complementarity have not yet been explored. In this thesis the focus has been on complementarity in terms of activities. A general overview of the sectoral division of labour between cities in PURs was presented. This could be further extended with research into the functional division of labour between cities, e.g. the spread over cities of for instance headquarter versus production functions, front-office versus back-offices, high skill top-level functions versus low-skill routine functions etc. Duranton and Puga (2003) have argued that cities are increasingly distinguished by their functional specialisation rather than by their sectoral specialisation. In addition, the analysis of the sectoral division of labour was based on the perhaps rather rough two-digit level of the NACE classification. On the request of a referee of the paper in Chapter 3, additional analyses were carried out on the more detailed three-digit level for two of the three regions (not reported extensively here). Even though these analyses confirmed the conclusions drawn for the analysis on the two-digit level of detail, it seems worthwhile to perform similar analysis for a selection of even more detailed NACE sectors. This would enable a closer examination of complementarity in terms of, for instance, advanced business services, shops or amenities and facilities. As stated in the introduction, complementarity may refer not only to activities, but also to places such as business locations and residential environments (see also Musterd and Van Zelm, 2001). A further analysis could focus on this kind of complementarities in PURs. Next to exploring other facets of complementarity, research on exploring its link with several other phenomena such as spatial interaction, competitiveness and quality of life, as well as critical mass seems worthwhile from both a theoretical standpoint and because of its relevance for practice. Ullmann (1956) and Batten (1995) state that spatial interaction between places occurs because of complementarity. On the other hand, the case of two cities having different specialisations does not necessarily imply inter-centre trade within the PUR (Parr, 2004). It seems valuable to explore whether PURs in which there is a higher extent of complementarity, measured for various facets, also demonstrate a higher extent of spatial interaction. The link between complementarity and such constructs as competitiveness and quality of life also deserves our future attention. Is a PUR with a high extent of complementarity more competitive? Does it have a higher quality of life? As regards this latter question, it should be stressed that, while complementarity may lead to a more specialised array of urban functions at the regional scale, it may entail that on the local scale of cities some urban functions will be less present. This may have consequences for the accessibility of urban functions for less mobile groups in our society. The accessibility of hospital care is a case in point (see also Meijers, 2005). With respect to the research issue of the organising capacity in PURs, further attention is needed for the actual co-operation within the frameworks allowing for organising capacity. A more detailed insight into the ways regional issues could be made manageable is needed, which also includes proper mechanisms for balancing the gains and burdens of these issues for the participating actors. Finally, the main research question with respect to critical mass is the exploration of trends over time. In Chapter 6 it was found that in terms of the regional support base of city-regions, PURs have a disadvantage compared to monocentric city regions. However, what remains unknown is whether this gap is widening or whether it is closing, and the conditions under which the latter may take place. In general, this need for research involving time-series also holds for the research issues of complementarity and organising capacity. Another obvious question that builds on the findings of this thesis relates to the question of how easily generalisations can be made from them. Do they only hold for North West Europe, or do the findings also hold for other parts of Europe, for other parts of the western world such as the USA, Canada and Australia or even for the other continents? Empirical research involving other countries than those presented in this thesis would enable the findings reported here to be put in the right perspective.

A second and broad direction for further research concerns the spatial organisation of city-regions, and in particular whether or not there are general models of spatial organisation that hold for contemporary city-regions. Chapter 4 presented a major discussion in this respect on whether a network model of spatial organisation is replacing the criticised paradigm of central place theory, which would allegedly be the case particularly in PURs. In Chapter 4, the attention was focused on one of the main features of the network model, namely complementarity. Other features of the network model should be researched in an integral way to further explore this comprehensive research agenda of whether a network model of spatial organisation is developing. This includes trends with respect to features such as, for instance, size neutrality (the relative disconnection between size and function of places), the role of nodality versus centrality, the pattern of flows, and the evenness of the distribution of the population across the territory.

A third and important direction for pursuing further research is the empirical underpinning of the characteristics and the value of PURs. In the past decade, many contributions to the discussion on PURs have focused on clarifying the potential of such regions in a rather theoretical way. Roughly speaking, the idea is that the specific spatial-layout of PURs enables them to enjoy agglomeration advantages quite similar to their monocentric counterparts – their natural 'benchmark' region – while agglomeration disadvantages would be largely absent. However, claims in this respect have not yet been empirically substantiated. This lacuna should be considered the major challenge for research into PURs (see also Kloosterman and Musterd, 2001; Parr, 2004; Turok and Bailey, 2004). Attenion should particularly turn to claims with respect to the presence of agglomeration economies and agglomeration diseconomies in PURs. The discussion of claims relating to reaping the benefits of urban size in a PUR as presented in Chapter 6 of this thesis can be considered a first exercise for exploring this research agenda. Findings of such research will determine whether the PUR concept is able to maintain its current position in policy practice. However, given the many still unanswered questions surrounding the notion of a regional clustering of rather similar-sized cities, some of which are presented here, it seems highly probably that in the academic debate the concept of PURs is there to stay.

7.6 Final remarks

This thesis has questioned several assumptions with respect to PURs that have not been questioned before. This particularly holds for the assumption, widespread in policy documents and also found in many academic writings, that cities constituting a PUR complement each other, and would increasingly do so. Leaving aside some early attempts to get to grips with this concept many decades ago, this thesis presents, for the first time, a conceptual clarification of complementarity and has made it operational, also presenting correspondence analysis techniques as a measure to innovatively measure and visualise complementarity. Another assumption that was questioned is that a PUR provides a similar critical mass as a monocentric city region, an assertion often found in policy documents and brought forward in academic writings. Critical mass was made operational as the support base for amenities. For the first time, this assumed link between spatial structure and support base has been empirically explored in a quantitative way. This included new methods to analyse the extent of polycentricity of a PUR. Finally, explanations have been provided for the complexities in developing regional organising capacity in such regions. As such, these research findings have contributed to the scientific and policy debates on PURs and their spatial organisation, in particular also adding empirical evidence to the debate.

References

Asbeek Brusse, W., H. van Dalen and B. Wissink (2002) *Stad en land in een nieuwe geografie. Maatschappelijke veranderingen en ruimtelijke dynamiek*, WRR voorstudies en achtergronden V112. The Hague: Sdu Uitgevers.

Bailey, N. and I. Turok (2001) Central Scotland as a polycentric urban region: useful planning concept or chimera?, *Urban Studies*, 38, pp. 697-715.

Batten, D.F. (1995) Network Cities: Creative Urban Agglomerations for the 21st Century, *Urban Studies*, 32, pp. 313-327.

Camagni, R. (1993) From city hierarchy to city networks: reflections about an emerging paradigm, in: T.R. Lakshmanan and P. Nijkamp (Eds) *Structure and change in the Space Economy: Festschrift in honour of Martin Beckmann*, pp. 66-87. Berlin: Springer Verlag.

Capello, R. (2000) The City Network Paradigm: Measuring Urban Network Externalities, *Urban Studies*, 37, pp. 1925-1945.

Davies, W.K.D. (1998) Urban Systems Research: Unfulfilled Promises?, *Canadian Journal of Regional Science*, XXI, pp. 349-356.

Duranton, G. and D. Puga (2003) *From sectoral to functional urban specialisation*, Center for Economic Policy Research Discussion Paper 2971.

Hague, C. and K. Kirk (2003) *Polycentricity Scoping Study*. London: Office of the Deputy Prime Minister.

Hall, P. and K. Pain (Eds) (2006) *The Polycentric Metropolis: Learning from mega-city regions in Europe*. London: Earthscan.

Kamann, D. (1989) Actoren binnen netwerken, in: F. Boekema and D. Kamann (Eds) *Sociaal-economische netwerken*, pp. 29-84. Groningen: Wolters-Noordhoff.

Kloosterman, R.C. and B. Lambregts (2001), Clustering of Economic Activities in Polycentric Urban Regions: The Case of the Randstad, *Urban Studies*, 38, pp. 717-732.

Kloosterman, R.C. and S. Musterd (2001) The Polycentric Urban Region: Towards a Research Agenda, *Urban Studies*, 38, pp. 623-633.

Knaap, G.A. van der (2002) *Stedelijke bewegingsruimte, over veranderingen in stad en land*. The Hague: Sdu uitgevers.

Lambooy, J.G. (1998) Polynucleation and Economic Development: The Randstad, *European Planning Studies*, 6, pp. 457-466.

Lambregts, B., R. Kloosterman, M. van der Werff, R. Röling and L. Kapoen (2006) Randstad Holland: Multiple Faces of a Polycentric Role Model, in: P. Hall and K. Pain (Eds) *The Polycentric Metropolis: Learning from mega-city regions in Europe*, pp. 137-145. London: Earthscan.

Malecki, E.J. (2004) Jockeying for Position: What It Means and Why It Matters to Regional Development Policy When Places Compete, *Regional Studies*, 38, pp. 1101-1120.

Meijers, E., B. Waterhout and W. Zonneveld (2005) Polycentric development policies in European Countries: An Introduction, *Built Environment*, 31, pp. 97-102.

Meijers, E. (2002) Deltametropool gebaat bij duidelijker regionale identiteit Randstad, *Geografie*, 11, pp. 34-36.

Meijers, E. (2005) Spreiding van ziekenhuiszorg, *Rooilijn*, 38, pp. 403-407.

Meijers, E. (2006) Ruimtelijke spreiding van het hogeronderwijsaanbod: duplicatie of complementariteit?, *Tijdschrift voor Hoger Onderwijs*, 24, pp. 23-33.

Ministerie van Volkshuisvesting, Ruimtelijke Ordening en Milieubeheer (VROM) (2005) *Nota Ruimte, Ruimte voor Ontwikkeling*, deel 4: tekst na parlementaire instemming. The Hague: Ministerie van VROM.

Musterd, S. and I. van Zelm (2001) Polycentricity, Households and the Identity of Places, *Urban Studies*, 38, pp. 679-696.

Nuchelmans, A. (2005) Een felomstreden erfenis, Het Wertheimer-legaat als splijtzwam, *Boekman*, 63, pp. 68-76.

Oort, F. van, J. van Brussel, O. Raspe, M. Burger, J. van Dinteren and B. van der Knaap (2006) *Economische netwerken in de regio*. Rotterdam/The Hague: NAi Uitgevers/Ruimtelijk Planbureau.

Parr, J.B. (2004) The Polycentric Urban Region: A Closer Inspection, *Regional Studies*, 38, pp. 231-240.

Taylor, P., D. Evans and K. Pain (2006) Organization of the Polycentric Metropolis: Corporate Structures and Networks, in: P. Hall and K. Pain (Eds) *The Polycentric Metropolis: Learning from mega-city regions in Europe*, pp. 53-64. London: Earthscan.

Thissen, M., P. van de Coevering and H. Hilbers (2006) *Wegen naar economische groei*. Rotterdam/The Hague: NAi Uitgevers/Ruimtelijk Planbureau.

Turok, I. and N. Bailey (2004) The Theory of Polynuclear Urban Regions and its Application to Central Scotland, *European Planning Studies*, 12, pp. 371-389.

Ullmann, E.L. (1956) The Role of Transportation and the Bases for Interaction, in: W.L. Thomas (ed) *Man's Role in Changing the Face of Earth*, pp. 862-880. Chicago: The University of Chicago Press.

Wassenberg, A.F.P. (1980) Netwerken: rivaliteit en samenwerking tussen organisaties, in: A.F.P. Wassenberg (ed) *Netwerken: Organisatie en strategie*, pp. 17-47. Meppel: Boom.

Zonneveld, W. (1992) *Naar een beter gebruik van ruimtelijke planconcepten*, Planologische Verkenningen 64. Amsterdam: Planologisch en Demografisch Instituut Universiteit van Amsterdam.

Zonneveld, W. and F. Verwest (2005) *Tussen droom en retoriek, De conceptualisering van ruimte in de Nederlandse planning*. Rotterdam/The Hague: NAi Uitgevers/Ruimtelijk Planbureau.

Appendix A Interviewees

Mr. A.P. Bandel head housing department, Albert Schweitzer ziekenhuis
Mr. B. Broerse senior policy-making official higher education, Ministerie van Onderwijs, Cultuur en Wetenschappen
Mr. J.M.J. Collette interim-manager general and technical services department, Medisch Centrum Rijnmond-Zuid
Mr. J. Elbers chairman board of directors, Hogeschool INHOLLAND
Mr. L. Elting chairman board of directors, Vlietland ziekenhuis
Mr. R.J. de Folter chairman board of directors, Amphia ziekenhuis
Mr. P.P. Groenewegen researcher, Universiteit Utrecht/Netherlands Institute for Health Services Research (NIVEL)
Mr. W.G. Koppelaars chairman Adviescommissie Onderwijsaanbod 1993-2003
Mr. P.J.J. de Kubber member of the board of directors, Jeroen Bosch ziekenhuis
Mr. P.E. van der Meer member of the board of directors, Medisch Centrum Haaglanden
Mr. B. Misere manager location Waalwijk, Tweesteden ziekenhuis
Mr. L. Touwen chairman board of directors, Reinier de Graaf Groep
Mr. N.M. Verbraak chairman board of directors, Fontys Hogescholen

Samenvatting

Synergie in polycentrische stedelijke regio's: complementariteit, organiserend vermogen en kritische massa

Evert Meijers

Inleiding

Steden kunnen niet als geïsoleerde ruimtelijke verschijnselen worden bestudeerd. Stromen van informatie, kapitaal, goederen en personen verbinden ze met andere steden, daarbij gebruik makend van een verscheidenheid aan infrastructurele netwerken. Alhoewel het actoren als bedrijven, organisaties, huishoudens en individuen zijn die deze relaties onderhouden, is het ook mogelijk om op een abstracter schaalniveau te spreken van relaties tussen steden. Deze vormen het aggregaat van de relaties van al deze actoren. In de hedendaagse wetenschappelijke literatuur wordt een grote betekenis toegekend aan dergelijke relaties tussen steden voor het verklaren van het economisch, sociaal en cultureel functioneren van die steden.

Deze interstedelijke relaties staan centraal in dit proefschrift, waarbij het ruimtelijke object van studie een specifiek type regio betreft, namelijk de polycentrische stedelijke regio. Een polycentrische stedelijke regio kan gedefinieerd worden als een regio waar meerdere historisch gezien op zichzelf staande en bestuurlijk en politiek onafhankelijke steden op korte afstand van elkaar liggen – zeg binnen maximaal een uur reistijd van elkaar – en goed verbonden zijn door infrastructuur, terwijl geen van de steden de andere sterk domineert. Klassieke voorbeelden van dergelijke regio's zijn de Randstad en het RijnRuhrgebied, maar ook op lagere ruimtelijke schaalniveaus kunnen polycentrische stedelijke regio's worden geïdentificeerd. De in de *Nota Ruimte* genoemde stedelijke netwerken zijn hiervan een voorbeeld. Niet alleen in Nederland richt strategisch ruimtelijk en regionaal beleid zich op polycentrische stedelijke regio's, maar ook in veel andere Europese landen is dit het geval. Net als in Nederland is 'stedelijk netwerk' hierbij de gangbare beleidsterm voor de polycentrische stedelijke regio, waarbij de netwerkmetafoor uiteraard gebruikt wordt om de vermeende of gehoopte sterke samenhang tussen de steden uit te drukken.

Het beleidsdebat geeft extra urgentie aan het wetenschappelijke debat waarin de aandacht voor het concept van de polycentrische stedelijke regio de laatste jaren sterk is toegenomen. Dit debat is sterk theoretisch van aard. De empirische validatie van de vele assumpties ten aanzien van polycentrische stedelijke regio's ontbreekt vooralsnog. Deze assumpties bouwen vaak op de specifieke ruimtelijke structuur van polycentrische stedelijke regio's. Zo zou het mogelijk zijn om allerlei agglomeratievoordelen te behalen, net als in monocentrische stedelijke regio's, terwijl de uiteengelegde stedelijke structuur ervoor zou zorgen dat agglomeratienadelen (als congestie, hoge huren en huizenprijzen, gebrek aan ruimte, milieuvervuiling) relatief beperkt blijven. De verwachting is dat steden in polycentrische stedelijke regio's zich op een zodanige manier tot elkaar verhouden dat er synergie ontstaat. Of, en in welke mate, dit het geval is, is echter niet of nauwelijks onderzocht. Dit proefschrift richt zich dan ook op het – deels – voorzien in deze kennisleemte.

Traditioneel worden relaties tussen steden in termen van hiërarchie uitgedrukt. Dit is terug te voeren op de centraleplaatsentheorie zoals in de jaren dertig en veertig van de vorige eeuw ontwikkeld door Christaller en Lösch. Tegenwoordig wordt algemeen onderschreven dat stedelijke systemen in geavanceerde economieën in de praktijk in veel opzichten niet meer voldoen aan een dergelijke strikte hiërarchie in centra en markten. Echter, terwijl de gebreken van de centraleplaatsentheorie vaak aangetoond zijn, is deze niet vervangen door een andere set van duidelijk omschreven hypothesen over de ruimtelijke organisatie van stedelijke systemen. Sinds begin jaren negentig hebben verschillende onderzoekers echter wel de suggestie gedaan dat een zogenaamd netwerkmodel van ruimtelijke organisatie in toenemende mate een betere duiding van deze ruimtelijke organisatie geeft dan een hiërarchisch model. Dit netwerkmodel is in essentie het tegenovergestelde van het centraleplaatsenmodel. Deze laatste benadrukt onder meer de kenmerken centraliteit, een sterke koppeling tussen omvang van een stad en de functies in die stad, een toenemende hiërarchie tussen steden, een dominantie van eenzijdig gerichte verplaatsingsstromen, een vast aantal ruimtelijke schalen en een gelijkmatig verspreide bevolking in een regio. Het netwerkmodel daarentegen benadrukt de kenmerken nodaliteit, een relatieve ontkoppeling tussen omvang van een stad en de stedelijke functies ervan, toenemende complementariteit tussen steden, dubbelzijdige kriskras verplaatsingsstromen, een variabel aantal ruimtelijke schalen en een ongelijkmatige verdeling van de stedelijke bevolking. Het interessante nu is dat dit netwerkmodel zich het meest zou manifesteren in polycentrische stedelijke regio's. Echter, ook hier geldt dat dergelijke beweringen nauwelijks empirisch onderbouwd zijn. Dit is dan ook de tweede kennisleemte waarop dit proefschrift zich richt.

Doelen en onderzoeksvragen

Doel van dit proefschrift is om –deels- te voorzien in de twee genoemde kennisleemten. Dit betekent in de eerste plaats dat het onderzoek ten doel heeft om het concept van de polycentrische stedelijke regio verder theoretisch te verhelderen en om een invulling te geven aan de empirische onderbouwing van de assumpties met betrekking tot de ruimtelijke structuur, meer in het bijzonder die ten aanzien van de relaties tussen de steden in een dergelijke regio. In de tweede plaats is het doel om de kenmerken van het netwerkmodel van ruimtelijke organisatie theoretisch te verhelderen en de empirische houdbaarheid ervan te testen voor polycentrische stedelijke regio's. Beide doelstellingen zijn sterk aan elkaar gerelateerd aangezien de assumpties over interstedelijke relaties in polycentrische stedelijke regio's in sterke mate overeenkomen met de kenmerken van het netwerkmodel. Het overkoepelende onderzoeksthema van dit onderzoek is dan ook of de steden die tezamen een polycentrische stedelijke regio vormen zich tot elkaar verhouden op een manier die tot synergie leidt. Met andere woorden, tot op welke hoogte is een polycentrische stedelijke regio meer dan de som der delen?

Gezien de breedte van dit onderzoeksthema en de twee onderliggende onderzoeksagenda's is er een noodzaak om het onderzoek te richten op een aantal thema's op deze agenda's. Daartoe is het overkoepelende onderzoeksthema gesplitst in drie onderzoeksvragen die verband houden met drie dominante thema's op deze agenda's:

1. complementariteit
2. organiserend vermogen
3. kritische massa

Voor elk van deze thema's is een onderzoeksvraag opgesteld:

1. *Tot op welke hoogte is er sprake van een toenemende complementariteit binnen polycentrische stedelijke regio's en is dit nastrevenswaardig?*
2. *Welke kansen biedt een regionaal gecoördineerde planning binnen polycentrische stedelijke regio's en welke factoren bevorderen danwel hinderen de ontwikkeling van regionaal organiserend vermogen in dergelijke regio's?*
3. *In welke mate beïnvloedt de polycentrische ruimtelijke structuur van polycentrische stedelijke gebieden het draagvlak voor stedelijke functies in dergelijke regio's?*

Deze vragen worden in een vijftal wetenschappelijke artikelen beantwoord, welke gebundeld zijn in dit proefschrift.

Complementariteit
Onderzoeksvraag 1: *Tot op welke hoogte is er sprake van een toenemende complementariteit binnen polycentrische stedelijke regio's en is dit nastrevenswaardig?*

De onderzoeksvraag betreft zowel de waarde die aan complementariteit gehecht moet worden als de trends met betrekking tot complementariteit in de praktijk. Daarnaast is aandacht besteed aan de conceptualisering van dit begrip. De hoofdstukken 2, 3 en 4 gaan in op deze onderzoeksvraag. Hoofdstuk 2 bevat een artikel dat eerder in *Urban Studies* verscheen (Meijers, 2005). Hoofdstuk 3 zal medio 2007 verschijnen in *Regional Studies*, terwijl hoofdstuk 4 begin 2007 is verschenen in het *Tijdschrift voor Economische en Sociale Geografie* (Meijers, 2007).

Alhoewel er in het verleden enige voorzichtige pogingen zijn gedaan om complementariteit te conceptualiseren, is het desondanks een met enige vaagheid omkleed begrip gebleven. Dit terwijl het begrip in toenemende mate, zij het veelal terloops, terugkeert in zowel wetenschappelijke geschriften als in beleidsdocumenten. Het gebrek aan conceptuele helderheid verklaart deels waarom het concept tot op heden nog maar nauwelijks empirisch geanalyseerd is. In dit proefschrift is getracht een nadere invulling te geven aan het concept complementariteit, en wel in de context van polycentrische stedelijke regio's.

Complementariteit refereert aan het idee dat steden binnen een polycentrische stedelijke regio verschillende functies vervullen en herbergen, terwijl deze ook ten goede komen aan bedrijven en huishoudens uit andere steden dan waarin de functies te vinden zijn. In die zin is complementariteit dus het resultaat van differentiatie in het aanbod van 'activiteiten' (stedelijke functies) en 'plaatsen' (denk aan woon- en werkmilieus), gecombineerd met een integratie van de markten – in ruimtelijke zin – waarop deze actief zijn. Dit laatste wil zeggen dat de vraag naar deze gedifferentieerde activiteiten en plaatsen niet alleen lokaal, maar zeker ook regionaal is. Gezien het multidimensionele karakter van complementariteit was het noodzakelijk om in dit onderzoek een aantal aspecten ervan centraal te stellen. Het onderzoek beperkt zich dan ook tot complementariteit met betrekking tot activiteiten en stedelijke functies. In hoofdstuk 2 staan economische activiteiten en daarmee de verschillende rollen van steden in de regionale economie centraal. In hoofdstuk 3 richt de analyse zich op complementariteit in de dienstverlenende sector, terwijl in hoofdstuk 4 complementariteit in een tweetal voorzieningensectoren – hoger onderwijs en ziekenhuiszorg – centraal staan. Alhoewel erkend wordt dat differentiatie tussen steden niet voldoende is om van complementariteit te kunnen spreken, daarvoor is immers ook integratie van markten nodig, zijn de analyses in deze hoofdstukken met name gericht op het aspect differentiatie. Dit facet van complementariteit is immers het vertrekpunt voor het ontstaan van complementariteit. In de literatuur is het idee geopperd dat uit deze differentiatie vanzelfsprekend ruimtelijke interactie, en daarmee integratie, volgt.

Complementariteit moet positief beoordeeld worden. Wanneer twee steden elkaar complementeren, dan kunnen de inwoners en bedrijven van de ene stad profiteren van de diverse andere functies die de andere stad te bieden heeft en vice versa. Deze functies kunnen dan meer gespecialiseerd en gediversificeerd zijn aangezien het draagvlak waarop zij bouwen groter is. Complementariteit is daarmee sterk verwant aan agglomeratieeconomieën, al zou er, gezien de fysieke scheiding tussen de steden, in dit geval beter gesproken kunnen worden van 'regionale externaliteiten'. De waarde van complementariteit is in theoretische zin verkend in hoofdstuk 2, waarin het idee van synergie in netwerken werd geanalyseerd. Hieruit kwam naar voren dat complementariteit tot synergie leidt, in het bijzonder in zogenaamde 'web' type netwerken. Complementariteit leidt hierbinnen tot verticale synergie via een specialisatieproces waarin activiteiten aan de deelnemende actoren worden toegedeeld op basis van hun competenties. De mogelijkheid om zich te concentreren op hun kerncompetenties leidt tot een betere prestatie van de individuele actoren en daarmee van het geheel. Polycentrische stedelijke regio's lijken op dergelijke 'web' type netwerken wanneer de steden in dergelijke regio's verschillende economische rollen vervullen, of complementaire stedelijke voorzieningen en economische activiteiten herbergen, welke dan ten goede komen aan de gehele regio. De verdeling van deze stedelijke functies en activiteiten zou dan zodanig moeten zijn dat deze het beste aansluiten bij de lokale comparatieve voordelen van de steden, bijvoorbeeld volgens het principe van clustering.

In de introductie op dit proefschrift is de vraag of er sprake is van een trend naar complementariteit in polycentrische stedelijke regio's benaderd via een analytisch micro-macro model. Zowel hoofdstuk 2 als 3 analyseren trends in de ruimtelijk-functionele structuur op macro-niveau. De analyse in hoofdstuk 2 heeft betrekking op alle economische activiteiten die te vinden zijn in de 14 grootste steden in de Randstad. Doorgaans hebben uitspraken over complementariteit in de Randstad, zoals bijvoorbeeld in beleidsstukken, betrekking op de verdeling van deze activiteiten over de steden. In dit proefschrift wordt correspondentie-analyse gepresenteerd en gebruikt als een geschikte techniek om de relatieve differentiatie van steden ten opzichte van elkaar te onderzoeken, zowel in kwantitatieve als in visuele zin. Deze correspondentie-analyse wordt in hoofdstuk 2 toegepast op een dataset verkregen uit de LISA-database. In deze dataset zijn gegevens over het aantal banen (geclassificeerd volgens de SBI-indeling op tweecijferig niveau) voor de 14 grootste gemeenten in de Randstad opgenomen. Analyses zijn uitgevoerd voor een drietal sets van steden: de vier grote steden in de Randstad; de steden in de Noordvleugel; en de steden in de Zuidvleugel. De analyse bevestigt de wijdverspreide opvatting dat er een duidelijke taakverdeling bestaat tussen de belangrijkste steden in de Randstad, in het bijzonder tussen de grootste drie. Ruwweg komt deze er op neer dat Amsterdam het centrum is voor commerciële dienstverlening, Rotterdam voor industrie, transport en logistiek, terwijl Den Haag het overheidscentrum is. Ten opzichte van deze steden kent Utrecht een lichte specialisatie in handel en onderwijs. De differentiatie in economische profielen van steden in de Noordvleugel bleek substantieel hoger dan in de Zuidvleugel. Echter, deze taakverdeling tussen steden in de Randstad of zijn vleugels gaat steeds minder op. In de periode 1996-2002 nam de differentiatie van de grote vier steden ten opzichte van elkaar met bijna 13% af.

In hoofdstuk 3 is eveneens gebruik gemaakt van correspondentie-analyse voor een internationale vergelijking tussen de Randstad, de Vlaamse Ruit en het RijnRuhrgebied voor wat betreft de differentiatie tussen de steden in de dienstensector in iedere regio. Het idee achter deze focus op alleen de dienstensector is dat het voor dergelijke activiteiten aannemelijker is dat deze ook betekenis hebben voor bedrijven en huishoudens in andere steden dan voor bedrijvigheid in de primaire en secundaire sectoren. Deze laatste sectoren zijn relatief vaker gerelateerd aan het nationale en internationale schaalniveau dan aan het regionale schaalniveau. Een analyse van de dienstensector komt daarom meer tegemoet aan de tweede voorwaarde om te kunnen spreken van complementariteit, namelijk integratie (naast differentiatie). Uit de vergelijking bleek dat de verdeling van taken tussen de vier grootste steden in de Randstad en in de Vlaamse Ruit veel sterker is dan tussen de vier grootste steden in het RijnRuhrgebied. Daarmee is het hoogstwaarschijnlijk dat de complementariteit in de Randstad en de Vlaamse Ruit veel groter is, zelfs twee keer zo groot. Een deel van de verklaring hiervoor ligt in de verschillende historie van de gebieden wat betreft stedelijke ontwikkeling. De polycentrische structuur van de Randstad en de Vlaamse Ruit is door de eeuwen heen gevormd als gevolg van het voortbestaan van gefragmenteerde politieke en bestuurlijke structuren, terwijl onderlinge rivaliteit de opkomst van een voortdurend dominante stad voorkomen heeft. Grootschalige stedelijke ontwikkeling in het RijnRuhrgebied vond pas veel later plaats, tijdens de industriële revolutie, en is vanzelfsprekend gerelateerd aan de in grote mate aanwezige grondstoffen als kolen en ijzererts. De steden in deze regio kenden daardoor dezelfde bloeitijd, terwijl in de Randstad en de Vlaamse Ruit de dominantie van steden varieerde per tijdsgewricht. Een opvallende uitkomst uit de analyse is voorts dat de mate waarin sprake is van een onderlinge taakverdeling tussen de steden in de Randstad en in de Vlaamse Ruit in snel tempo afneemt, terwijl dit nagenoeg stabiel is in het RijnRuhrgebied. Dit duidt er op dat steden zich steeds minder onderscheiden in aangeboden werkmilieus en bedrijfsomgevingen, waardoor er lokaal minder clusters van gespecialiseerde dienstverlening zijn. Clusterformatie lijkt plaats te hebben op supralokaal, mogelijk zelfs regionaal schaalniveau in plaats van lokaal. Het lijkt er dan ook op dat lokale competitieve voordelen in toenemende mate geregionaliseerd worden. De afname in sectorale specialisatie van steden is overigens een vrij algemene trend. In dat licht is de neerwaartse trend in differentiatie tussen de steden in de Randstad en de Vlaamse Ruit wellicht ook niet verwonderlijk. Vermoed wordt dat de functionele specialisatie van steden (bijvoorbeeld hoofdkantoren in de ene plaats, en backoffices ergens anders) wel toeneemt.

Hoofdstuk 3 stelt ook de vraag aan de orde of een verdere polycentrische ontwikkeling op regionaal schaalniveau, dus op het niveau van polycentrische stedelijke regio's, overeen komt met polycentrische ontwikkeling op lokaal schaalniveau, dus op het niveau van een enkele polycentrische stad, voor wat betreft de taakverdeling tussen centra. Er blijkt een groot verschil te zijn. In tegenstelling tot het lokale schaalniveau waar de opkomst van nieuwe centra naast het stadscentrum gepaard gaat met een toenemende specialisatie van die centra, is er op het regionale schaalniveau sprake van een afname van deze taakverdeling. Hiermee is wederom aangetoond dat begrippen als polycentriciteit en polycentrische ontwikkeling dan wel van toepassing verklaard kunnen worden op uiteenlopende schaalniveaus, maar dat ze een verschillende betekenis hebben op elk van deze schaalniveaus.

Hoofdstuk 4 richt zich op het analyseren van de micro-aspecten van een mogelijke trend naar complementariteit. Daarbij gaat het dus om het gedrag van individuele actoren en hun ruimtelijk handelen, en hoe condities op macro-niveau deze individuele handelingsruimte op micro-niveau beïnvloeden. De focus hierbij is op een tweetal typen consumentgerichte voorzieningen: hogescholen en ziekenhuizen. De analyse van complementariteit richt zich op meerlokatiehogescholen en -ziekenhuizen. 'Meerlokatie' wil zeggen dat deze organisaties hun activiteiten verspreid hebben over lokaties in verschillende, doorgaans nabijgelegen, steden. Als gevolg van veel recente fusies zijn er steeds meer meerlokatiehogescholen en -ziekenhuizen ontstaan. In plaats van lokaal, opereren deze organisaties daardoor steeds meer op een regionaal schaalniveau. Er wordt een analogie verondersteld tussen deze meerlokatie-organisaties en polycentrische stedelijke regio's: relaties tussen lokaties van deze organisaties zouden exemplarisch kunnen zijn voor relaties tussen steden. De vraag die gesteld wordt is of deze organisaties, na recent gefuseerd te zijn, overgaan op een andere verdeling van ziekenhuiszorg respectievelijk studie-opleidingen over de lokaties. Is er een trend naar complementariteit of juist naar duplicatie?

Alle meerlokatiehogescholen waarvoor data voorhanden waren, bleken gevestigd te zijn in de zes door de rijksoverheid in de *Nota Ruimte* onderscheiden polycentrische stedelijke regio's (stedelijke netwerken). De onderzochte meerlokatiehogescholen bevinden zich in de Zuidvleugel en Brabantstad. Voor de analyse van de hogescholensector is gebruik gemaakt van verschillende jaargangen van het CROHO register van de Informatie Beheer Groep, waarin alle bachelor-opleidingen aan hogescholen geregistreerd staan. Dit maakte een correspondentie-analyse mogelijk. Aanvullende informatie werd verzameld tijdens interviews met managers van hogescholen en andere betrokkenen in het veld. Voor de ziekenhuizen bleken geen openbare registraties van zorgtaken op lokatieniveau beschikbaar. Informatie werd verzameld tijdens een serie interviews met managers van meerlokatieziekenhuizen en uit secundaire literatuurbronnen als jaarverslagen en beleidsdocumenten.

Binnen meerlokatieziekenhuizen is een duidelijke trend naar meer complementariteit waarneembaar. In de oude situatie van voor de fusie had iedere stad zijn eigen ziekenhuis waarbinnen zoveel mogelijk medische specialisaties vertegenwoordigd waren als maar mogelijk was op basis van de omvang van het verzorgingsgebied. Fusies tussen ziekenhuizen in verschillende steden leiden er in veel gevallen toe dat managers naar schaaleconomieën zoeken door een profilering van de lokaties door te voeren. Een specialisatie van de ene lokatie in complexe en acute zorg en van een andere lokatie in relatief eenvoudige, planbare of electieve behandelingen is daarbij het meest gangbaar. Een dergelijke profilering van lokaties wordt mede afgedwongen door macro-condities. In het geval van ziekenhuizen stelt de overheid voorwaarden aan de kosten van de zorg, wat ziekenhuizen dwingt tot financiële efficiëntie. De tendens naar meer complementariteit gaat in het bijzonder op in sterk verstedelijkte regio's, waar veel ziekenhuisorganisaties relatief dicht bij elkaar gevestigd zijn en waar de concurrentie om het verzorgingsgebied dientengevolge groot is. Aangezien fusies tussen ziekenhuizen tot op heden altijd hebben plaatsgevonden tussen ziekenhuizen waarvan de verzorgingsgebieden in meer of mindere mate reeds overlappen, lijkt het zo te zijn dat aan beide voorwaarden voor complementariteit – differentiatie én integratie – wordt voldaan.

Alhoewel de macro-context voor hogescholen sterk vergelijkbaar is met die voor ziekenhuizen, verschilt hun micro-gedrag aanzienlijk. Uit de kwantitatieve analyses volgt dat meerlokatiehogescholen doorgaans tenderen naar een duplicatie van het onderwijsaanbod op hun locaties, in plaats van naar complementariteit. Een deel van de verklaring hiervoor is dat de kosten van duplicatie betrekkelijk laag zijn, dit in tegenstelling tot ziekenhuizen. Bovendien zijn veel aankomende studenten niet bereid ver te reizen of te verhuizen voor hun studie. Om zoveel mogelijk studenten, en daarmee financiering, aan te trekken is het zinvol om opleidingen zo dicht als maar mogelijk bij de potentiële student aan te bieden. Binnen deze consumentgerichte voorzieningensectoren kunnen zodoende tegengestelde trends worden gevonden. Of er een trend naar duplicatie of naar complementariteit is, bleek afhankelijk van sectorspecifieke efficiëntie-eisen, de bereidheid van consumenten om te reizen en de mate van regionale competitie.

Vanwege de multidimensionaliteit van het concept complementariteit hebben de analyses zich gericht op een beperkt aantal facetten ervan. Complementariteit tussen steden werd gevonden in termen van hun economisch profiel, evenals tussen lokaties van meerlokatieziekenhuizen. Echter, trends wijzen op een daling van complementariteit, waarbij de ziekenhuissector vooralsnog de uitzondering op de regel lijkt.

Organiserend vermogen

Onderzoeksvraag 2: *Welke kansen biedt een regionaal gecoördineerde planning binnen polycentrische stedelijke regio's en welke factoren bevorderen danwel hinderen de ontwikkeling van regionaal organiserend vermogen in dergelijke regio's?*

De hoofdstukken 2 en 5 bevatten artikelen eerder gepubliceerd in *Urban Studies* (Meijers, 2005) en *European Urban and Regional Studies* (Meijers en Romein, 2003). Hierin worden de bevindingen ten aanzien van het thema organiserend vermogen gepresenteerd. Op basis van theorie wordt in hoofdstuk 2 geconcludeerd dat samenwerking in belangrijke mate tot synergie tussen de steden kan leiden, in het bijzonder in het geval van netwerken van het 'club' type, waarbinnen actoren een gezamenlijk doel en/of gezamenlijke activiteiten delen en overeenkomende belangen hebben. Samenwerking leidt dan tot zogenaamde horizontale synergie door middel van schaaleconomieën en positieve netwerkexternaliteiten. In hoofdstuk 5 worden een drietal concrete thema's voor samenwerking geïdentificeerd die van bijzonder belang zijn voor polycentrische stedelijke regio's: 1) het bundelen van middelen om zodoende faciliteiten te delen en om kritische massa te verkrijgen; 2) het ontwikkelen en benutten van complementariteiten; en 3) het optimaliseren van ruimtelijke diversiteit, in het bijzonder gericht op het waarborgen van de kwaliteit van de tussen de steden gelegen open ruimte. Regionale coördinatie en samenwerking ten aanzien van deze thema's biedt veel grotere voordelen dan een aanpak op lokaal niveau.

Overheden zijn doorgaans georganiseerd op een territoriaal-hiërarchische manier. Echter, samenwerking in polycentrische stedelijke regio's vereist dat verschillende bestuurslagen, op diverse ruimtelijke schaalniveaus, erbij betrokken zijn. Dergelijke 'multilevel governance' vereist bovendien dat ook private actoren en maatschappelijke belangengroepen betrokken zijn bij de besluitvorming. Daarbij moet voorts rekening gehouden worden met het feit dat, in het ideale geval, voor ieder specifiek (ruimtelijk) vraagstuk er andere allianties van actoren met uiteenlopende (ruimtelijke) bevoegdheden moeten worden gevormd, terwijl de levensduur van dergelijke allianties samenhangt met de oplossing van het vraagstuk en dus variabel is. Hieruit volgt dat regionale coördinatie en samenwerking in polycentrische stedelijke regio's niet alleen samenwerking tussen steden betreft. Een veel bredere benadering is nodig: regionaal organiserend vermogen moet tot stand gebracht worden. Dit concept, regionaal organiserend vermogen, is geïntroduceerd in hoofdstuk 5. Het refereert aan het vermogen om regionale ontwikkelingen te coördineren door middel van in meer of mindere mate geïnstitutionaliseerde kaders waarbinnen regionale samenwerking, debat, onderhandeling en besluitvorming kan plaatsvinden aangaande gezamenlijke regionale belangen. Zowel publieke als private actoren en maatschappelijke belangengroepen moeten hier een plaats in hebben. Alhoewel regionaal organiserend vermogen beschouwd moet worden als een *conditio sine qua non* voor regionale coördinatie en samenwerking, is de effectiviteit ervan afhankelijk van de wijze waarop gebruik gemaakt wordt van deze kaders en het functioneren van actoren daarbinnen. De bereidheid om het gezamenlijke regionale belang leidend te laten zijn in plaats van lokale belangen is daarbij doorslaggevend. De analyse in hoofdstuk 5 heeft zich toegespitst op de eerste stap om tot effectieve regionale coördinatie en samenwerking te komen, namelijk op de ontwikkeling van regionaal organiserend vermogen. Ondanks de ogenschijnlijk duidelijke voordelen die regionale coördinatie en samenwerking bieden om het potentieel van polycentrische stedelijke regio's optimaal te benutten, zijn voorbeelden van dergelijke regio's waarin regionaal organiserend vermogen is ontwikkeld dun gezaaid. Op basis van de empirie in een viertal polycentrische stedelijke regio's in Noordwest Europa – de Randstad, de Vlaamse Ruit, het RijnRuhrgebied en Centraal Schotland – is geconcludeerd dat de ruimtelijk-functionele context, de politiek-institutionele context en de culturele context bepalend zijn voor de ontwikkeling van regionaal organiserend vermogen. Bij de ruimtelijk-functionele context is met name de functionele rationaliteit achter het identificeren van een polycentrisch stedelijk gebied als een eenheid van belang. Die functionele rationaliteit komt met name tot uiting in het ruimtelijk bereik van markten (zoals de arbeidsmarkt, afzetmarkten van bedrijven), de verbondenheid door infrastructuur en in het bijzonder de verplaatsingsstromen. Een gebrek aan sterke en zichtbare functionele interacties in polycentrische stedelijke regio's, of het voortdurend ter discussie stellen ervan, bleek een belangrijke barrière voor de ontwikkeling van regionaal organiserend vermogen in de vier cases. Belangrijke factoren binnen de politiek-institutionele context zijn de houding en visie van bestuurders met betrekking tot regionale samenwerking en hun leiderschap daarin. Daarnaast speelt de mate waarin de bestaande bestuurlijke opzet ruimte biedt aan een regionale invulling van multilevel governance een belangrijke rol. Bij de culturele context moet gedacht worden aan factoren als de mate waarin men zich met elkaar verbonden voelt en de mate waarin culturele elementen dit gevoel van eenheid versterken. Denk bijvoorbeeld aan het delen van een gemeenschappelijke historie, normen en waarden. Soms komen er binnen polycentrische stedelijke regio's bronnen van conflict voor op cultureel gebied, zoals verschillen met betrekking tot taal, etniciteit, religie en politieke preferenties. Deze maken de ontwikkeling van regionaal organiserend vermogen vaak tot een uiterst moeizame opgave. Voorts maakt ook de regionale identiteit van een polycentrische stedelijke regio deel uit van de culturele context. 'Regionale identiteit' is een gelaagd, sociaal geconstrueerd fenomeen, dat wil zeggen dat er sprake is van verschillende regionale identiteiten, bijvoorbeeld op buurt-, lokaal, regionaal en nationaal niveau en dat deze dynamisch zijn. Welke identiteit op een bepaald moment dominant is, wordt met name bepaald door interacties met anderen. Of er van een polycentrische stedelijke regio ook een identificerende kracht uitgaat is afhankelijk van een aantal zaken. Hoe duidelijk is het bijvoorbeeld wat wel en wat niet tot het gebied behoort? Zijn er symbolen gekoppeld aan de regio? Gebruiken organisaties (publiek, privaat, maatschappelijk) de regio als territoriaal organiserend principe, daarmee de regio reproducerend in het dagelijks leven? Is de polycentrische stedelijke regio ook een politieke arena, zijn er bijvoorbeeld media op het schaalniveau van dergelijke regio's? Al deze factoren kunnen zowel positief als negatief uitwerken op het regionaal organiserend vermogen. De belangrijkste factoren die het regionaal organiserend vermogen negatief beïnvloeden in de vier cases bleken te zijn: bestuurlijke fragmentatie; een interne oriëntatie van (mogelijke) sleutelfiguren in het regionale debat, zoals politici en beleidsmakers; en, een gebrek aan identificatie met de regio. In vergelijking met de Vlaamse Ruit, het RijnRuhrgebied en Centraal Schotland scoort de Randstad aanzienlijk beter waar het regionaal organiserend vermogen betreft. Dit blijkt het meest duidelijk uit het ontstaan van de Vereniging Deltametropool en het Bureau Regio Randstad.

Kritische massa

Onderzoeksvraag 3: *In welke mate beïnvloedt de polycentrische ruimtelijke structuur van polycentrische stedelijke gebieden het draagvlak voor stedelijke functies in dergelijke regio's?*

In hoofdstuk 6 is onderzocht of de kritische massa die georganiseerd kan worden in een polycentrische stedelijke regio, even groot is als in een qua bevolkingsomvang vergelijkbare monocentrische stedelijke regio. Kritische massa is daarbij geoperationaliseerd als en ingeperkt tot het draagvlak voor supralokale culturele, vrijetijds- en sportvoorzieningen. Bestaat er een verband tussen een polycentrische ruimtelijke structuur en het draagvlak voor deze voorzieningen? Om deze vraag te beantwoorden werd geïnventariseerd welke culturele voorzieningen (zoals bioscopen, theaters, musea, concertzalen, poppodia), overige vrijetijdsvoorzieningen (zoals casino's, restaurants) en sportvoorzieningen (schaats-, ski- en klimhallen, kartbanen, stadions) er aanwezig zijn in 42 Nederlandse regio's. Dit betreft de zogenaamde WGR-samenwerkingsgebieden. Dit zijn regio's die afgebakend zijn binnen de Wet Gemeenschappelijke Regelingen. Deze regio's zijn afgebakend door lokale bestuurders vanuit de veronderstelling dat het zin heeft om bovenlokale issues op dat regionale schaalniveau aan te pakken. Op een indirecte manier betreft het dus een afbakening van functioneel samenhangende regio's. Andere belangrijke voordelen van deze regio-indeling ten opzichte van andere regionale indelingen zijn dat deze zich niet hoeft te houden aan oude administratieve grenzen en dat deze betrekkelijk recent is. Voor iedere regio is de aanwezigheid van de genoemde voorzieningen geïndexeerd, met andere woorden, uitgedrukt in één score. Deze score fungeerde als de afhankelijke, te verklaren variabele in een multivariate regressie-analyse. Als onafhankelijke, verklarende variabelen waren opgenomen: de bevolkingsomvang van een regio; het aantal bezoekers per regio (op basis van het gemiddelde aantal bezette hotelbedden); het gemiddelde huishoudensinkomen in de regio en een waarde die de mate van polycentriciteit van de regio weergeeft. Voor de bepaling van deze laatste waarde is gebruik gemaakt van een innovatieve meetmethode welke het mogelijk maakte het stedelijk systeem in iedere WGR-regio te scoren op een schaal lopend van (zeer) polycentrisch tot (zeer) monocentrisch. De meting baseerde zich op de log lineaire 'rank-size distribution'; de distributie van de omvang van de vijf belangrijkste plaatsen per regio op basis van hun rangorde. De helling van de regressielijn die het best past bij deze distributie is opgenomen als indicator voor de mate van polycentriciteit. Hoe vlakker deze lijn, dus hoe gelijker de plaatsen zijn qua bevolkingsomvang, hoe polycentrischer. Een steile regressielijn werd uiteraard verkregen in het geval een of twee steden in een regio de andere sterk domineerden qua omvang (dus: monocentrisch). De multivariate regressie-analyse resulteerde in de constatering dat er, gecorrigeerd voor verschillen tussen regio's in termen van bevolkingsomvang, het aantal bezoekers en het gemiddelde huishoudensinkomen, in polycentrische stedelijke regio's significant minder voorzieningen zijn dan in monocentrische regio's. Hoe polycentrischer, hoe minder culturele, vrijetijds- en sportvoorzieningen. Of andersom, hoe monocentrischer, hoe meer dergelijke voorzieningen present zijn. Juist de specifieke polycentrische ruimtelijke structuur zorgt er dus voor dat polycentrische regio's niet in dezelfde mate profiteren van het aanwezige bevolkingspotentieel als monocentrische regio's, tenminste voor wat betreft het draagvlak voor culturele, vrijetijds- en sportvoorzieningen. Agglomeratievoordelen gaan dus minder op voor een collectie van steden. De verklaring voor het mindere draagvlak in polycentrische stedelijke regio's moet gezocht worden in de noodzaak tot langere reistijden tussen de steden, een minder gemakkelijke informatie-uitwisseling en een gebrek aan een metropolitaan stedelijk milieu. Bovendien, wanneer je een stel steden samen neemt, is de kans op duplicatie groot, terwijl het onderzochte type voorzieningen ook sterk geworteld blijkt te zijn in de lokale context. De conclusie kan niet anders zijn dan dat het centrale onderzoeksthema van dit onderzoek te positief geformuleerd is: steden in een polycentrische stedelijke regio verhouden zich niet tot elkaar op een manier die ertoe leidt dat zij meer dan de som der delen zijn, integendeel, waar het culturele, vrijetijds- en sportvoorzieningen betreft, zijn zij zelfs minder dan de som der delen.

Synergie in polycentrische stedelijke regio's

De drie onderzoeksthema's in dit proefschrift refereren alle aan synergie tussen steden. De positieve waarde van complementariteit is reeds behandeld: het leidt tot regionale externaliteiten, oftewel agglomeratievoordelen gerelateerd aan specialisatie en diversificatie. Dit geldt ook voor het thema kritische massa. Wanneer er in een polycentrische stedelijke regio sprake is van een regionale markt in plaats van een splitsing in deelmarkten, zal de regio profiteren van een grotere kritische massa, wat bijvoorbeeld naar voren komt in de aanwezigheid van hoogwaardige voorzieningen. Ten slotte, regionaal organiserend vermogen en daarmee feitelijke regionale coördinatie en samenwerking leidt tot synergie gerelateerd aan schaalvoordelen bij het aanpakken van gemeenschappelijke issues, en kan de ontwikkeling van complementariteit en een regionaal draagvlak bevorderen door het bundelen van krachten. Een toename van complementariteit, regionaal organiserend vermogen en kritische massa leidt zodoende tot betere prestaties van de regio als geheel, al vergroot het wel de afhankelijkheidsrelaties tussen de steden. Tussen de drie thema's bestaan sterke verbanden. Bijvoorbeeld, complementariteit en een kritische massa gebaseerd op de regio verhogen de afhankelijkheid van de steden van elkaar en zodoende de noodzaak voor organiserend vermogen. Het lijkt er sterk op dat complementariteit, een regionaal gebaseerde kritische massa en organiserend vermogen elkaar versterken, zodoende leidend tot steeds meer synergie in polycentrische stedelijke regio's.

Of er sprake is van een dergelijke opwaartse spiraal in polycentrische stedelijke regio's is ter discussie gesteld in dit onderzoek. Daartoe is een theoretisch gefundeerd onderscheid gemaakt tussen polycentrische stedelijke regio's en stedelijke netwerken. Een polycentrische stedelijke regio kan geidentificeerd worden aan de hand van min of meer structurele kenmerken zoals de lokatie van historisch gezien afzonderlijke steden dicht bij elkaar met een behoorlijk gelijke bevolkingsomvang. Stedelijke netwerken kunnen beschouwd worden als een geavanceerd type polycentrische stedelijke regio. Polycentrische stedelijke regio's kwalificeren zich als stedelijk netwerk wanneer de steden met elkaar in relatie staan op een manier zoals beschreven in het netwerkmodel van ruimtelijke organisatie. Dus, om het predikaat 'stedelijk netwerk' te rechtvaardigen, moet er sprake zijn van onder meer: een bepaalde mate van functionele integratie, een relatieve ontkoppeling tussen omvang en functies van steden, complementariteit, een kris-kraspatroon van ruimtelijke interactie en een regionaal gebaseerde kritische massa die leidt tot specialisatie. Dit onderscheid tussen polycentrische stedelijke regio en stedelijk netwerk maakt het mogelijk om alle polycentrische stedelijke regio's te scoren op een schaal met als, wellicht hypothetische, extremen aan de ene kant een losse verzameling nabijgelegen steden (zonder synergie ertussen), en, aan de andere kant, het stedelijk netwerk (met veel synergie).

De vraag die dan rijst is waar de case studie gebieden geplaatst moeten worden op deze schaal: in welke mate hebben deze polycentrische stedelijke regio's zich ontwikkeld tot stedelijke netwerken? Dit onderzoek kan een voorzichtig eerste antwoord geven op deze brede vraag, al heeft het zich gericht op slechts enkele aspecten die deze transitie kenmerken, en zijn er voor deze verschillende aspecten bovendien verschillende case studie gebieden gebruikt. De algemene indruk op basis van de resultaten is echter dat er nog veel te winnen valt voor polycentrische stedelijke gebieden in hun ontwikkeling naar stedelijke netwerken. Het lijkt er op dat polycentrische stedelijke regio's slechts enige eerste stappen hebben gezet op het pad naar stedelijke netwerken.

De achtergrond van bovenstaande vraag wordt uiteraard gevormd door het wetenschappelijke debat of er sprake is van een netwerkmodel van ruimtelijke organisatie dat het hierarchische centraleplaatsenmodel verdringt. Dit theoretische debat kwam uitgebreid aan de orde in hoofdstuk 4, en empirisch bewijs met betrekking tot één belangrijk kenmerk van het netwerkmodel – complementariteit – was verzameld door een vergelijking te maken tussen polycentrische stedelijke regio's en meerlokatie-organisaties in de ziekenhuissector en de hogescholensector. De ziekenhuissector voldoet in toenemende mate aan dit netwerkmodel, echter voor de hogescholen gaat dit niet op. Toch geldt voor hogescholen dat er dan weliswaar geen sprake is van een toename van complementariteit, maar dat dit nu ook weer niet betekent dat het centraleplaatsenmodel van toepassing is. Zelfs in een situatie met weinig complementariteit binnen een meerlokatiehogeschool is het niet zo dat op de grootste lokatie ook alle opleidingen gedoceerd worden. Op kleinere lokaties worden soms unieke opleidingen gegeven, hetgeen dan weer overeenstemt met het kenmerk van het netwerkmodel dat er een ontkoppeling is tussen omvang en functie van een lokatie.

Implicaties voor strategisch regionaal beleid in stedelijke netwerken

In veel Europese landen wordt beleid gemaakt ten aanzien van de ruimtelijke en economische ontwikkeling van polycentrische stedelijke regio's, welke doorgaans worden aangeduid als stedelijke netwerken. De effectiviteit van dergelijk beleid is mede afhankelijk van de juistheid van de assumpties waarop dit beleid stoelt. In veel gevallen komen deze stedelijke netwerken in het beleid naar voren als zijnde een ruimtelijke werkelijkheid. Soms ook is het een nastrevenswaardig toekomstperspectief, terwijl in veel andere gevallen het een beleidskader vormt om te anticiperen op verwachte toekomstige ruimtelijke ontwikkelingen. Hier is geconstateerd dat er, in theoretische zin, eigenlijk niet van stedelijke netwerken kan worden gesproken, omdat de relaties tussen de steden niet van dien aard zijn. Er moeten dan ook vraagtekens gezet worden bij de juistheid van het schaalniveau waarop het beleid, en de uitvoering ervan, zich richt indien er uitgegaan wordt van het stedelijk netwerk als een bestaande werkelijkheid. In ieder geval verdient het aanbeveling om niet één regionaal schaalniveau – zoals het stedelijk netwerk – te benoemen, maar voor ieder ruimtelijk issue het relevante ruimtelijk schaalniveau na te gaan, respectievelijk te bepalen.

Alhoewel de thema's van dit onderzoek – complementariteit, organiserend vermogen en kritische massa – veelvuldig terug te vinden zijn in beleidsdocumenten als nastrevenswaardige beleidsdoelen, en dit proefschrift de waarde ervan benadrukt, is het hoogst onzeker of beleid substantieel kan bijdragen aan een verhoging ervan. Dit onderzoek werpt enig licht op de wijze waarop complementariteit en respectievelijk regionaal organiserend vermogen tot stand komen. Uit hoofdstuk 4 volgt dat het antwoord op de vraag of er zich al dan niet complementariteit ontwikkelt in een meerlokatie-organisatie afhankelijk is van een complexe interactie tussen voorwaarden op macro-niveau (zoals wet- en regelgeving, publieke investeringen en maatschappelijke trends) met overwegingen, beweegredenen en belangen van organisaties op micro-schaalniveau. Deze laatste volgen doorgaans de wetten van de markt. Meestal betreft het actoren die niet publiek zijn, hun eigen agenda nastreven en niet gecommitteerd zijn aan een eventuele ruimtelijke doelstelling als het verhogen van de complementariteit. De invloed van de overheid blijft daarmee beperkt tot het sturen op macrocondities, en de bepaling daarvan wordt zelden gedomineerd door ruimtelijke overwegingen.

Overigens moet duidelijk zijn dat in polycentrische stedelijke regio's het streven niet in de eerste plaats moet zijn om te komen tot meer complementariteit, maar dat het hierbij feitelijk gaat om het verhogen van de mate van specialisatie en diversificatie, wat betrekking kan hebben op dienstverlening, voorzieningen, woon- en werkmilieus. Het gaat er om dat het 'top'- of metropolitane specialisatieniveau tot stand gebracht wordt, welke ruimtelijke vorm dit aanneemt is een tweede. Dit kan door een enigszins gelijkmatige verdeling van gespecialiseerde 'top'-activiteiten en omgevingen over de steden in de regio (dus door complementariteit), maar even goed kan het zijn dat dit topniveau geclusterd is in één plaats in de regio. Ook in dat geval kan de hele regio ervan meeprofiteren. Het lijkt er op dat de eerste manier, dus complementariteit, kansrijker is in polycentrische stedelijke regio's, aangezien de steden doorgaans aan elkaar gewaagd zijn en niet voor elkaar onder willen doen. De tweede optie, concentratie op één plek, impliceert de ontwikkeling van een hiërarchie. Dit lijkt echter moeilijk samen te gaan met de historische stedelijke ontwikkeling van polycentrische stedelijke regio's. Welke optie het meest mogelijk is wordt met name bepaald door de concurrentie- en krachtsverhoudingen tussen de steden.

Aanbevelingen voor verder onderzoek

Een drietal richtingen voor verder onderzoek kan worden onderscheiden. In de eerste plaats betreft dit onderzoek dat dichtbij de thema's in dit proefschrift blijft en dat verder gaat waar dit proefschrift eindigt. Zo zijn er verschillende facetten van het thema complementariteit nog niet verkend. Hierbij moet gedacht worden aan: analyse van de functionele specialisatie van steden in plaats van de sectorale specialisatie; analyse van een gedetailleerdere uitsplitsing van de sectorale specialisatie van steden, bijvoorbeeld gericht op 'advanced producer services', winkelvoorzieningen en een uitgebreider analyse van het voorzieningenpakket in steden; en analyses van complementariteit tussen steden voor wat betreft woonlokaties, kantoorlocaties en bedrijfsterreinen. Verder verdient het aanbeveling om het verband tussen complementariteit en respectievelijk ruimtelijke interactie, concurrentiekracht, 'quality of life' en kritische massa nader te verkennen. In hoeverre heeft een toename van complementariteit op regionaal schaalniveau bijvoorbeeld ook gevolgen voor de toegankelijkheid en beschikbaarheid van stedelijke functies op lokaal niveau? Wat betreft het thema 'organiserend vermogen' is verder onderzoek nodig naar het daadwerkelijk functioneren van de coördinatie en samenwerking binnen de kaders die zorgen voor organiserend vermogen. Een beter inzicht in wijzen waarop regionale issues hanteerbaar kunnen worden gemaakt, en hoe regionale voordelen en lasten verdisconteerd kunnen worden op lokaal niveau is noodzakelijk. Ten slotte, met betrekking tot het thema 'kritische massa' verdient het aanbeveling om de ontwikkeling in de tijd te meten. We weten nu dat er in een polycentrisch stedelijk systeem minder draagvlak voor culturele, vrijetijds- en sportvoorzieningen aanwezig is in vergelijking tot monocentrische stedelijke regio's, maar of dit gat groter of kleiner wordt, en onder welke condities, is onbekend. Tot slot is het uiteraard nodig om de generaliseerbaarheid van de bevindingen in dit proefschrift naar polycentrische stedelijke regio's in andere delen van Europa en de wereld te toetsen.

Een tweede onderzoeksagenda betreft de ruimtelijke organisatie van stedelijke regio's, meer in het bijzonder de vraag of er al dan niet sprake is van algemeen toepasbare modellen van ruimtelijke organisatie zoals het netwerkmodel. In dit proefschrift kwam slechts één aspect van dit model aan de orde – complementariteit – maar het netwerkmodel kent meer kenmerken. Onderzoek zou zich bijvoorbeeld moeten richten op trends aangaande de koppeling tussen omvang van een stad en de stedelijke functies daarbinnen, op het belang van nodaliteit ten opzichte van centraliteit, op het ruimtelijk patroon van ruimtelijke interacties en op de manier waarop de bevolking over een regio verdeeld is.

Ten slotte, een derde en belangrijke onderzoeksrichting betreft de empirische validatie van de claim dat polycentrische stedelijke regio's wel profiteren van agglomeratievoordelen, gelijk aan monocentrische stedelijke regio's – hun natuurlijke tegenhanger –, maar dat agglomeratienadelen in vergelijking daarmee beperkt blijven. Hoofdstuk 6 van dit proefschrift kan beschouwd worden als een opmaat voor dergelijk onderzoek. De uitkomst van dergelijk onderzoek bepaalt de toekomst van het concept polycentrische stedelijke regio's als beleidsconcept. Echter, gegeven de vele vragen die nog onbeantwoord zijn, is het hoogstwaarschijnlijk dat de polycentrische stedelijke regio een blijvende positie in het wetenschappelijk debat zal krijgen.

Slotopmerkingen

Dit proefschrift heeft verschillende veronderstellingen met betrekking tot polycentrische stedelijke regio's ter discussie gesteld en deze naar mijn weten voor het eerst daadwerkelijk empirisch onderzocht. Dit geldt in het bijzonder voor de wijdverspreide assumptie dat steden die een polycentrische stedelijke regio vormen elkaar complementeren, en wel in toenemende mate. Voor het eerst is complementariteit als concept nader uitgewerkt en geoperationaliseerd. Correspondentie-analyse is gepresenteerd als innovatieve methode om complementariteit te meten en te visualiseren. Ook het verband tussen de stedelijke structuur van een regio en het draagvlak voor voorzieningen is voor het eerst onderzocht. Dit vereiste de ontwikkeling van nieuwe methoden om de mate van mono- danwel polycentriciteit te bepalen. Tot slot zijn verklaringen aangedragen voor het al dan niet ontstaan van regionaal organiserend vermogen. Deze lijken generaliseerbaar voor niet onderzochte polycentrische stedelijke regio's. De onderzoeksresultaten van dit promotieonderzoek dragen zodoende bij aan het wetenschappelijke debat over polycentrische stedelijke regio's en de ruimtelijke organisatie ervan. Daarbij richt dit proefschrift zich met name op het vullen van het empirische gat dat deze debatten tot op heden kenmerkt – overigens, zonder de pretentie dat hierover het laatste woord is gezegd.

Curriculum Vitae

Evert Meijers was born on 6 October 1975 in Veere. In 1994 he received his VWO diploma from the Christelijke Scholengemeenschap Walcheren in Middelburg, and commenced his university education at the Katholieke Universiteit Nijmegen where he obtained the Dutch equivalent of a Bachelors degree in Policy Sciences in 1996. He further specialised in Spatial Planning and received his Masters degree in 1999. Afterwards, he became a junior researcher at the same Spatial Planning department of the Katholieke Universiteit Nijmegen. In 2000 he joined OTB Research Institute for Housing, Urban and Mobility Studies at Delft University of Technology. As a researcher, he has worked on a variety of international collaborative research projects such as EURBANET, GEMACA II and various ESPON projects. In 2003 he also started his PhD research. He has published some 50 journal articles, book chapters, research reports and conference proceedings. This includes the co-editing and co-authoring of two books on 'Polycentric Urban Regions in North West Europe' and on 'Policy integration in practice', as well as a special issue of *Built Environment* on 'Polycentric development policies in European countries'.

Sustainable Urban Areas

1. Beerepoot, Milou, **Renewable energy in energy performance regulations. A challenge for European member states in implementing the Energy Performance Building Directive**
2004/202 pages/ISBN 90-407-2534-9
2. Boon, Claudia and Minna Sunikka, **Introduction to sustainable urban renewal. CO_2 reduction and the use of performance agreements: experience from The Netherlands**
2004/153 pages/ISBN 90-407-2535-7
3. De Jonge, Tim, **Cost effectiveness of sustainable housing investments**
2005/196 pages/ISBN 90-407-2578-0
4. Klunder, Gerda, **Sustainable solutions for Dutch housing. Reducing the environmental impact of new and existing houses**
2005/163 pages/ISBN 90-407-2584-5
5. Bots, Pieter, Ellen van Bueren, Ernst ten Heuvelhof and Igor Mayer, **Communicative tools in sustainable urban planning and building**
2005/100 pages/ISBN 90-407-2595-0
6. Kleinhans, R.J., **Sociale implicaties van herstructurering en herhuisvesting**
2005/371 pages/ISBN 90-407-2598-5
7. Kauko, Tom, **Comparing spatial features of urban housing markets. Recent evidence of submarket formation in metropolitan Helsinki and Amsterdam**
2005/163 pages/ISBN 90-407-2618-3
8. Kauko, Tom, **Between East and West. Housing markets, property prices and locational preferences in Budapest from a comparative perspective**
2006/142 pages/ISBN 1-58603-679-3
9. Sunikka, Minna Marjaana, **Policies for improving energy efficiency in the European housing stock**
2006/251 pages/ISBN 1-58603-649-1
10. Hasselaar, Evert, **Health performance of housing. Indicators and tools**
2006/298 pages/ISBN 1-58603-689-0
11. Gruis, Vincent, Henk Visscher and Reinout Kleinhans (eds.), **Sustainable neighbourhood transformation**
2006/158 pages/ISBN 1-58603-718-8
12. Trip, Jan Jacob, **What makes a city? Planning for 'quality of place' The case of high-speed train station area redevelopment**
2007/ISBN 978-1-58603-716-1

13. Meijers, Evert, **Synergy in polycentric urban regions. Complementarity, organising capacity and critical mass**
2007/182 pages/ ISBN 978-1-58603-724-6

Copies can be ordered at www.dupress.nl.